German & Austro-Hungarian Aero Engines of WWI

Vol. 2

Michael Düsing

Great War Aviation Centennial Series #65

Acknowledgements

For our aviation books, please see our website at: www.aeronautbooks.com

I am looking for photographs of the less well-known German aircraft of WWI for this series. For questions or to help with photographs you may contact me at jherris@me.com

Interested in WWI aviation? Join The League of WWI Aviation Historians (www.overthefront.com), Cross & Cockade International (www.crossandcockade.com), and Das Propellerblatt (www.propellerblatt.de).

ISBN: 978-1-953201-52-2

Design and layout: Jack Herris
Cover design: Aaron Weaver
Digital photo editing: Jack Herris

Aeronaut Books

Books for Enthusiasts by Enthusiasts
www.aeronautbooks.com

2

Table of Contents

4

Above: Albatros D.I prototype D.384/16 at Johannisthal in September 1916. The Albatros D.I was the first fighter powered by the 160 hp Mercedes D III engine. With their power, performance, and twin synchronized machine guns, the Albatros fighter family immediately gained superiority over existing Allied fighters. The Mercedes D.III/D.IIIa was a very reliable engine which became the most popular engine used in German fighters until the end of the war. Introduction of the over-compressed BMW IIIa finally provided better performance than the Mercedes and spurred Daimler to develop improved derivatives of their D IIIa engine.

3.16 Daimler Motoren Gesellschaft Untertürkheim (Mercedes)

3.16.0 General

The Daimler Motoren Gesellschaft (DMG) Stuttgart-Untertürkheim and Berlin is the oldest automobile factory in the world. Gottlieb Daimler, born on March 17, 1834, was primarily active in the field of mechanical engineering after completing his multifaceted professional education at various locations and with different orientations. His comprehensive engineering knowledge was recognized by Nicolaus August Otto, the inventor of the 4-stroke gasoline engine, when Daimler was appointed Technical Director of Gasmotorenfabrik Deutz (Cologne) in August 1872. In this position he succeeded in recruiting his childhood friend Wilhelm Maybach (later his own industrialist) as a development engineer. As a result of disagreements with Otto, Daimler and Maybach left the company and moved to Cannstadt, where Daimler purchased a disused factory site and set up his test workshop in November 1890. It was here that Maybach became his technical director and in the years that followed played a major role in the further development of the automobile in Germany.

Since the four-stroke technique was still protected by the Otto patent, both worked in secret until 1886 and expected the end of patent protection. In the following year, the first Daimler car taxi drove through the city of Esslingen.

Inspired by Renard's famous attempt at a motorized airship, Gottlieb Daimler developed a light petrol engine in Cannstatt in 1886. In 1887, Daimler personally offered his invention to the Imperial Airship Department for use in an airship and gave a practical demonstration of it on a

Above: Inclined cylinder Daimler engine from 1888. This arrangement was already used and patented by Gottlieb Daimler in 1888 (see D.R.P. No. 50 839 of June 9, 1889). This is a gasoline engine with surface carburetor and glow tube ignition, whose two cylinders are inclined towards each other in a V-shape. "Grandfather clock" design. A surface carburetor is a carburetor in which the air is passed over the surface of a liquid, like fuel. [M55]

Above: Advertisement 1914. [J4,1914]

Above: First Daimler two-cylinder V-type motor (1888). [B30]

motorboat on Lake Rummelsburg near Berlin. But the military personnel present had neither the mandate nor the necessary means to independently evaluate these experiments.

In 1888, Daimler Motoren Gesellschaft supplied a water-cooled 4 hp single-cylinder engine for the balloon of the bookseller Dr. Wölfert in Leipzig. Wölfert's airship first took off directly from Daimler's factory site on the Seelberg in Cannstadt on September 1, 1888. Curiously, Dr. Wölfert appeared to be too heavy for the small balloon, which meant that the somewhat lighter mechanic was allowed to make the maiden journey alone. In the following days, too, it became apparent that the balloon was too small to be able to make longer flights than 4-5 km. After several more or less unsuccessful attempts, the manufacturer Riedinger from Augsburg took up the matter. Immediately a 6 hp four-cylinder engine was installed according to the drawings of DMG. Years later, in the meantime the motorised balloon was exhibited at the Industrial Fair held in Berlin in 1896, Wölfert undertook a test flight from Tempelhofer Feld together with

his mechanic. The balloon reached a height of 1000 m when it suddenly caught fire. A technical malfunction forced Wölfert to make an early landing, for which gas had to be released. But they forgot to extinguish the engine's pilot flame first.

In 1890 the company got into difficulties because it could not sell enough vehicles. In order to restructure the business, Gottlieb Daimler founded Daimler-Motoren-Gesellschaft (DMG), in which the industrialists Max Duttenhofer and Wilhelm Lorenz held shares alongside him and Wilhelm Maybach. Because of disputes with Lorenz, Daimler left the company in 1893. In the meantime, he had developed the first two-cylinder engine (model Sch 1891) together with Maybach in 1892.

But also, the airmen like David Schwarz, engineer W. Kreß and Lebaudy frères used Daimler engines.

Since 1898 the Austrian Wilhelm Kress worked on the design of a seaplane. After completion of his "flying ship" in 1901 and after providing the financial means for a 35 hp Daimler aircraft

Year	85 hp DF 80	D.I 100 hp DF 100	D.II 120 hp DF 120	D.III 160 hp DF 160	D.IIIa 170 hp DF 170	D.IV 220 hp DF 220	D.IVa 260 hp DF 260	Half Year Total
Production of Daimler Aeroengines Between 1 July 1914 and 31 December 1918								
1914 VIII–XII	16	557	18	11				602
1915 I–VI	1	1108	219	201		2		1531
1915 VII–XII		11	383	1011		120		1525
1916 I–VI		50		1475		248	42	1815
1916 VII–XII				882		27	1456	2365
1917 I–VI				1623		2	560	2185
1917 VII–XII			87	2580		24	876	3567
1918 I–VI			109	2230	4	1	1004	3348
1918 VII–XII			85	1828	446		617	2976
Total	17	1726	901	11841	450	424	4555	19914

engine, Kress undertook first flight tests on the Wienerwaldsee. This aircraft can be regarded as the first aircraft with a combustion engine. The Viennese "Allgemeine Sport-Zeitung" reported on February 10, 1901: "As we hear, Mr. engineer Kress has now ordered a Mercedes engine of 35 horsepower from Daimler in Cannstadt for his flying ship. These engines are said to be the lightest and most reliable ones available at present, but only in two sizes, of 16 and 35 horsepower. Since 16 horsepower is too limited for Kress' flying ship, he had to decide on 35 horsepower. ..."

However, the attempts were unsuccessful and had to be stopped after the aircraft capsized and was destroyed on 3 October.

Gottlieb Daimler died in March 1900. In the same year 185,000 m² of new terrain was purchased for a new engine factory in Untertürkheim.

On July 29, 1902, Daimler-Motoren-Gesellschaft took over Motorfahrzeug- und Motorenfabrik Berlin AG (MMB) in Marienfelde near Berlin as a branch office, after Daimler members of the board of directors of DMG had already used Motorenfabrik Adolf Altmann & Co. in Marienfelde to build motor cars according to the Daimler system in 1899. In 1902, DMG registered the name **"Mercedes"** as a patented brand name.

A major fire in the Cannstatt factory buildings in 1903 destroyed all production machinery and 93 finished Mercedes vehicles; as an interim solution, production began prematurely at the Untertürkheim plant in December 1904. In the following year, the complete move from Cannstatt to Untertürkheim took place.

In 1909 the trident star, the symbol of the company, was designed by the artist Otto Ewald and made available to Daimler.

Other German airship men such as Major von Parseval, and the Military Airship Department in Berlin used Daimler engines. In a competition for the best engine for powered airship purposes, which was held by the Motorluftschiff-Studiengesellschaft in Berlin in 1908, a 60 hp Daimler (Mercedes) four-cylinder engine came out as the winner (see later Type TH 1907/08).

However, the Daimler engines in the service of airships have gained the greatest interest because it is closely related to the work and successes of Count von Zeppelin.

Even during his attempts to determine the most favorable form of propellers, Count v. Zeppelin used a Daimler engine which, installed in a boat, had to operate two powerful wind blades that moved the boat forward.

The fact that ever greater engine power was desired can be clearly seen from a list of engines which Graf v. Zeppelin purchased from Daimler-Motorengesellschaft. First there were two 12 hp engines and a reserve engine of the same power for his airship LZ 1, which were delivered in 1899. In 1905, two 90 hp Daimler engines were used for the airship later called "Zeppelin I". In 1907 the airship LZ 4 received two 100 HP engines, which were installed in the airship "LZ II" after repair. In 1909 another two 115 hp Mercedes engines were ordered for the airship "LZ III".

The total number of Daimler airship engines built is very considerable in contrast to the number of aircraft engines supplied. In the years between 1890 and 1913, the number did not exceed 50 units.

International Relationships (American licences)

In 1888, Gottlieb Daimler established a cooperation with the German-born piano maker William Steinway in Astoria, Queens, later New York City, to build stationary and marine engines for gas and petroleum, and later on, 1892, also to build cars as full copies of the German design. The engines and cars were produced in Steinway's premises of the "Rikers plant" opposite of Rikers Island which is in use for piano production until nowadays. This business was sold after William Steinway died in 1896.

Other arrangements have been established all over the world. See table on facing page.

3.16.1   Airship Engines of Daimler-Motoren-Gesellschaft

3.16.1a   Single-cylinder 2 hp airship engine Model P (1888)

This single-cylinder motor, developing 2 hp at 720 rpm had a mass of 84 kg. The first aeroengine built by Daimler for aviation, was used by Dr. Wölfert for

Above: 1888: Bookseller Dr. Wölfert. Wölfert's airship first took off directly from Daimler's factory site. 4-stroke single cylinder motor. [J9, 1912]

Specification Daimler Airship Engine P	
Year:	1888
Cylinder:	1
Bore:	80 mm
Stroke:	120 mm
Displacement:	0,6 l
Power (max./norm.):	2 hp @720 RPM
Weight:	84 kg
Used by Dr. Wölfert (Leipzig) in his powered balloon.	

Above: Daimler single-cylinder 2 hp airship engine Model P (1888). [L21]

Overview of Delivered Aero-Engines of Daimler-Motoren-Gesellschaft Stuttgart-Untertürkheim in the Years 1890 until 1911*		
1890	1 piece	5 hp 4-cyl. engine for an airship developed by Dr. Wölfert, München
1892	1 piece	5 hp 4-cyl. engine for an airship developed by David Schwarz, Agram
1895	1 piece	2 hp 2-cyl. engine for an airship developed by Dr. Wölfert, München
1896	1 piece	6 hp 2-cyl. engine for an airship developed by Dr. Wölfert, München
1896	1 piece	10 hp 4-cyl. engine for an airship developed by David Schwarz, Agram
1898	1 piece	10 hp 4-cyl. engine for test by Graf von Zeppelin
1899	2 pieces	12 hp 4-cyl. engine for Zeppelin airship No. 1
1899	1 piece	12 hp 4-cyl. engine for Zeppelin airship No. 1
1900	1 piece	6 hp 2-cyl. engine for an airship developed by Militärluftschiffer-Abteilung, Berlin
1901	1 piece	35 hp 4-cyl. engine for the Ing. W. Kress aeroplane, Wien
1901	1 piece	35 hp 4-cyl. engine for an airship, Lebaudy Frères, Paris
1905	2 pieces	90 hp 4-cyl. engine for airship Zeppelin Z I
1906	1 piece	90 hp 4-cyl. engine for airship Parseval No. 1
1907	2 pieces	100 hp 4-cyl. engine for airship Zeppelin Z II
1908	1 piece	115 hp 4-cyl. engine for airship of Motor-Luftschiff-Studien-Gesellschaft Berlin.
1909	2 pieces	115 hp 4-cyl. engine for airship Zeppelin Z III
1909	4 pieces	115 hp 4-cyl. engine for airship of Siemens-Schuckertwerke AG, Berlin
1909	2 pieces	240 hp 8-cyl. engine for Schütte-Lanz airship (J8L)
1909	1 piece	115 hp 4-cyl. engine for aeroplane developed by Major v. Parseval
1909	1 piece	25 hp 4-cyl. engine r for an airship developed by Major v. Parseval
1909	1 piece	115 hp 4-cyl. for an aeroplane developed by Degn's Flugmaschinen-Ges., Bremen
1909	2 pieces	40 hp 4-cyl. engine for Dir. Boris Loutzky, Berlin
1909	1 piece	40 hp 4-cyl. engine for an aeroplane developed by Otto Widmann, Berlin
1909	1 piece	18 hp 4-cyl. engine for an aeroplane developed by Rudolf Eipperle, Eßlingen
1909	1 piece	20 hp 4-cyl. engine for an aeroplane developed by W. Jochems, Gravenhage
1910	3 pieces	120 hp 4-cyl. for a Zeppelin airship
1910	2 pieces	120 hp 4-cyl. for a Parseval airship
1911	2 pieces	240 hp 8-cyl. engine for Schütte-Lanz airship (J8L), Danzig
* This list is not exhaustive! Several engines are missing.		

his airship in 1888. "Grandfather clock" (Standuhr) type. Upstanding controlled exhaust valve, hanging uncontrolled intake valve (flutter valve). Crankcase as fresh air scavenge pump with membrane inlet. Maybach float carburetor, hot-tube ignition.

Wölfert was looking for a light, powerful propulsion system for the latest stage of development of his airship – he had electric and gas engines in mind, among others, but none of the engines examined seemed suitable. Then Gottlieb Daimler contacted Wölfert and recommended his high-speed four-stroke gasoline engine, developed together with Wilhelm Maybach, as the airship's power source.

Daimler saw Wölfert's airship project as an opportunity to finally realize his dream of motorizing vehicles on land, water and in the air. His two-cylinder engine was already working reliably in the "Reitwagen" of 1885 (the world's first vehicle with an internal combustion engine and also a forerunner of today's motorcycle) and in the world's first four-wheeled motor vehicle presented in 1886. These were joined by the "Marie" motorboat, the four-seater "Motor-Draisine" and the "Motor-

Above: Replica of engine gondola with control station of the airship *"Deutschland"* by Dr. Karl Wölfert, 1896 (Source: Mercedes-Benz Museum Stuttgart) [A4]

Above: Daimler Modell P1890 used by Wölfert and Schwarz (1890). [L4]

Waggonet" narrow-gauge tramway (all 1887).

The 84-kilogram engine was installed in the airship's nacelle, which was constructed of wooden slats and strings and hung below a cigar-shaped fuselage. A control lever allowed the pilot to apply engine power to a vertical propeller (for forward motion) or to a horizontal propeller (to control altitude). The 1.5 hp / 2 hp engine drove the propellers at up to 720 revolutions per minute. The airship was steered by means of a large rudder at the bow of the gondola, which was covered with cloth like the two propellers.

This fast-running Daimler light engine, which already operated with a kind of compressor, was admittedly not an "aircraft engine" in today's terms, but it was the first gasoline aircraft engine in the world.

3.16.1b Four-Cylinder 5,9 hp Airship Engine Model P (P1890)

Dr. Wölfert received from Daimler a twin engine installation in 1890, consisting of two coupled of these four-cylinders engines Model P.

In terms of effect, Wölfert had an eight-cylinder engine for his tests, with each cylinder having its own exhaust pipe. The valves were controlled, the carburetor and ignition were as on the single cylinder, but without flushing pump. Due to the use of aluminium for the crankcase for the first time here, the power-to-weight ratio was reduced to 56 kg/hp. With this Daimler eight-cylinder aviation engine, Dr. Wölfert initially conducted further tests together with the Augsburg balloon factory August Riedinger.

A second single four-cylinder "P"-type engine of 5.9 hp at 590 min^{-1} with mass approx. 150 kg were

Specification Daimler Airship Engine P1890

Year:	1891
Cylinder:	2 x 4
Bore:	80 mm
Stroke:	120 mm
Displacement:	2 x 2,4 l
Power (max./norm.):	10 hp @590 RPM
Weight:	84 kg

delivered in the same year again to Dr. Wölfert but to David Schwarz as well.

3.16.1c Four-Cylinder 12,9 hp Airship Engine P (P1895/96)

As already reported on the previous page, David Schwarz ordered 2 different engines from DMG. The practical trials showed that the weaker 5,9 hp-engine was not suitable for use as an airship engine.

Specification Daimler Airship Engine P1890

Year:	1890
Cylinder:	4
Bore:	80 mm
Stroke:	120 mm
Displacement:	2,4 l
Power (max./norm.):	5,9 hp @590 RPM
Weight:	84 kg

Above: David Schwarz aluminium airship (1898), powered by 12 hp Daimler motor.

Above: David Schwarz in his airship's gondola.

Specification Daimler Airship Engine P1895/96

Year:	1895
Cylinder:	4 in line
Cooling:	Water
Bore:	110 mm
Stroke:	160 mm
Displacement:	6,08 l
Power (max./norm.):	12 hp
@ max. RPM	480
Empty Weight:	320 kg
Fuel consumption:	0,42 kg/hp/hr
Used in Schwarz airship.	

Above: Daimler 12,9 hp 4-cylinder in-line motor model P1895/96 used in Schwarz airship.

On March 28, 1896, Daimler delivered a simple 10-hp 4-cylinder engine for Schwarz's airship, which had now been improved in some details and was equipped with all the proven improvements and had a power-to-weight ratio of only about 25 kg/hp. Four single cylinders (in a crankcase of aluminium) produced the same power as Daimler's so-called eight-cylinder engine of 1890. The engines were built according to the system of the Phoenix engines; the cooling water circulation was operated by a vane pump and the spray nozzle carburetor controlled the fuel supply. A Schwarz airship equipped with this new engine made its first ascent on November 3, 1897, at Tempelhofer Field near Berlin; however, it was caught and crushed by a sudden gale-force wind.

The stronger Daimler engine had also 4 cylinders and the well-known patented glow tube ignition. The engine effectively produced 12 hp at 480 rpm.

Petrol with a relative weight of 0,70 g/cm³ was used for operation. The fuel consumption was 0,42 kg/hph. The engine was made of aluminium as far as possible and had a weight of 320 kg.

The power transfer was accomplished by means of Daimler's patented drive and reversing device, as shown in the adjacent figure. The principle of this was that a cone was pressed into the engine flywheel, causing the drive shaft to rotate in the same direction as the engine. If the direction of rotation of the propeller is to be changed, the cone is disengaged by means of a hand lever and two lateral conical discs are brought into contact with the flywheel and at the same time with a third conical disc mounted on the drive shaft, whereupon the drive shaft moves in the opposite direction to the engine crank axle.

Water or another liquid was necessary to cool the cylinders. The hot cooling water runs from the engine into an upper vessel, where it gives off its heat, while it drains through the connecting pipes into the lower vessel.

3.16.1d Two-Cylinder 7,1 hp Airship Engine P1896

In 1896, Gottlieb Daimler supplied Wölfert with a 7 hp two-cylinder Phoenix engine with a light metal crankcase for his airship "Deutschland". Wölfert undertook various successful test flights with this airship until he and his mechanic crashed fatally in Berlin in June 1897 after the balloon burst into flames. The causes of the catastrophe were any lack of a safety device on the gasoline carburetor, so that when the balloon climbed, the gas flowing out of the valve, which, by the way, was placed Wölfert himselfs very low, became explosive when mixed

Above: Daimler two-cylinder airship engine 1894, 2 hp at 700 rpm (additional air supercharging). It is not certain that this engine is related to the P1896 described here. [A1]

Specification Daimler Airship Engine P1896

Year:	1896
Cylinder:	2 in line
Cooling:	Water
Bore:	104 mm
Stroke:	160 mm
Displacement:	2,7 l
Power (max./norm.):	7,1 hp
@ max. RPM	535
Empty Weight:	108 kg

Above: Wölfert's airship "*Deutschland*" (1896).

Below: Engine nacelle and control station of the airship "*Deutschland*" by Dr. Karl Wölfert, 1896.

with the atmospheric air and ignited.

The engine itself was a two-cylinder in-line motor, developing 7,1 hp at 535 min⁻¹, mass 108 kg. Improved design as "Phoenix" engine. Cast cylinder block, valve arrangement and control as for the "grandfather clock" single cylinder, but without flushing pump.

3.16.1e Two-Cylinder 2,6 hp Airship Engine Type Sch (Sch1891)

Two-cylinder in-line, stationary water-cooled engine developed by Daimler engineer Max Schrödter. Valve arrangement and control were similar to the "grandfather clock" single cylinder. Used in 1894/95 by Dr. Wölfert for balloon tests.

Above: Daimler aircraft engine from 1891: Model Sch with excentric control system [A1]

Right: Carburetor side of Daimler model Sch 1891. [L21]

Specification Daimler Airship Engine P1891

Year:	1891
Cylinder:	2 in line
Cooling:	Water
Bore:	75 mm
Stroke:	120 mm
Displacement:	1,1 l
Power (max./norm.):	2,6 hp
@ max. RPM	660 RPM
Empty Weight:	152 kg

3.16.1f Four-Cylinder 12 hp Airship Engine N (N1898)

Daimler brought a 10 hp four-cylinder engine of the Phoenix model to Lake Constance in June 1898 for Count Zeppelin's experimental airship. Four upright cylinders cast together in pairs were installed in a crankcase made of aluminium. Gottlieb Daimler also used these engines for his propeller boat to test the Bosch magnetic low voltage break-away ignition system. The engine was equipped with a water-cooled exhaust manifold due to fire hazard on board of airships. The engine was mainly used for experiments by Daimler on a propeller test boat, to establish the best propeller parameters for the first Zeppelin airship.

Above: Daimler's airscrew - (propeller) - experimental boat on Lake Constance. [L21]

Specification Daimler Airship Engine P1898

Year:	1896
Cylinder:	4 in line
Cooling:	Water
Bore:	90 mm
Stroke:	130 mm
Displacement:	3,3 l
Power (max./norm.):	12 hp
@ max. RPM	660 RPM
Empty Weight:	320 kg

3.16.1g Four-Cylinder 16 hp Airship Engine N1899, NL 1

In 1899, Gottlieb Daimler completed development work on two engines for Count Zeppelin's LZ 1 airship. They produced an effective 16 hp at 760 rpm and a power-to-weight ratio of only 20 kg/hp. The four upright cylinders were cast together in pairs; the crankcase was made of aluminium. The overhead intake valve was automatic, the upright exhaust valve cam-controlled. A centrifugal governor controlled the fuel supply. The spray-nozzle carburetor was developed to the highest degree of perfection; lube oil pumps guaranteed controlled lubrication. The cooling water circulation was operated by vane pumps; the exhaust pot was water-cooled. On the test stand, these Zeppelin engines were still equipped with glow-tube ignition. Before they were installed in the nacelles of the airship, however, they were fitted with the now perfected Bosch electric spark ignition system. Count Zeppelin made his first successful voyages with these engines in his LZ 1 on July 2, 1900. The Zeppelin airship LZ1 was equipped with two 16 hp Daimler petrol engines of the "Phoenix" type in a more powerful version

Above: 16 hp airship engine for use in Graf v. Zeppelin's first airship. [L14]

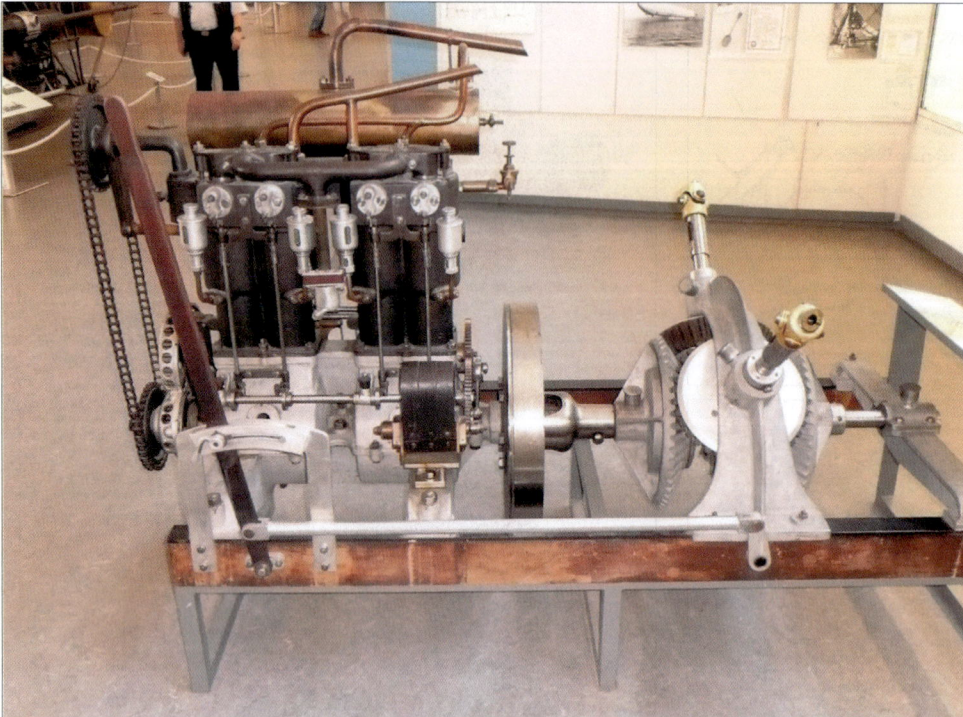

Left: Daimler N/L1 16 hp "Balloon engine" 1900 model N1899 as used in Zeppelin LZ1. (exhibit in the Deutsches Museum Munich)

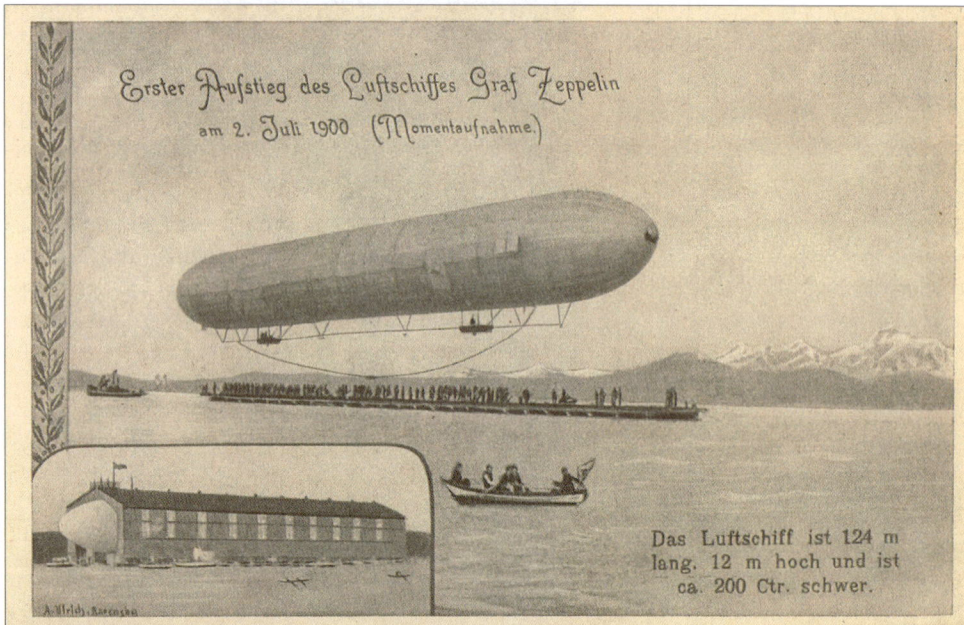

Left: Postcard showing the airship Zeppelin LZ I.

Below Left: Stamp showing Zeppelin LZ I.

with 16 hp at 760 min⁻¹. Two of the 385 kg heavy engine have been installed on the first Zeppelin airship LZ 1. The engines had water-cooled exhaust manifold (because of the fire hazard).

Both engines were installed in separate nacelles at the foredeck and the rear of the airship, with two propellers each being driven simultaneously via a bevel gear.

At 680 rpm the engine reached its maximum power of 16 hp.

During several trips on Lake Constance, first a single engine, then two engines were tested

Left: Exhaust side of Daimler NL 1 16 hp airship engine.

Above: One of the 16 hp airship engines, gear with 2 propeller shafts. [J4, 1925]

Specification Daimler NL1 (N1899)

Year:	1899/1900
Cylinder:	4 in line
Cooling:	Water
Bore:	100 mm
Stroke:	140 mm
Displacement:	4,4 l
Power (max./norm.):	16/12 hp
@ max. RPM	760/680
Weight:	340 kg
Fuel comsumption:	0,4 kg/hp/h

Used in Zeppelin LZ 1.

Specification Daimler N1899

Year:	1899
Cylinder:	2 in line
Cooling:	Water
Bore:	100 mm
Stroke:	140 mm
Displacement:	2,2 l
Power (max./norm.):	8 hp
@ max. RPM	700
Weight:	153 kg

simultaneously at full load.

The bore of the cylinders was 100 mm, the stroke was 140 mm. The fuel consumption of the engine was 400 gr/hp/h, which means that at full load each engine used 6.4 kg of petrol per hour.

This engine was developed by Karl Maybach. Because of the increased fire risk on airships, a Bosch low-voltage cut-off ignition and a water-cooled exhaust manifold were specially developed for this engine type.

3.16.1h Two-Cylinder 8 hp Airship Engine N1899

Also under the designation N1899, Daimler-Motoren Gesellschaft brought out a two-cylinder according to the "Phoenix" design described above. In the practical version, it was a "half" NL 1. This engine was used for powered balloon tests by the Military Airship Department (1899).

3.16.1i Four-Cylinder 40/35 hp Aero-Engine N/LF

After Daimler's death, the 35 hp Mercedes engine (with only 7 kg/hp) was also installed by the Austrian Wilhelm Kreß in the world's first experimental airplane with an internal combustion engine. However, since Kreß had this powerful engine, which easily reached 950 rpm, run at just under 500 rpm on October 3, 1901, and instead of 35 hp at the most, got only 15 hp out of the machine, the intended airplane attempts failed. This is the only reason why the Wright brothers retain the fame of having performed the first flight of 12 seconds in an airplane on September 17, 1903.

The same Mercedes engine, admittedly with somewhat increased power, was delivered to the Lebaudy brothers on June 9, 1901 for the first French guided airship. The Lebaudy brothers wrote enthusiastically after one of their successful ascents "that they were pleased to have recognized the

Specification Daimler N-LF

Year:	1901
Cylinder:	4
Bore:	116 mm
Stroke:	140 mm
Displacement:	5,9 l
Power (max./norm.):	35/25 hp
@ max. RPM	950/800
Weight:	230 kg

Used in Kreß' flying boat and French airship *Lebaudy*.

Daimler-Mercedes engine, which had proved itself in the best possible way both on water and on land, as the most excellent power engine for conquering the air.

The engine for the first time had cast iron cylinder blocks cast together in pairs, aluminium crankcase, bottom controlled valves. Low voltage break-away ignition.

Below: French airship *Lebaudy*.

Left: First aircraft in the world powered by a combustion engine (1900/01). The water plane designed by the Austrian Wilhelm Kreß with a 35 hp 4-cylinder engine from Daimler Motoren Gesellschaft. [J3, 1942]

Below: Daimler four-cylinder 35 hp aero-engine N/LF.

Above: 35 hp 4-cylinder Aircraft engine, delivered in 1901 to Kress for his flying boat. [A1]

Right: Kress aroplane fuselage with 35 hp engine installation.

3.16.1k Four-Cylinder 90 and 105 hp Airship Engine H4L

August von Parseval, the well-known German designer of semi-rigid airships, was the head of the Berlin-based Motor Airship Study Company, which in turn set itself the goal of promoting airship aviation in Germany. As technical director of the Studiengesellschaft Parseval developed several airships. Although Parseval had an affinity for Maybach engines, the experimental airship "P V" (V = Versuch) from 1906 and PL 1 (1909) and PL 2 (1908) were equipped with Daimler engines. It should be remembered here that at this time Maybach was still employed by Daimler as Technical Manager and had a major influence on engine development.

Two different H4L four-cylinder water-cooled airship engine models developed by W. Maybach are recorded. The basic design was similar to their predecessors, the valves were controlled by pushrods.

DMG delivered a total of four of these 90 hp engines to Friedrichshafen in 1904 for installation in the Zeppelin airships LZ 2 and LZ 3.

Above: Mercedes H4L, 100 hp airship engine.

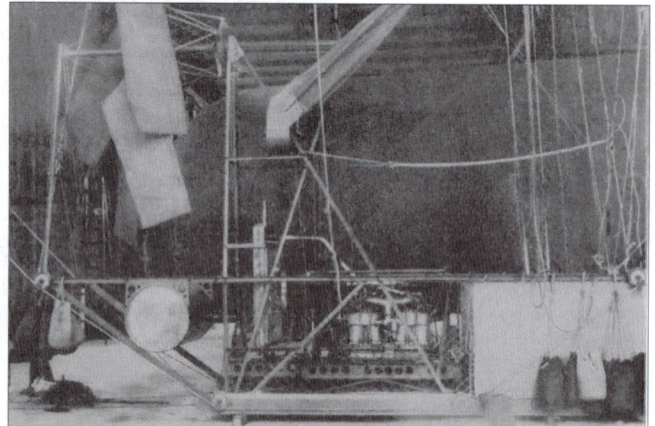

Above: 1906: Parseval airship gondola with Mercedes 4B4L.

Specification Daimler H4L

Year:	1904/1905
Cylinder:	4 in-line
Cooling	Water
Bore:	165 mm
Stroke:	140 mm
Displacement:	12 l
Power (max./norm.):	90 hp
@ max. RPM	1050 RPM
Weight:	360 kg

Used in Zeppelin LZ 2 and LZ 3, Parseval PV (1908) and PL 1 (1909).

Above: Gondola, with engine, fuel tank, propeller blades (System Parseval). [B31]

The new H4L, with an approximately 20 percent larger displacement, already had an output of 105 from a displacement of 14.0 liters and initially replaced the weaker Daimler H4L engine in the Parseval airships PV and PL 1 and was also used in the Parseval airship PL 2.

The Parseval's propellers were unusual: non-rigid propellers, the blades stiffened and deployed to their operating mode under centrifugal force. When not in use, they hung limp, as seen here in the Museum. The PL-airships were a so-called "blimp" design with no rigid internal airframe. The shape of the frame (balloon) was maintained by gas pressure.

Specification Daimler H4L

Year:	1905/1906
Cylinder:	4 in-line
Cooling	Water
Bore:	175 mm
Stroke:	146 mm
Displacement:	14 l
Power (max./norm.):	105 hp
@ max. RPM	1100 RPM
Weight:	410 kg

Used in Parseval PL 2 (1908).

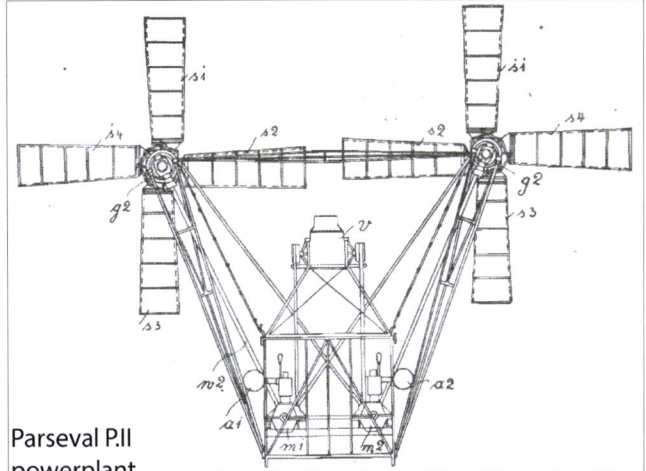

Parseval P.II powerplant installation, 2 Mercedes 90 hp, Type 4H4L.

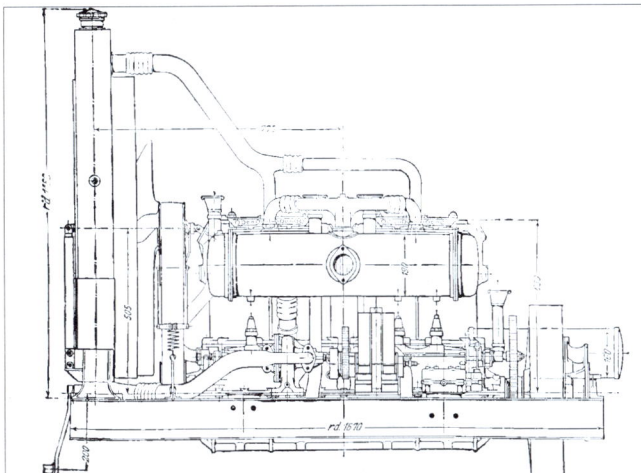

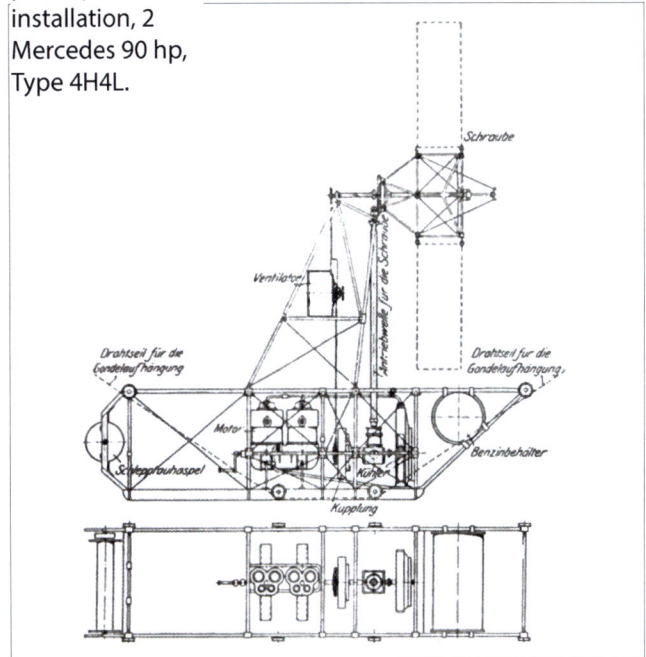

Above: Side view, exhaust side, M4L 115 hp airship engine.

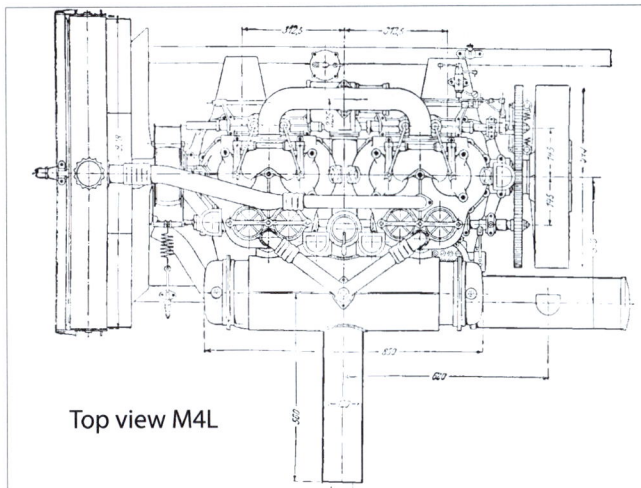

Top view M4L

Above: Parseval blimp in the air.

Above: Parseval car with engine prepared for test runs. [B32]

Above: Parseval P.II powerplant installation, 2 Mercedes 90 hp, Type 4H4L. [B25]

3.16.1l Four-Cylinder 110/100 hp Airship Engine M4L

The M4L engine was the first airship engine developed by Paul Daimler in 1907. The cylinders were cast in pairs from gray iron. The valves were controlled by pushrods. The M4L had a light alloy case, cast iron pistons, fresh oil central lubrication, a Mercedes Soden carburetor, low voltage breakaway dual ignition (2 separate ignition systems (low voltage ignition and high voltage ignition magnetos). Installed in the airship LZ 4. After the fire disaster of the airship LZ 3, the engine was overhauled and used again in LZ 5.

The basic design was taken over from the H4L, whereby the bore and stroke were increased up to 175 mm and 150 mm, respectively.

Two of these engines have been installed in airships like Zeppelin LZ 4 and LZ 5, but also in LZ 3 after its rebuilding.

As can be seen, they work with four cylinders cast in pairs, the cylinders themselves being made of grey cast iron, while the housing enclosing the crankshaft is made of cast aluminium.

The intake valves are located on the vertical axis of the cylinders directly above them, so that the steering has to be done by means of a crossbar and rocker arm.

Above: Mercedes 115/105 hp airship engine M4L.

Facing Page, Below: 115 hp M4L airship engine, carburetor side. [B15, V2]

Above: Forward gondola of the Reichsluftschiff Z II with built-in 100 hp Daimler engine. Clearly visible the exhaust pipe a, the power transmission shaft b-c, the ball bearing transmission at c and the three-bladed propeller, d. [M55]

Left: Carburetor and exhaust sides of Mercedes M4L engine, used initially in Zeppelin LZ IV. Later installed in LZ V.

Specification Daimler H4L

Year:	1907
Cylinder:	4 in-line
Cooling	Water
Bore:	175 mm
Stroke:	150 mm
Displacement:	14,4 l
Power (max./norm.):	100 hp
@ max. RPM	1200 RPM
Weight:	410 kg
Used in Zeppelin LZ4 and 5.	

3.16.1m Eight-Cylinder 110 hp Airship Engine M8L

In 1909 the Daimler Motoren Gesellschaft (DMG) offered an eight-cylinder in-line engine for the use in airships. To reach 240 hp two M4L engines have been combined in one. The engine with a bore of 175 mm and a stroke of 150 mm had a displacement of 28,8 liter.

It is not known whether such engine was in practical use. No drawings or pictures are available so far.

3.16.1n Four-Cylinder 70 hp Airship Engine T.H.

In 1908 this type won the tender of the Motorluftschiff-Studiengesellschaft. The basic design was similar to that of the M4L, but the geometric

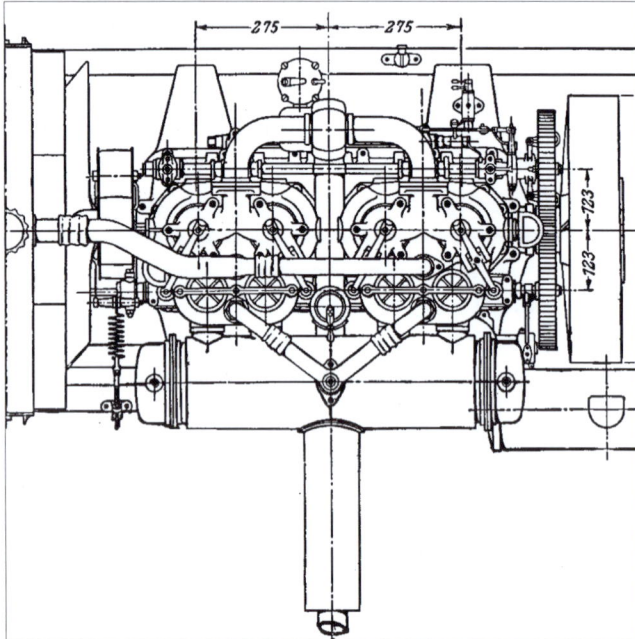

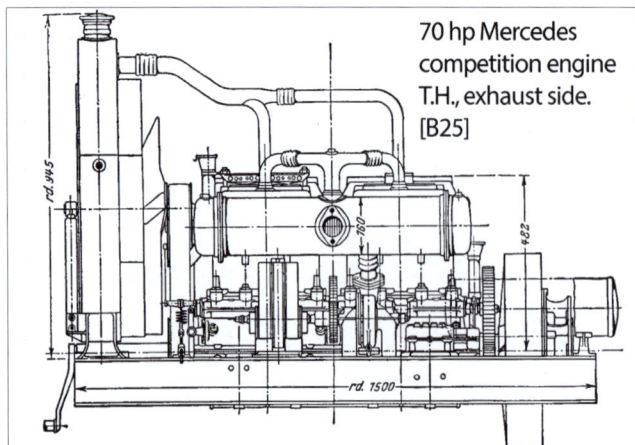

70 hp Mercedes competition engine T.H., exhaust side. [B25]

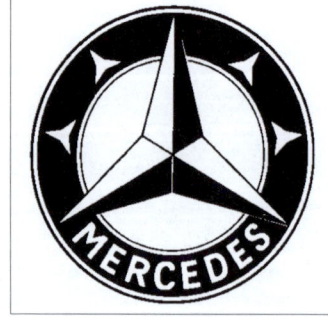

Specification Daimler T.H.

Year:	1907/1908
Cylinder:	4 in-line
Cooling	Water
Bore:	140 mm
Stroke:	129,8 mm
Displacement:	8,0 l
Power (max./norm.):	70/60 hp
@ max. RPM	1300/1200 RPM
Weight:	280 kg
Fuel consumption:	0,26 kg/hp/h

dimensions were smaller.

It can be assumed that this engine was built for competition only and no practical use was intended.

Left: Drawing of the DMG airship engine T.H., top view. 4 cylinders in a row, two cast together. Intake valves controlled by rocker arms on top, exhaust valves on the side.

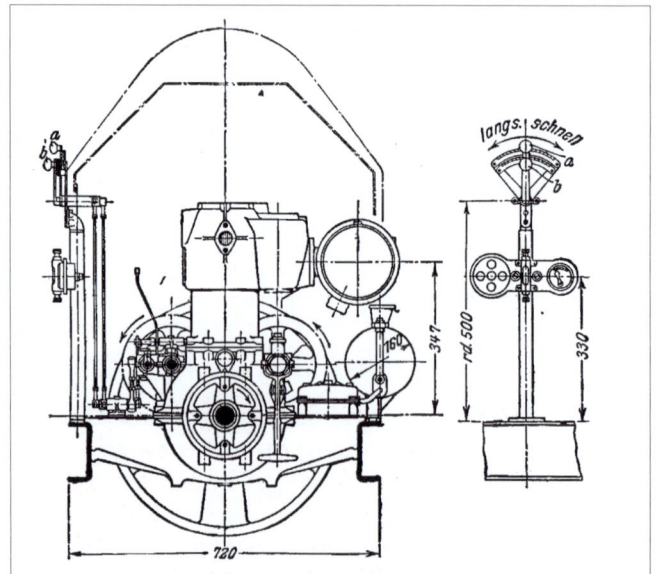

Above: Drawing of the airship engine, view from the front, on the right the oiler and regulating lever, radiator removed. [B25]

Above: 100 hp 4H4L used in both Zeppelin and Parseval airships. [J4, 1909]

Above: 100 hp 4H4L carburetor side. [J4, 1909]

Below: Dutch airship "*Duindigt*", equipped with 30 hp Mercedes engine (1909).

3.16.1o Four-Cylinder 30 hp Airship Engine B4L

The airship PL 5, which was constructed by the Motorluftschiff Studiengesellschaft in Berlin-Reinickendorf and built by LFG in Bitterfeld, represented the smallest type, and was primarily intended for private individuals and clubs. The test runs have shown that the ship, with a maximum diameter of 7,7 m, is about 40 m long and displaces

Specification Daimler B4L

Year:	1909
Cylinder:	4 in-line
Cooling:	Water
Bore:	90 mm
Stroke:	140 mm
Displacement:	3,6 l
Power (max./norm.):	30/25 hp
@ max. RPM	1200 RPM
Weight:	130 kg
Fuel consumption:	0,27 kg/hp/h

Used in Parseval PL 5 and Dutch airship *Dunidigt*.

1450 m³, and is capable of carrying three persons in addition to the sufficiently large amount of ballast at a speed of no less than 9 m/sec. for 6-7 hours.

The nacelle, which was composed of steel tubes, was designed as a framework structure with compression bars and tension rods. It offered space for four people with a length of 4.5 m, a width of 0.75 m and a frame height of 1 m. In the front part the guide has had place, at the rear end all mechanical equipment is arranged.

The 30 hp Daimler engine with four cylinders and about 1200 rpm, equipped with overhead valves with pushrod control, a Mercedes piston slide carburetor, consumed about 270 g gasoline for 1 hp/hour at full power. The ignition is provided by a high voltage magneto. The flywheel is designed as a radiator fan and at the same time as a pulley to drive the balloonet fan. The radiator is located behind the engine. The three-bladed screw of 3 m diameter, mounted on a trestle above the engine, is driven by a roller chain with a transmission ratio of approx. 4 : 1.

3.16.1p Four-Cylinder 50 hp Airship Engine E4L (L1244)

The "E" series airship engines discussed in this section are not part of the official "Mercedes-Benz" engine list. The smallest engine is a water-cooled 60/50 HP airship engine.

The cast iron cylinders were cast together in pairs. The inlet valve was controlled from above, the outlet valve from below. The flywheel was equipped with a spring band clutch.

In this 4-cylinder engine, the cylinders are arranged in pairs in a line next to each other. The cylinder heads are cast individually and bolted to the cylinders. The material chosen for the cylinders is grey cast iron, while the housing enclosing the crankshaft, which is divided in its longitudinal direction, is made of cast aluminium.

Ventilation of the housing is provided by vents at the front and rear, which are fitted with a mesh to make it more difficult for dirt to penetrate.

The screwed-on cylinder heads support the inlet valve seats, the oscillating lever bearings and the connection pieces for the gas mixture line and the cooling water line. The cooling water is fed through this latter line to the double walls of the working cylinders and cylinder heads. The cooling water is re-cooled by a so-called honeycomb cooler (Daimler patent), the effect of which is supported by an additional propeller which rotates directly behind the cooler and is driven from the crankshaft by means of a belt drive and tension pulley.

A patented Mercedes carburetor is used to

Specification Daimler E4L

Year:	1910
Cylinder:	4 in-line
Cooling	Water
Bore:	120 mm
Stroke:	140 mm
Displacement:	6,3 l
Power (max./norm.):	60/50 hp
@ max. RPM	1300/1200 RPM
Weight:	190 kg
Fuel consumption:	0,26 kg/hp/h

generate an explosive gas mixture. In this cooler the preheated primary and secondary air is sucked in through a common pipe and can be adjusted by means of regulating valves, actuated by the machine operator, so that it enters only as warm air from the heat pipe via the exhaust pipe or only as fresh air or also at any intermediate temperature. If the amount of mixture supplied is changed by moving the regulating piston via the mixture lever on the steering wheel, the amount of additional air supplied also changes at the same time.

The gas mixture is ignited by an electromagnetic Bosch ignition device.

The airship engines of the "E" series are complemented by the 6-cylinder E6L (L1246) engine and the eight-cylinder E8L (L1248).

It is not known in which airships these engines were used.

3.16.1q Six-cylinder 75 hp and 125 hp Airship Engines E6L (L1246) and E8L (L1248)

The E6L (also built in 1910) was a direct development of the E4L. This 6-cylinder engine had an output of 75 hp.

Using the assemblies already tested on the 6-cylinder E6L engine, a further 8-cylinder water-cooled airship engine with lower power output was tested, but not developed to production readiness. The E8L was created by combining two E4L engines.

Specification Daimler E8L

Year:	1910
Cylinder:	8 in-line
Cooling	Water
Bore:	120 mm
Stroke:	140 mm
Displacement:	12,7 l
Power (max./norm.):	140/125 hp
@ max. RPM	1350/1250 RPM

The engine was to deliver 140/125 hp at 1350/1250 rpm. The bore was as said 120 mm, the stroke was 140 mm.

The further development of this airship engine was abandoned in favour of aircraft engines.

3.16.1r Four-Cylinder 75 hp Airship Engine F4L

An F4L airship model is listed in Bruno Lange's book „*Typenhandbuch der deutschen Luftfahrttechnik*" as an four-cylinder airship engine. According to this book the engine produced 75 hp at 1150 min⁻¹ and is prescribed as a stronger version of the E4L.

According to the engine classification schematic this engine had a bore of 130 mm. More information is not given.

Example of engine designation between 1904 until 1912:

B 4 L

     L – airship, F – aeroplane
     4 -number of cylinder
     Bore in mm (see below)

Letter	B	C	D	E	F	G	H	J
Bore [mm]	90	100	105-110	120	130	140	160-165	170-175

3.16.1s Four-Cylinder 120 thru 150 hp Airship Engines J4L

The J4L engine was built in three variants, by keeping the same design but having different cylinder dimensions.

This four-cylinder Mercedes engine, known also

Specification Daimler E6L

Year:	1910
Cylinder:	6 in-line
Cooling	Water
Bore:	120 mm
Stroke:	140 mm
Displacement:	6,3 l
Power (max./norm.):	75 hp
@ max. RPM	1200 RPM

Above: J4L 125 hp engine presented in the Daimler-Benz-Museum in Stuttgart.

Above: Mercedes 120 hp engine for Zeppelin LZ6. [J9, 1910]

Above: Daimler 120 hp type J4L 1908, water-cooled muffler, Bosch high-voltage plug ignition. [A1]

Above: Mercedes J4L carburetor side. [A1]

Above: Mercedes airship engine J4L, 150 PS, 1909, bore/stroke: 175 mm/172 mm, carburetor modified. [A1]

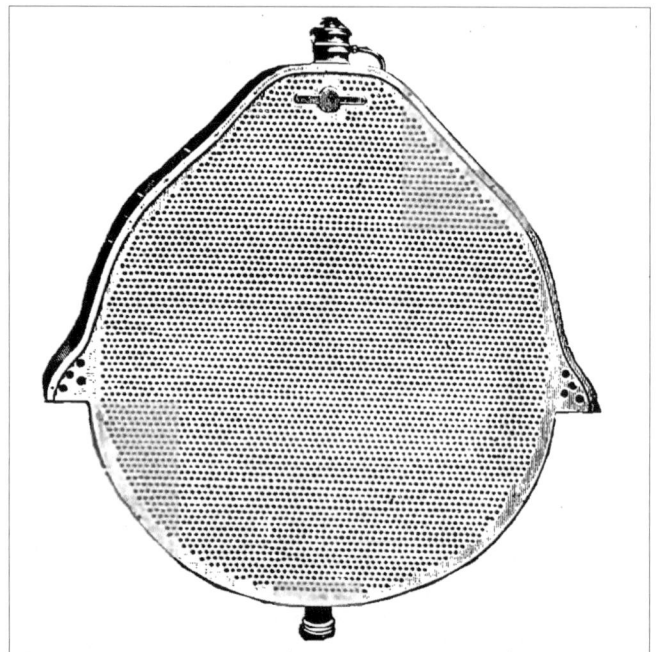

Above: Engine honeycomb-type radiator (built at Basse & Selve) for use on airships. [J8, 1911]

in the literature as Type 4J4L, had a 175 mm bore, 160 thru 172 mm stroke, and a total displacement of up to 16,6 litres. The most powerful variant was rated to 150 hp at 1200 rpm and said to weigh 320 kg. The cylinders were constructed in pairs from cast-iron, and one inlet and two exhaust valves, standing vertically in each cylinder head, were operated by means of push rods and rockers.

The four-cylinder (4)J4L engine was used in airships from 1908, including the Zeppelin passenger airships LZ 6 to LZ 8. With its good power-to-weight ratio of 3 kg/hp, overhead camshaft and Bosch high-voltage ignition, it was a very modern engine.

The engine was started by hand using a normal crank handle. By moving the control shaft, auxiliary cams are placed under the exhaust valve spindles, thus reducing compression in the cylinders and

Above: J4L 125hp in Siemens-Schuckert airship SSW1 first take-off. [J8, 1911]

making starting easier.

The non-encapsulated gears on the control and ignition shaft are located near the flywheel and are made of fibre, while the gear on the crankshaft is made of steel. The gear wheel on the ignition shaft contains the Regulator attached.

The suction valves are very large and are actuated by rocker arms, which receive their movement from push rods from the control shaft mounted in the crankcase. The rods are connected to the rocker arms and to the pushrods by ball joints. The exhaust valves are normally actuated directly from the

Above: Siemens-Schuckert-Werke SSW 1 airship in the air (First Take-off).
Facing Page, Below: Airship gondola of Siemens-Schuckert SSW1 equipped with Mercedes J4L, large radiator, exhaust pipes, small 4-blade propeller. [J8, 1911]

Specification Daimler J4L

Year:	1908
Cylinder:	4 in-line
Cooling	Water
Bore:	175 mm
Stroke:	160 mm
Displacement:	15,4 l
Power (max./norm.):	120 hp
@ max. RPM	1100 RPM
Weight:	320 kg

Used in Zeppelin LZ 6, Siemens-Schurkert SS1, Mercedes racing car 1910, ship engine.

Specification Daimler J4L

Year:	1908
Cylinder:	4 in-line
Cooling	Water
Bore:	175 mm
Stroke:	165 mm
Displacement:	15,9 l
Power (max./norm.):	139 hp
@ max. RPM	1200 RPM
Weight:	320 kg

Used in Zeppelin LZ 6 (after remodelling), different other airships.

Specification Daimler J4L

Year:	1909/1910
Cylinder:	4 in-line
Cooling	Water
Bore:	175 mm
Stroke:	172 mm
Displacement:	16,6 l
Power (max./norm.):	150 hp
@ max. RPM	1200 RPM
Weight:	320 kg
Fuel consumption:	0,245 kg/hp/h

Used in Zeppelin LZ 8, PL 8, and Veeh.

control shaft by means of pistons.

The Mercedes airship carburetor differs from the usual carburetors for cars in that it operates without additional air. The "air" sucked in by the engine is passed through the muffler in front of the carburetor and thus preheated effectively.

The very short, casted exhaust pipe leads into a muffler directly attached to the engine, which is cooled with water with respect to the inflammable balloon gases. This ensures that the exhaust gases are discharged at low temperature.

The spark ignition, which is common to all Mercedes engines, is fed by a low-voltage magnetic inductor (Bosch system).

The cooling water is kept in motion by a centrifugal pump. The pump and solenoid are driven by a common shaft, which receives its rotation from the control shaft through a pair of spur gears located in the centre of the motor housing. The water is fed to the so-called honeycomb type water cooler ("Bienenwabenkühler"), behind which a three-bladed fan with wide blade surfaces is arranged; it is moved by the crankshaft through a belt which can be tensioned by a roller.

The engine is provided with central lubrication, which is operated from the control shaft.

a) 120 hp J4L

Further development by Paul Daimler, first with Bosch high-voltage spark plug ignition; overhead valves with pushrod control. First used in the LZ 6 airship (1908/09). After its conversion in 1910, the more powerful version of the J4L (139 hp) was installed.

b) 139 hp J4L

The increase in stroke by 5 mm led to a power increase

of 19 hp. Same design as the predecessor engine.

c) 150 hp J4L

Third variant with further increased stroke (172 mm). The engine reached 150 hp.

3.16.1t Six-Cylinder 150 hp Airship Engines J6L

This engine is part of the production list provided by the Daimler-Benz Museum Stuttgart. This engine was developed in 1908 as a derivative of the smaller J4L with a Stroke of 160 mm. According to the a.m. list this engine developed 150 hp at 1100 rpm.

3.16.1u Eight-Cylinder 240 hp Airship Engines J8L

In January 1913 the British magazine "Flight" reported on new airship engines, including an 8-cylinder Mercedes engine with 240 hp. In fact, DMG took advantage of their positive experience with the J4L engine by combining two of these engines into one overall propulsion system.

Indeed, Gottlieb Daimler had died in the meantime and Maybach had left Daimler Motorengesellschaft, DMG developed its most powerful airship engine under the direction of Paul Daimler, Gottlieb Daimler's eldest son. An engine of 240/225 hp was developed, two of which were used in the airship Schütte-Lanz SL1 and thus provided the airship with 480 hp.

The rotational speed of the crankshaft was 1100 rpm. The fuel consumption was 220 g/hp/h. Each cylinder had two exhaust valves and one intake valve; in the crankcase an eight-cranked crankshaft is supported in white metal shells at 6 points; two cylinders each form a common casting with a common water jacket.

The regulation of the revolutions is effected by a regulator, which can be adjusted in such a way that the number of revolutions and the power can be varied within narrow limits.

The circulation of the cooling water is effected by two centrifugal pumps, which are dimensioned so large that a very extensive cooling can take place. Temperature sensors are also installed in the cooling water pipes so that the temperature of the cooling water can be checked at the thermometers at any time. Piston cooling is provided to prevent any possibility of malfunction.

The exhaust was on the right side. The gas-air-mixture was produced in a double carburetor, which was located on the left side of the engine. Cylinders 1, 2, 7 and 8 as well as cylinders 3, 4, 5 and 6 were each supplied by one carburetor part. The carburetor

Above: 240 hp Mercedes 8-cylinder airship engine J8L, carburetor side. [J9, 1912]

Above: 240 hp Mercedes 8-cylinder airship engine J8L, exhaust side. [J9, 1912]

itself was controlled manually by a hand lever and additionally by a flywheel. The latter was done to keep the engine speed constant by adjusting the control pistons.

Each cylinder had two spark plugs, which received their current through twin Eisemann magnetos. These magnetos were driven by two flexible

Above: J8L engine fixed to a propeller on a test bench.

Specification Daimler J8L

Year:	1912
Cylinder:	8 (2 x 4) in-line
Cooling	Water
Bore:	175 mm
Stroke:	165 mm
Displacement:	31,6 l
Power (max./norm.):	260/240 hp
@ max. RPM	1200/1100 RPM
Weight:	780 kg
Fuel consumption:	0,245 kg/hp/h

Used in Schütte-Lanz SL 1.

couplings of shafts of two centrifugal pumps with double impellers installed on the left side of the engine. The order of ignitions is 1, 5, 2, 6, 4, 8, 3, 7, since two normal 4-cylinder crankshafts are in series, the second of which is offset 90 degrees from the first.

To reduce the risk of fire, the mufflers were water-cooled.

For larger individual engines with more than 150 hp, starting devices were absolutely necessary. These additional aggregates were not of great importance compared to the overall system. For example, the 240 hp 8-cylinder engine for the Schütte airship with such a device, which weighed only about 9-10 kg including the manual ignition device. The gas-air-mixture was fed to 2 cylinders by means of a hand mix pump with the appropriate adjustment of the engine and then ignited by means of a manual ignition device.

Eisemann-Ignition system

In order to solve the problem of automatic ignition moment adjustment, the Eisemann company

Below: Schütte-Lanz airship, aft powerplant gondola. [J4, 1911]

used several patents from abroad as early as 1905, which had nothing to do with the automatic part of the ignition adjustment but solved the problem constructively.

With the earlier Eisemann igniters, the plunger had to be brought into a certain position to the pole shoes by manually pulling a lever. This was done from the operator's seat (engine operator), which in turn required a complicated linkage from the magneto to the control panel. If the armature was not in its optimal position, this made it difficult to start the motor, or even led to injuries to the mechanic while the motor was being started-up by hand.

This operation, which up to now had to be carried out by the machine operator according to his own feeling, was carried out by a small weight regulator on the drive axle of the new Eisemann magneto apparatus. Depending on the increase in engine speed, the armature connected to the regulator shifted in the direction of pre-ignition, and as soon as less fuel was supplied to the engine, it automatically adjusted itself back to post-ignition. In this way the adjustment of the ignition point was exactly

Right: Schütte-Lanz airship SL I under construction. [J4, 1911]

Below: SL I airship forward motor gondola with 8-cylinder Mercedes 8J8L installed. [B26]

Above: 240 hp Mercedes 8-cylinder airship engine J8L (with gear) as delivered for SL 1 airship. [B35]

Above: Improved Eisemann magneto Modell 1910 with automatic ignition time control. [J9, 1910]

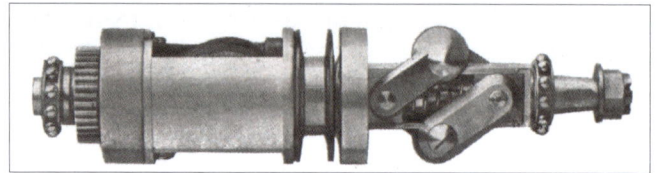

Above: Magnetic Anchor together with regulator. [J9, 1910]

Above: Advertisment Eisemann ignition. [J9, 1911]

Above: Mercedes J8L installed in Schütte-Lanz airship SL 1. [B26]

proportional to the engine speed.

As a result, engine operation was enormously simplified, fuel consumption was reduced, and a smoother running of the engine was achieved.

3.16.1v Six-Cylinder 200 hp Airship Engines H6L (L1676)

In 1913 and 1915, Daimler Motoren-Gesellschaft, under the management of Paul Daimler, expanded its range of engines for airships by adding further 6-cylinder in-line engines for airships by combining proven double-cylinder modules to form 6-cylinder engines. In the meantime, DMG had already been quite successful as a supplier for aircraft engines. However, these airship engines were no longer so successful, for in the meantime Maybach had successfully conquered the airship market by founding "Luftfahrzeug-Motorenbau G.m.b.H." in Bissingen on the Enz together with the Count of Zeppelin, and "Luftschiffbau Zeppelin" procured its engines exclusively from Maybach.

The Information about these engines is very poor because they were not used practically airships.

Above: 160 hp Mercedes 6-cylinder experimental engine (L1676), first edition.

Above: 160 hp Mercedes 6-cylinder experimental engine (L1676), first edition, exhaust side. [B12]

The development on further airships ended at this stage. Paul Daimler and his engineering staff concentrated exclusively on aircraft engines.

Left: 160 hp Mercedes 6-cylinder experimental engine (L1676), first edition. [A1]

Specification Daimler H6L

Year:	1913
Cylinder:	6 in-line
Cooling	Water
Bore:	160 mm
Stroke:	170 mm
Displacement:	20,5 l
Power (max./norm.):	200/185 hp
@ max. RPM	1200/1100 RPM
Weight:	470 kg
Used in Schütte-Lanz airships.	

Above: L1676, Second edition, with twin magneto.

| Type | T/O Power | RPM | Cylinder | | | Displ. [L.] | Wt. [kg] | Year | Remarks & Information |
			No.	Bore, mm	Stroke, mm				
	2	720	1	80	120	0,6		1888	Built into a steerable balloon of the bookseller Dr. Wölfert, Leipzig
P 1890	5,9	590	4	80	120	2,4	210	1890	Built into a large balloon by Dr. Wölfert and in the airship Schwarz (first rigid airship)
	10	590	8	80	120	4,8		1891	Built into a large balloon by Dr. Wölfert
P 1895/96	12,9	670	4	110	160	6,08	320	1895/1896	Built into a large balloon and in the aluminium airship from Schwarz in Agram (2,12 hp/l)
P 1896	7,1	535	2	104	160	2,7	140	1896	Airship "Deutschland" Wölfert (2,63 hp/l)
Sch 1891	2,6	660	2	75	120	1,1	152	1891	Dr. Wölfert, airship test trials 1895
N 1898	12	670	4	90	130	3,3	320	1898	Used for test trials on a boat for first airship from Graf Zeppelin; low voltage breakaway ignition; water-cooled exhaust manifold due to fire hazard on board of airships.
N 1899 [NL 1]	16	700	4	100	140	4,4	325	1899	Zeppelin LZ 1 (20 kg/hp)
N 1899	8	700	2	100	140	2,2	153	1899	Trials at Militär-Luftschiff-Abteilung
N 1899	33	950	4	116	140	5,9	230	1900/1901	Kress aeroplane
	40	1260	4	116	140	5,9	230	1901/1902	French airship Lebaudy
[E4L] [L1244]	60	1200	4	120	140	6,3	190	1910	Inlet valve top controlled, outlet valve bottom controlled
[E6L] [L1246]	75		6	120	140	9,5		1910	
[E8L] [L1248]			8	120	140	12,7			2 x E4L
H4L	90	1050	4	165	140	12,0	360	1904/05	LZ 2, LZ 3
	105	1100	4	175	146	14,0	410	1905/06	Parseval airships PLa, PLb, PL 1, PL 2

Summary of Daimler/Mercedes Airship Engines (Source: Daimler-Benz-Museum, Stuttgart)

Summary of Daimler/Mercedes Airship Engines (Source: Daimler-Benz-Museum, Stuttgart) (continued)									
Type	T/O Power	RPM	Cylinder			Displ. [L.]	Wt. [kg]	Year	Remarks & Information
			No.	Bore, mm	Stroke, mm				
Grand Prix 1907 [M4L]	110	1200	4	175	150	14,4	410	1907	LZ 4, LZ 5: Light metal housing, cast iron pistons, fresh oil central lubrication, two separate ignition systems (low voltage ignition and high voltage ignition magnetos). After the fire catastrophe the engine was overhauled and reused in the LZ 5.
TH 1907/08 [F4L]	60 [85/75]	1200 [1050]	4 [4]	140 [140]	129,8 [130]	8,0	280	1907/08	Competition Motorluftschiff-Studiengesellschaft
	140	1100	6	165	140	18,0	475	1908	Airship engine
	150	1100	6	175	160	25,0		1908	Airship engine
	120	1100	4	175	160	16,0	320	1908/07	LZ 6, SS 1, Mercedes race car 1910, aluminium pistons
J4L	139	1200	4	175	160	16,1	368	1908	LZ 6 (repair), SS 1, SL 1
B4L	30	1400	4	90	140	3,6	130	1909	Parseval PL 5, Dutch airship "Duindigt", Luftfahrzeug-Ges. Bitterfeld (4 kg/hp)
J4L	135	1200	4	175	165	16,1		1908/09	LZ 7, Luftfahrzeug-Ges. Bitterfeld
J4L	150	1200	4	175	172	16,5		1909/10	LZ 8, PL 8, airship "Veeh"
J8L L175/658	360	1200	8	175	165	31,7		1910/11	Installed in Schütte-Lanz SL 1. 1 inlet valve, 2 outlet valves per cylinder; fresh oil lubrication.
H6L L1676	200	1200	6	160	170		430		2 variants built, 2,1 kg/hp; Schütte-Lanz
J6L L1246	190	1100	6	124	140				Modified D I engine
L1248	140	1350	8	120	140				Combination of two 4-cylinder engines

Notes:
1) Cursive written data/information were added by author.
2) In some literature the names of the engines are also written with 4 digits, e.g. B4L = 4B4L or J8L = 8J8L.

Daimler Motoren Gesellschaft Aircraft Engines

Left: 50 hp 4-cylinder watercooled aeroengine for Fiedler's monoplane. [J9, 1910]

Below: Mercedes test engine system Schiske; 4-cylinder radial engine. Built by Daimler, had two counter-rotating thumbshafts instead of the crankshaft and therefore counter-rotating propellers. [A1]

With the leaving of Maybach and the foundation of Maybach Motorenbau GmbH in Friedrichshafen, the development of further aircraft engines was initially suspended. In addition to the already mentioned 35/25 hp 4-cylinder in-line engine (model N1899) for the Austrian aviator Wilhelm Kreß, Daimler Motoren-Gesellschaft did not attempt to build engines for aircraft again until around 1908/09. The first step was an experimental engine based on the patent of the Schiske spark plug factory in Vienna. This 4-cylinder radial engine developed 20 hp. Although the two opposing "thumbshafts" made it possible to realize a non-reactive operation, this concept was not pursued further and logically one returned to the construction methods commonly used in automobile and airship construction.

The real restart in the aircraft engine business began in 1909 with the construction of a 30 hp 4-cylinder in-line engine.

The construction of this 30 hp water-cooled in-line engine (model B4F) with a piston diameter of 90 mm and a stroke of 140 mm had a weight of about 130 kg.

3.16.2 Four-cylinder 160 hp in-line aircraft engine (J4F)

As previously mentioned, around 1900 Daimler Motoren Gesellschaft supplied the Austrian Kress with a 5.9-liter four-cylinder aircraft engine of 33 hp derived from an automobile. A little later Daimler also offered his J4L airship engine to the

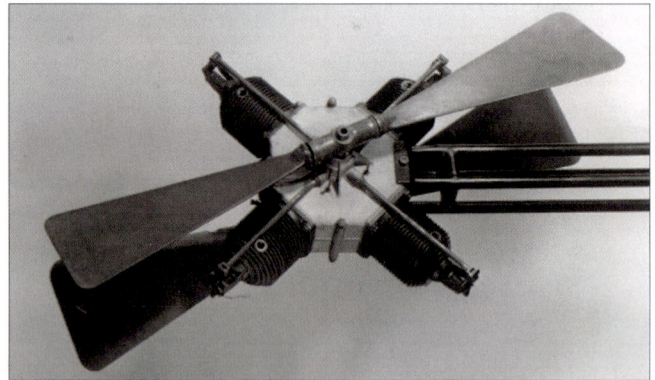

Above: 125 hp in-line engine, developed in 1908/09. This engine was rejected by the military administration due to the high power. [A1]

Engine Datasheet	
Daimler Motoren Gesellschaft, Stuttgart-Untertürkheim	
Designation	**Mercedes 160 hp 4 cylinder in-line (J4F)**
Year:	1908/09
Purpose:	Aircraft engine
Number of Cylinders:	4
Arrangement of Cylinders:	Inline piston engine
Bore [mm]:	175
Stroke [mm]:	165
Displacement [l]:	15,9
Compression [Ratio]	
RPM [min-1]: norm./max.	1600
Power [hp]: norm./max.	160
Power per displacement [hp/l]:	7,9
Carburetor(s)	
No.:	1
Type:	
Fuel consumption per hp per hour [g]:]	240
Oil Pump	
No.:	
Oil consumption per hp per hour [g/PS/h]:	15
Ignition No.:	
Type:	
Firing order:	
Cooling	Water
Weight of complete engine (dry) & ext. masses	
Total [kg]:	290
Weight per displacement [kg/l]:	17,6
Weight per hp [kg/hp]:	2,24
Remarks:	

test department of the transport troops with minor modifications as the J4F aircraft engine with up to 160 hp take-off power. What was not expected: this engine was rejected because of too high performance. A few years later the Benz company with its Bz DV (for further information see section 3.11) suffered the same fate.

The first four-cylinder Mercedes engine, known as Type J4F, had a 175 mm bore, 165 mm stroke, and a total displacement of 15,9 litre. This engine was rated 125 hp at 1100 rpm, and said to weigh 290 kg, or 2,24 kg per rated hp. The consumption of fuel and

Above: 125 hp aero-engine J4L, exhaust view. [A1]

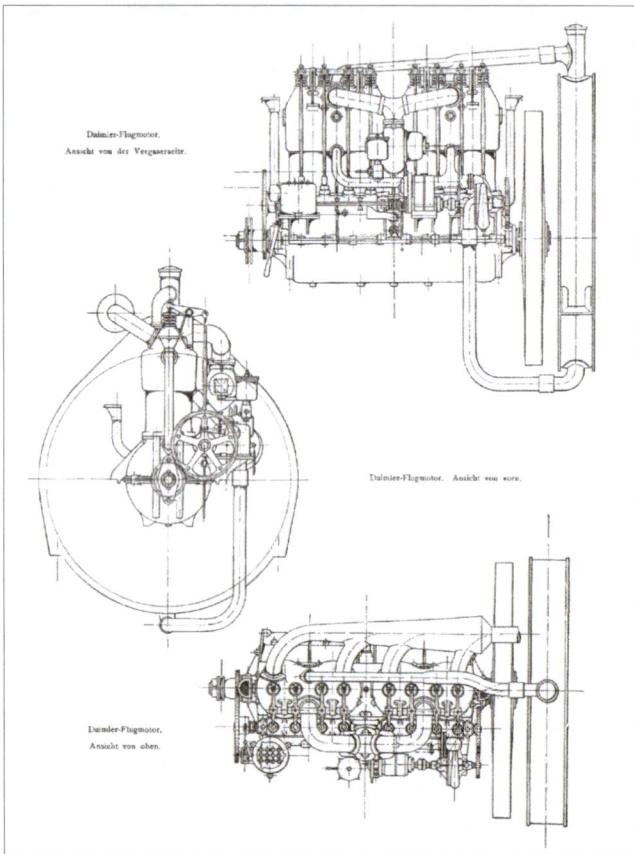

Above: Drawing of Mercedes J4F. [J8, 1910]

oil was reported as 240 grams and 15 grams per hp-hr, respectively. The cylinders were constructed in pairs from cast-iron, and one inlet and two exhaust valves, standing vertically in each cylinder head, were operated by means of push rods and rockers.

The basic design is the same as of the airship engine J4L and similar to the "Simplex"-automotive-engine.

All moving parts are located on the carburetor side of the engine. Inlet and exhaust valves are driven by a common control shaft. The valves are opened by means of push rods and rocker arms. The valves are inserted through the cylinder from below because experience shows that even with the usual arrangement of inserting the exhaust valves, the cylinders had to be removed anyway when replacing the exhaust valves.

To vent the housing, 3 vent pipes are foreseen, the openings of which are protected against the penetration of debris by wire meshes.

The control shaft was laterally movable in order to bring the lifting rollers of the valve rods under the auxiliary cams sitting on the shaft, which prevent the exhaust valves from closing completely and thus make a strong compression impossible. This decompression device is activated by a hand lever when the engine is to be started. During regular operation, this decompression device is not in operation.

3.16.3 Four-cylinder 60/50 hp in-line aero-engine (F 1144, D4F)

Paul Daimler, Gottfried Daimler had passed away in the meantime, and his engineers were aware that with aircraft engines, in addition to reliability, the dead weight in particular had to be taken into account to an even greater extent than with airship engines. Just as important and justified was the requirement to ensure that the associated equipment, such as the ignition system, oil pump, cooling water pump and carburetor, were accommodated as inexpensively as possible due to the limited space available in the aircraft.

With the D4F, DMG also developed the first true aircraft engine in which the above-mentioned requirements were solved to satisfaction.

The Mercedes engine fleet series starts with a 50 hp four-cylinder engine (see also the pre-series model, delivered to Mr. Fiedler), which already has a larger oil reservoir for several hours of operation in the engine housing. The control shaft on the side has still open spur gear drive from the rear end of the crankshaft. The magnetic dynamo (magneto) and pump are located next to the engine one behind the other and are also driven from the control shaft by overhead gears. Recirculating lubrication is compulsory; part of the oil lines is still outside the crankcase, exposed to the air flow, and can therefore easily freeze. The carburetor with water heating has relieved rotary slide valves, forced main and secondary air supply.

The D4F had been successfully used until 1912

Above: D4F, 50 hp Mercedes 4-cylinder engine, version as tested in the Kaiserpreis competion 1912. [B36, 1912–13]

Above: D4F, view from behind on magneto, valve control linkages. [B36, 1912–13]

Engine Datasheet	
Daimler Motoren Gesellschaft, Stuttgart-Untertürkheim	
Designation	**Mercedes 60/50 hp 4 cylinder in-line (D4F)**
Year:	1909/12
Purpose:	Aircraft engine
Number of Cylinders:	4
Arrangement of Cylinders:	Inline piston engine
Bore [mm]:	110
Stroke [mm]:	140
Displacement [l]:	5,3
Compression [Ratio]	
RPM [min-1]: norm./max.	1200/1400
Power [hp]: norm./max.	50/60
Power per displacement [hp/l]:	11,1
Carburetor(s)	
No.:	1
Type:	
Fuel consumption per hp per hour [g]:]:	224
Oil Pump	
No.:	
Oil consumption per hp per hour [g/PS/h]:	13
Ignition No.:	
Type:	
Firing order:	
Cooling	Water
Weight of complete engine (dry) & ext. masses	
Total [kg]:	173
Weight per displacement [kg/l]:	23,7
Weight per hp [kg/hp]:	2,5
Remarks: Company designation: F 1144.	

Above: D4F (F1144) 55hp Mercedes engine. [A1]

Left: D4F, 50 hp Mercedes 4-cylinder engine, one of the most popular pre-war engines. [A1]

in various aircraft types of Albatros, Otto, and many others. The E4F, an engine of the same basic design, appeared in 1911 as the successor engine.

3.16.4 Four-Cylinder 65/70 hp In-line Aero-Engine (F1244, E4F)

The 70 hp engine has four-cylinders with a bore of 120 mm and a stroke of 140 mm. Its normal output at 1250 - 1400 rpm is 65 - 70 hp, the total weight is approx. 125 kg.

The structural design already shows a much smoother construction.

The cylinders are cast together in pairs in the conventional form one behind the other and are provided with cooling water chambers. Each cylinder has one inlet and one outlet valve, which are installed vertically above the piston. The valves are actuated by a common control shaft with the help of push rods and rocker arms and a coil spring arranged above each valve. The front gear drive of the control shaft is installed between the pairs of cylinders.

The mixture is formed by a Mercedes rotary vane carburetor with adjustable hot water heating, which results in relatively low fuel consumption at high

Above: Mercedes aero-engine E4F, 1910 (F1244) 70 PS, First variant of E4F with front solenoid actuation, hanging valves with push-rod actuation. [A1]

Above: E4F from 1910, the Bosch magneto is very remarkable. [A1]

Above: Hellmut Hirth on Rumpler-Etrich-Taube with Daimler engine before departure to Munich. [J3, 1911]

Mercedes-Daimler-Motoren

für

Luftschiffe und Flugmaschinen

Gewinner des Kathreinerpreises im Fernflug München-Berlin

70 PS Mercedes-Flieger-Motor

Anerkannt bester Deutscher Fliegermotor im Deutschen Rundflug

Daimler-Motoren-Gesellschaft

Stuttgart-Untertürkheim.

✳

Prospekt und Preislisten stehen Interessenten gerne zur Verfügung.

Above: Advertisment 1911. [J3, 1911]

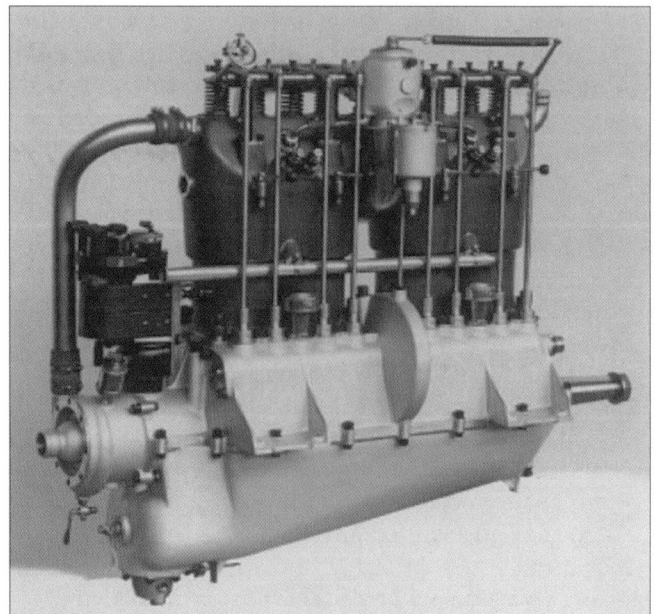

Right: 69 hp 4-cylinder Mercedes E4F (Model 1912), The lower part of the engine bay of this engine already has the typical central pointed shape of the next 6-cylinder engines. [A1]

Right: Example of engine installation (pusher) on Albatros Militär-Doppeldecker (biplane). [J6, 1912]

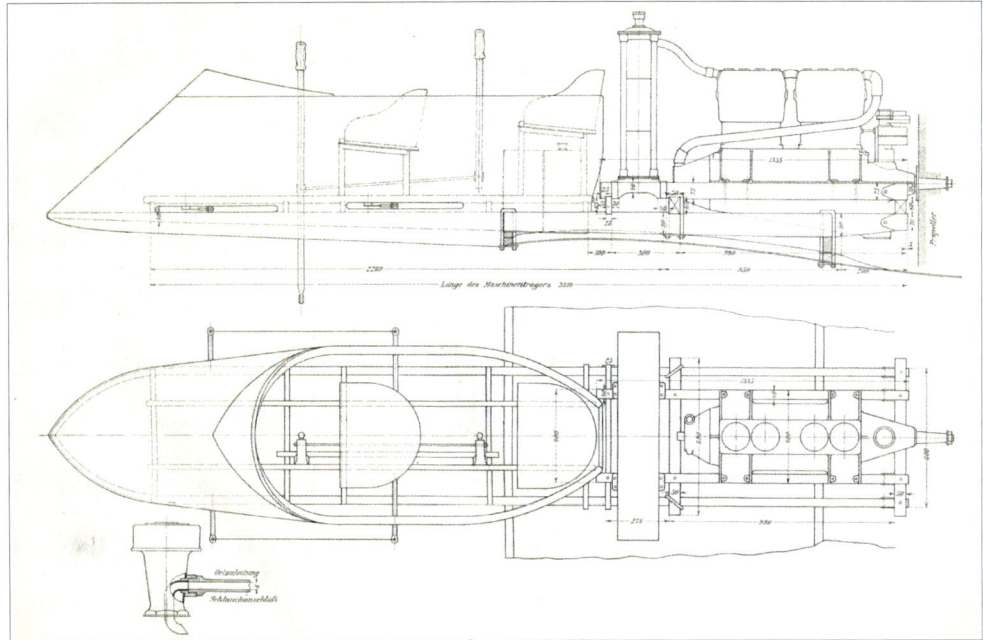

Right: Mercedes 70 hp 4-cylinder aeroengine E4F (Model 1911), Hirth won the Kathreiner Prize on his Taube equipped with this E4F engine. [J6, 1912]

Above: 70 hp 4-cylinder Mercedes E4F (Model 1912), The lower part of the engine bay of this engine already has the typical central pointed shape of the next 6-cylinder engines. [B36]

Above: Carburetor side of 70 hp Mercedes E4F (Model 1912), E4F like participated on the Kaiser-Preis competition in 1912. [B36]

Engine Datasheet	
Daimler Motoren Gesellschaft, Stuttgart-Untertürkheim	
Designation	**Mercedes 70/65 hp 4 cylinder in-line (E4F)**
Year:	1910
Purpose:	Aircraft engine
Number of Cylinders:	4
Arrangement of Cylinders:	Inline piston engine
Bore [mm]:	120
Stroke [mm]:	140
Displacement [l]:	6,4
Compression [Ratio]	
RPM [min-1]: norm./max.	1250/1350
Power [hp]: norm./max.	65/70
Power per displacement [hp/l]:	11,0
Carburetor(s)	
No.:	1
Type:	Mercedes rotary valve carburetor
Fuel consumption per hp per hour [g]:]:	230
Oil Pump	
No.:	1
Oil consumption per hp per hour [g/PS/h]:	15–20
Ignition No.:	1 HT magneto
Type:	System Eisemann or Bosch
Firing order:	
Cooling	Water
Weight of complete engine (dry) & ext. masses	
Total [kg]:	142
Weight per displacement [kg/l]:	20,5
Weight per hp [kg/hp]:	1,9
Remarks: Built in several variants between 1910 and 1912. Applications*: Albatros WMZ.2, Euler B.I. * Listing has no claim to completeness!	

Above: Mercedes E4F at the Deutsche Technikmuseum Berlin. [Author]

Above: Engine detail: valve springs on E4F. [Author]

Above: Side view of 70 hp 4-cylinder Merceeds E4F (1912). [A1]

rpm and high output. Ignition was by means of a high-voltage magnet with automatic ignition torque adjustment system Eisemann.

The control shaft drives encapsulated spur gears located between the pairs of cylinders, leaving both ends of the motor free for driving the auxiliary devices and direct attachment of the propeller. This is also where the arrangement of two magnetos and water pump at the rear of the engine, as well as the crankcase, which is recessed towards the middle of the engine, where it carries compulsory lubricating oil pumps, are found. The smaller one is for fresh oil, the larger one for circulating oil. Both pumps press into a common distribution line, which is isolated from the cold air flow inside the crankcase. The carburetor is located much higher, which saves on piping, but at the same time virtually eliminates the possibility of fuel supply under natural gradient in the aircraft. Although the weight of this motor

has been significantly reduced, in order to ensure reliable and safe operation, all bearing points and friction surfaces are so generously dimensioned that rapid wear was not to be feared. Special care has been taken in the design of the sealing points of the cooling water pipes and the cooling water jackets on the cylinders, so that in this respect too, a disruption of operation was almost impossible.

The motors were mainly used in the Rumpler Tauben, with which Hellmuth Hirth was successful in several competitions, thus ensuring the popularity of this motor.

It should be mentioned that the London-based company Messrs. Milnes-Mercedes, a public limited company in which Daimler holds a majority stake, took over the distribution of this engine, as well as that of a 6-cylinder engine (DF80), in Great Britain.

3.16.5 Four-Cylinder 65/70 hp In-line Aircraft Engine (E4uF)

In 1912, Daimler Motoren-Gesellschaft (DMG) competed for the Kaiserpreis for the best German aircraft engine with a total of 7 different aircraft engines. Two of these engines, unlike all the others, had inverted cylinders.

With this design, the Daimler company had made the remarkable attempt to run their 65 hp four-cylinder E4F engine in a suspended position, i.e. with the cylinders pointing downwards. This was intended to achieve a number of advantages: on the one hand a clear view for pilots and observers, and on the other hand a lower position for the aircraft's centre of gravity. The carburetor, which was now located quite low, also made it easier to supply fuel under natural gravity; the cooling water supply was also more favourable, because the hottest parts of the cylinder were located lowest, i.e. in the coldest water, and any steam bubbles could escape upwards

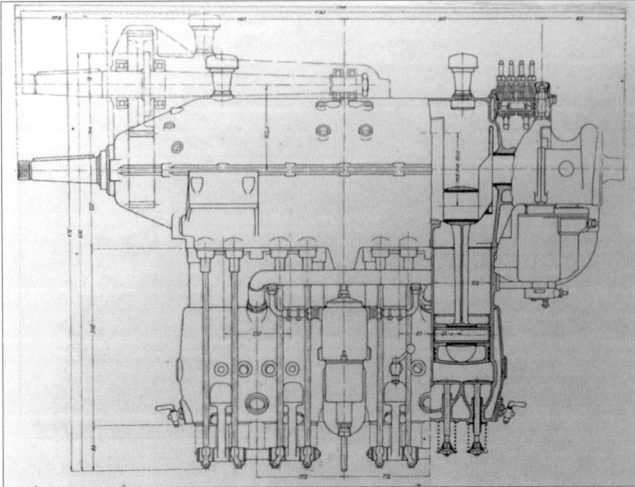

Above: Mercedes 65 hp aero-engines (E4uF variant with higher positioned prop shaft shown as dotted line). [J6, 1913]

Above: Mercedes E4uF 65 hp 4-cylinder aeroengine, carburetor side. [B36, 1912–13]

Above: Mercedes E4uF variant with gear box, carburetor side. [B36, 1912–13]

Above: Mercedes E4uF 65 hp 4-cylinder aeroengine, right side. [B36, 1912–13]

unhindered. Finally, the aircraft crew was no longer bothered by the exhaust fumes and the oil that was now ejected deep down.

The main influence of this innovation is the lubrication. The crankcase, which has been converted into an oil reservoir, has been replaced by a straight one; the recirculating lubrication has been replaced by pure fresh oil lubrication, and a four-way distributor leads oil to all bearings as well as to the cylinder sliding surfaces. The repeated use of the oil, as with recirculating lubrication, is therefore no longer necessary. However, this would not even be necessary with other types of crankcase design; the relatively high oil consumption of this engine is therefore by no means an unavoidable disadvantage of the suspended design.

The water pump was directly linked to the crankshaft, and the magnet was located under the crankshaft. It is worth noting that the spark plugs have not failed due to oiling, as was often feared with the suspended design. No particular disadvantages of the suspended design have been mentioned.

With the second engine of the same design and performance, they have gone one important step further. The inverted motor is equipped with a gear shaft for the propeller, which has a slow transmission ratio. This aims to increase the motor speed, i.e. to get more performance output from the given motor weight, and to reduce the speed of the propeller to improve its efficiency. The flywheel, which was otherwise considered necessary with a geared propeller drive, has been abandoned; this also seems to be proving its worth; no technical problems whatsoever were encountered during the tests.

Considerations were made to let a machine gun

Engine Datasheet	
Daimler Motoren Gesellschaft, Stuttgart-Untertürkheim	
Designation	**Mercedes 70/65 hp 4 cylinder in-line (E4uF)**
Year:	1911
Purpose:	Aircraft engine
Number of Cylinders:	4
Arrangement of Cylinders:	Inline piston engine
Bore [mm]:	120
Stroke [mm]:	140
Displacement [l]:	6,4
Compression [Ratio]	
RPM [min-1]: norm./max.	1250/1350
Power [hp]: norm./max.	65/70
Power per displacement [hp/l]:	10,3
Carburetor(s)	
No.:	1
Type:	
Fuel consumption per hp per hour [g]:]:	230
Oil Pump	
No.:	
Oil consumption per hp per hour [g/PS/h]:	20
Ignition No.:	
Type:	
Firing order:	
Cooling	Water
Weight of complete engine (dry) & ext. masses	
Total [kg]:	144
Weight per displacement [kg/l]:	22,7
Weight per hp [kg/hp]:	2,2
Remarks: Built in two variants (with or without gear box).	

shoot through the free-standing engine shaft.

The particularly strong design of the spur gear transmission is striking. In the experience of motor vehicle construction, it is designed with such accuracy that even after 16 hours of running under full load, no play between the tooth flanks could be detected.

Both types of the Mercedes E4uF took part in the 1912 Kaiser Prize competition for the best German aircraft engine and won 4th prize.

Above: Mercedes E4uF 4-cylinder 65 hp, exhaust side, gear box. [B36, 1912–13]

Above: Rumpler Monoplane with cowling for Mercedes E4uF with hanging cylinders. [J6, 1913]

Above: Mercedes 70 hp 4-cylinder aeroengine E4F (Model 1911), Hirth won the Kathreiner Prize on his Taube equipped with this E4F engine. [J6, 1912]

Facing Page, Left Middle: Carburetor side E4uF. [A1]

Facing Page, Left Bottom: Exhaust side of E4uF. [A1]

Above: E4uF Mercedes engine powering a Baumann-Freytag biplane. [A1]

Left: Front view of Mercedes E4uF, 70 hp, 4-cylinder. [A1]

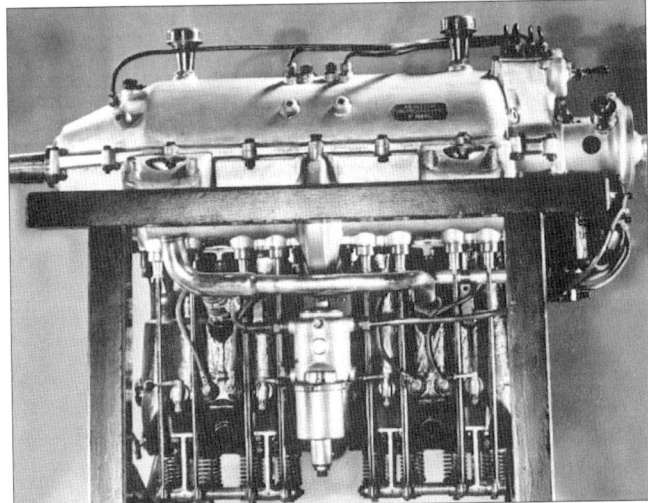

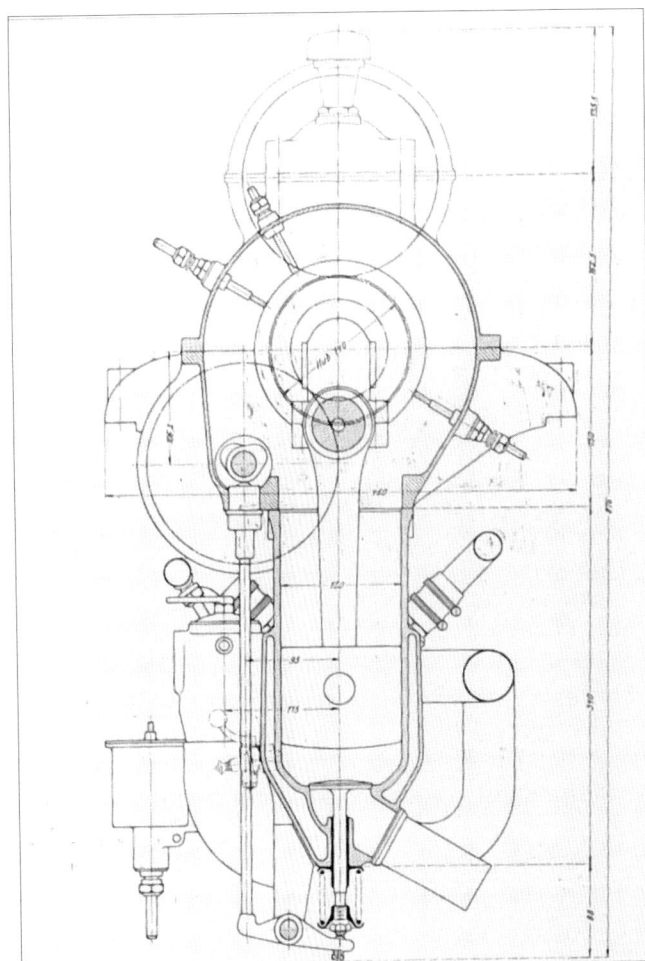

Above: Motorwagen 1913. [A1]

3.16.6 Four-Cylinder 45/50 hp In-line Aircraft Engine (F 1034, C4F) (1912/13)

Under the internal designation F1034, the DMG tested another 4-cylinder engine with small cylinder dimensions in 1911/12, the bore was only 100 mm, the stroke was 130 mm. At 1400 rpm the engine produced 50/45 hp. As can be seen in the illustrations, the camshaft was located at the top, so that any control linkage could be avoided.

This type of engine was not produced in series later, probably because the industry already needed stronger engines.

This is the first Daimler aircraft engine with an overhead camshaft, which was driven by an unencapsulated "Königswelle" ("king shaft") - vertical shaft with one bevel gear set each at the lower and upper end - located at the front of the engine. The C4F also had suspended valves.

This basic arrangement was subsequently (from 1913) implemented for all subsequent Mercedes aircraft engines, although the Königswelle moved in future more often to the upper end. The lower part of this engine which contains the oil pump has the same design as early E4F.Note on the designations of the Daimler engines, using the F1034 as an example:

F1034 Flugzeug (Airplane), **L** – Luftschiff (airship)

F**10**34 Bore: 100 mm

F10**3**4 Stroke:130 mm

F103**4** Cylinder: 4The fuel consumption was said to be 490 grams per hp-hr., and the weight 181 kg, or 2,01 kg/hp.

3.16.7 Four-Cylinder 90 hp In-line Aircraft Engine (F 1454, G4F)

The 90 hp four-cylinder engine differs from the earlier ones in that the control shaft is located upwards, centrally above the cylinder heads, and is driven by bevel gears and vertical intermediate shaft from the rear end of the engine. This arrangement makes it possible to increase the speed considerably due to the reduction of the moving masses of the control parts. The carburetor is lowered again, so that the fuel supply is possible under natural gradient. It has two separate jets, a small one on the side for low speed and a larger one in the middle for full speed. The relieved rotary slide valve with water heating is set up in such a way that it releases only one of the jets at full throttle; at the same time it serves to balance the secondary air. The

Above: Experimental Mercedes engine C4F (1913), carburetor side. [B37]

Above: 45 hp experimental Mercedes engine, exhaust side. [L4]
Below: 45 hp experimental Mercedes engine, exhaust side. [L4]

main and secondary air are sucked in at the same place, namely at the surface of the crankcase which is warm during operation; other preheating is not required, with the exception of the rotary valve heating mentioned above.

Engine Datasheet	
Daimler Motoren Gesellschaft, Stuttgart-Untertürkheim	
Designation	**Mercedes 50 hp 4 cylinder in-line (F 1034, C4F)**
Year:	1911
Purpose:	Aircraft engine
Number of Cylinders:	4
Arrangement of Cylinders:	Inline piston engine
Bore [mm]:	100
Stroke [mm]:	130
Displacement [l]:	4,1
Compression [Ratio]	
RPM [min-1]: norm./max.	1300/1400
Power [hp]: norm./max.	45/50
Power per displacement [hp/l]:	12,0
Carburetor(s)	
No.:	1
Type:	
Fuel consumption per hp per hour [g]:]:	490
Oil Pump	
No.:	
Oil consumption per hp per hour [g/PS/h]:	
Ignition No.:	1
Type:	Bosch magneto
Firing order:	
Cooling	Water
Weight of complete engine (dry) & ext. masses	
Total [kg]:	100
Weight per displacement [kg/l]:	24,5
Weight per hp [kg/hp]:	2,0

Remarks: For the first time with overhead camshaft and vertical drive ("king shaft", Königswelle). Experimental engine.

Engine Datasheet	
Daimler Motoren Gesellschaft, Stuttgart-Untertürkheim	

Designation	**Mercedes 100 hp 4 cylinder in-line (G4F)**
Year:	1912/13
Purpose:	Aircraft engine
Number of Cylinders:	4
Arrangement of Cylinders:	Inline piston engine
Bore [mm]:	140
Stroke [mm]:	150
Displacement [l]:	9,25
Compression [Ratio]	
RPM [min-1]: norm./max.	1200/1350
Power [hp]: norm./max.	85/95
Power per displacement [hp/l]:	9,7
Carburetor(s)	
No.:	1
Type:	
Fuel consumption per hp per hour [g]:]:	240
Oil Pump	
No.:	
Oil consumption per hp per hour [g/PS/h]:	
Ignition No.:	
Type:	
Firing order:	
Cooling	Water
Weight of complete engine (dry) & ext. masses	
Total [kg]:	180
Weight per displacement [kg/l]:	19,5
Weight per hp [kg/hp]:	2,0
Remarks: Participated in the Kaiserpreis competition.	

Above: 90 hp Mercedes G4F, open "Königswelle", capsuled control shaft above cylinder heads. [B36, 1912–13]

Below: Mercedes G4F exhaust side [B36, 1912–13]

3.16.8 Six-Cylinder 100 hp In-line Aircraft Engine (F 1246, E6F))

With the 100 hp six-cylinder E6F engine, which was derived from the E4F, the Daimler Works deviated for the first time from the previous four-cylinder arrangement in 1911, as it seemed brave to increase the cylinder dimensions even further out of

Above Right: Drawing E6F exhaust side. [B24]

Right: Drawing E6F carburetor side. [B24]

Above: 100 hp 6-cylinder MercedEs E6F. [J9, 1912]

Below: First Daimler 6-cylinder engine development E6F. [J9, 1912]

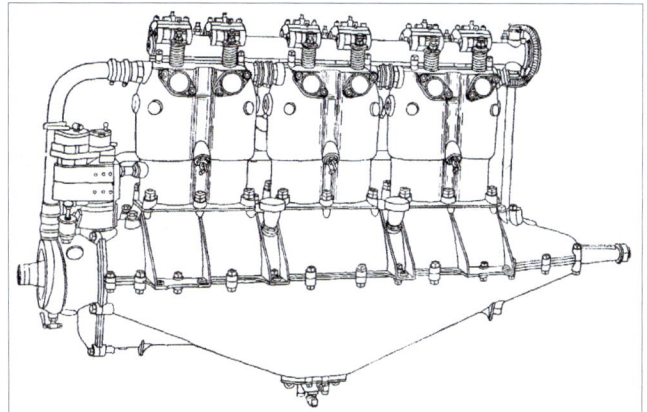

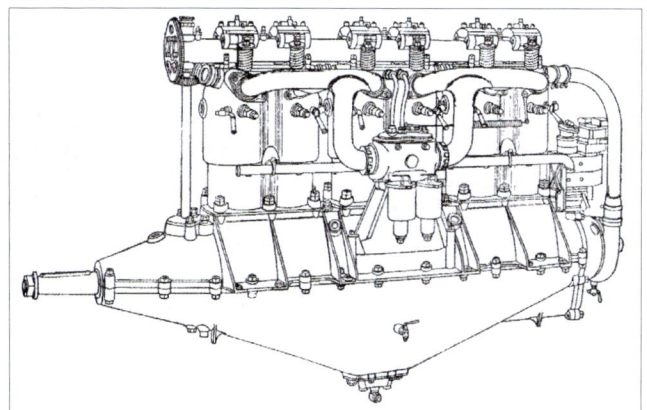

Engine Datasheet	
Daimler Motoren Gesellschaft, Stuttgart-Untertürkheim	
Designation	**Mercedes 100 hp 6 cylinder in-line (F 1246, E6F)**
Year:	1911 (1913)
Purpose:	Aircraft engine
Number of Cylinders:	6
Arrangement of Cylinders:	Inline piston engine
Bore [mm]:	120
Stroke [mm]:	140
Displacement [l]:	9,5
Compression [Ratio]	
RPM [min-1]: norm./max.	1200/1350
Power [hp]: norm./max.	95/105
Power per displacement [hp/l]:	9,5
Carburetor(s)	
No.:	1
Type:	Double Mercedes carburetor
Fuel consumption per hp per hour [g]:]	240
Oil Pump	
No.:	
Oil consumption per hp per hour [g/PS/h]:	15
Ignition No.:	1
Type:	Bosch ZH 6
Firing order:	1 – 5 – 3 – 6 – 2 – 4
Cooling	Water
Weight of complete engine (dry) & ext. masses	
Total [kg]:	200
Weight per displacement [kg/l]:	21,0
Weight per hp [kg/hp]:	2,22

Remarks: Can also be found as CF1246.
Applications*: Albatros Taube-EE & FT; Fokker M 1, M 2, M 3, M 3a; Kondor Taube Type B, Type C.
* Listing has no claim to completeness!

The winner of the long distance flight Berlin – Vienna. Hellmut Hirth and his passenger, Lieutenant Schoeffler, after landing on the airfield near Aspern. [J9, 1912]

Above: Open engine cowling on a DFW Mars aircraft. [J2, 1914]

Left: E6F H Hirth 6-cylinder. [B24]

shaft) allowed the disassembly or assembly of the control shaft by loosening or tightening a few screws, which is of major importance for aircraft engines, for the adjustment of the valves.

A double revolving disc carburetor causes the gas mixture to form when the engine is running. The intake air was led through the crankcase to cool the engine. At the same time this led to an improved mixture distribution due to the preheated air.

Further components such as the centrifugal water pump, oil pump and ignition are the same and are arranged in the same way as for the four-cylinder engine described above.

The E6F design later was used for the little bit more powerful engine with the military designation Daimler D I (power range 100 - 150 hp).

Applications of this engine (example wise): AEG B.I, G.I; Albatros B.I, G.I; Aviatik B.I; DFW B.I, Floh; Fokker D.I; LFG V 39, Roland Arrow; Stahlwerk-Mark R.V, Pfalz E.V.

3.16.9 Six-Cylinder 85/75 hp In-line Aero-Engine (F 10546, Da6F, DF 80)

Daimler Works finally made significant progress in a completely different direction with the 90 hp six-cylinder engine, which was therefore awarded second prize in the Kaiser-Preis competition 1912. With cast iron cylinders, the standardized performance of the cylinder capacity cannot be further increased. Compression ratio and effective piston pressure are already driven up to the achievable limit in most aircraft engines - the compression ratio is usually around 4 : 1 to 5 : 1, the piston pressure up to 7.6 kg/cm^2. At higher compression ratios self-ignition occurs, and this can only be avoided by much

consideration for operational safety.

Since one had made good experiences in the meantime with the use of the bevel shafts (see Mercedes C4F), this detail was taken over also with this engine, however the bevel shaft moved forward.

The six-cylinder design is unfavourable from the point of view of weight, but in addition to the better mass balance it also offers the advantage of a more steady torque, so that the vibrations generated by the engine are reduced. The arrangement of control shaft, magnets, pump and water pipe has been retained from the past. In order to avoid too uneven mixture distribution, however, two carburetors have been combined in one housing, which feed three cylinders each through separate pipes. With two carburetors, however, it is not possible to achieve such low fuel consumption as with one single one.

The cylinders of this engine from DMG have a bore of 120 mm and a stroke of 140 mm. The normal output at 1200 - 1250 rpm is 100 to 105 hp. Cylinders and valves are designed and arranged in the same way as the aforementioned engine, except that the latter are actuated here by a jointly encapsulated control shaft located above the cylinders, which is driven by a vertical shaft with pairs of bevel gears from the crankshaft. This arrangement of a so-called "Königswelle" (vertical

Above: Ingold's Aviatik-Pfeil biplane record aircraft with 100 hp Mercedes.

Left: Advertisement with DF80 Mercedes-Daimler [J4, 1914].

Above: 6-cylinder 85 hp Mercedes engine DF80, second winner of the Kaiser-Preis competion 1912. [B36, 1912–13]

stronger cooling than can be achieved with both wall thicknesses of cast iron cylinders. Therefore, steel cylinders have been used, namely all highly stressed parts subjected to high heat are made in one piece by relatively simple turning; cooling jacket, gas ducts etc. are welded to them, so that the welding joints are hardly stressed. In view of the numerous casting errors (at least 50 %) that were

Engine Datasheet	
Daimler Motoren Gesellschaft, Stuttgart-Untertürkheim	
Designation	**Mercedes 85/75 hp 6 cylinder in-line (F 10546, Dd6F, DF 80)**
Year:	1912/13
Purpose:	Aircraft engine
Number of Cylinders:	6
Arrangement of Cylinders:	Inline piston engine
Bore [mm]:	105
Stroke [mm]:	140
Displacement [l]:	7,27
Compression [Ratio]	4,6
RPM [min-1]: norm./max.	1200/1400
Power [hp]: norm./max.	75/85
Power per displacement [hp/l]:	10,3
Carburetor(s)	
No.:	1
Type:	Double Mercedes carburetor
Fuel consumption per hp per hour [g]:]:	240
Oil Pump	
No.:	1
Oil consumption per hp per hour [g/PS/h]:	25
Ignition No.:	2
Type:	Bosch ZH 6 magnetos
Firing order:	1 – 5 – 3 – 6 – 2 – 4
Cooling	Water
Weight of complete engine (dry) & ext. masses	
Total [kg]:	150
Weight per displacement [kg/l]:	20,6
Weight per hp [kg/hp]:	2,0

Remarks: Also known as Da6F.
Applications*: Gotha LE 1, Halberstadt Taube IV.
* Listing has no claim to completeness!

Above: DF80 exhaust side. [B36, 1912–13]

Above: DF80 carburetor side. [B36, 1912–13]

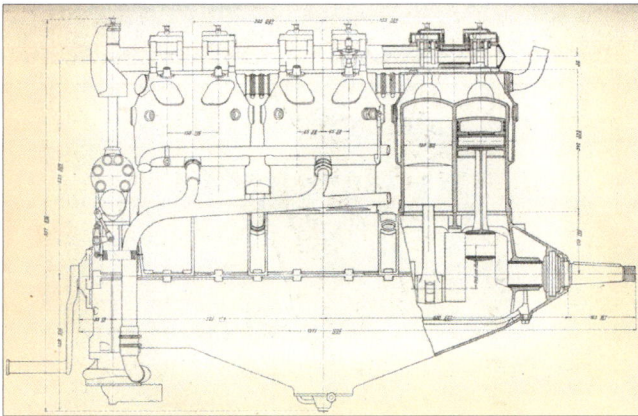

Above: DF80 engine drawing. [J6, 1913]

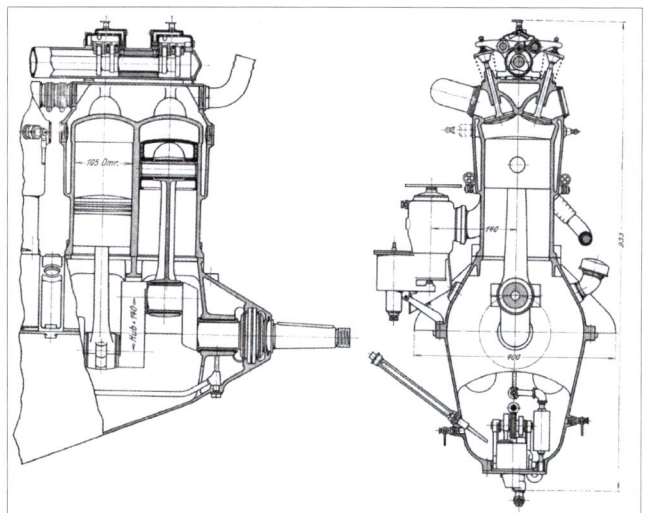

Above: Sectional view of DF80 Mercedes engine. [B36, 1912–13]

Above: Mercedes aircraft engine from 1913: DF 80 (Da6F, F10546) with 90 PS, rear camshaft drive, bevel shaft (Königswelle), dual ignition. [A1]

Above: Side view 85 hp Mercedes engine. (1913) [A1]

to be expected with cast cylinders, the production of steel cylinders in rows is unlikely to become more expensive. The well-known concerns about steel for cylinder construction appear to have been eliminated after the long competitive tests and the flight performances recently achieved with this engine (distance and duration world record with one passenger on 31 March 1913, 595 km in 6 hours 9 minutes). Because despite its high unit power of 12.39 hp/l and the extraordinarily high average piston pressure of 8.04 kg/cm^2, the engine had mirror-smooth running surfaces after the endurance tests.

By the way, general construction of this engine is quite similar to six-cylinder-engine E6F, but cylinder dimensions are much smaller. The valves are set at a slight angle so that they can be used from the inside with the largest possible plates, but the spindles have no bushes that affect their cooling. The crankshaft is mounted between 2 pairs of cylinders and at both ends. In the front, close behind the hub stub, there is a double thrust bearing. Another visible feature of the DF 80 is the uncovered bevel shaft, which, in contrast to the E6F, is now back again.

From this time on, Daimler plants also primarily used steel cylinders (and later aluminium cylinders) for other aircraft engines. Incidentally, the development of the Daimler engines shown here shows that they did not use designs with long piston strokes to achieve low weight and particularly low fuel consumption. The recent preference for six-cylinder engines also proves that the main aim is to achieve smooth running and uniform torque.

Among many other German pilots who used the DF80 engine, Lieutenant Canter should be mentioned. He used this engine shortly after the announcement of the winners of the 1st Kaiserpreis 1912 to set a new world record for cross-country flights on a Rumpler Taube on 31 March 1913. The exact total time that Canter flew through was 6 hours and 13 minutes, the average altitude was 750 to 800 m, the highest altitude reached was 950 m. Not taking into account the circular flights during take-off and landing, the distance covered was exactly 599 km, resulting in an average speed of 97.4 km. This cross-country flight of Canters with passenger was a particular success for German aviation and demonstrated that Germany need not fear comparison with other countries. Canter had by this achievement, this double world record, the so-called big guns of the foreign countries not with a special machine, but with a normal military machine smoothly outbid. The greatest achievement so far was: Lieutenant Baarigton Kennet on an English monoplane, type Neuport, 401.5 km in 4 hours 51 minutes. This means that the distance covered has also set an overland distance world record.

3.16.10 Six-Cylinder 105/95 hp In-line Aeroengine (DF 100, F1246, D I)

Found in *"The Aeroplane"*, 1914:
The Mercedes D I was like all Mercedes motors a water-cooled aircraft engine which developed 105/95 hp at 1400/1300 rpm.

After the successes in the 1st Kaiser Prize competition in 1912 for the best German aircraft engine, this engine was also used in the Mercedes Grand Prix cars that ran in 1913 using the inline-six aeroplane engine. They ran a four-cylinder, but also photos show two six-cylinder cars! Both on land... and in the air in 1913.. Using the larger cylinders of the E6F (bore/stroke: 120 mm/140 mm) and the basic design elements of the DF 80, the DF 100 was developed under DMG's internal project designation F1246. A little later, after type certification, the DF 100 was widely used in German warplanes under the military designation D I.

The lubrication system of the Mercedes D I is at least thorough, leaving nothing to chance. Practically the crankshaft itself forms the reservoir for the reciprocating parts, the cylinders, and all bearings ; the oil being originally delivered thereto – by a rotary type of pump driven from the vertical shaft – via the aftermost bearing in the conventional way of most systems of the kind. But the tubular casing of the vertical shaft forms a second main conduit – hence its ample diameter – for the valve gear; the oil being driven up through it into and through the hollow camshaft, which is duly perforated to allow the oil to reach its main bearings and to flow into the shaft casing. From the oil-bath

Above: The British company Milnes-Daimler, Ltd. Represented the DMG in UK. [J10, 1913]

Above: Mercedes D I installed in a Taube, Fuel tank between the wings, cooler on top of the engine, exhaust pipe located under the fuselage. [J4, 1914]

thus constituted, the cams and the rollers at the inner ends of the rockers are lubricated; and the little metal splash guards that project from the interior of the aluminium casing cover (one for each rocker) drop the oil into the hollow bodies of the rockers, and allow it to run to their bearings.

These bearings are also lubricated through the hollow lay-shafts on which the rockers are pivoted, from an oil box on the top of the camshaft casing. Finally, these layshafts return their oil into the forward end of the casing; from which the entire surplus runs down the return-pipe into the crank-chamber. Except for the little that inevitably gets through the ends of the rocker bearings, there is no wastage, and the top of the motor is thus kept clean.

Similarly, the water circulation is well thought

Above: The British company Milnes-Daimler, Ltd. Represented the DMG in UK. [J10, 1913]

Above: 6-cylinder D III Mercedes engine in an Albatros C III. Machine gun alongside to the engine. [J10, 1917]

Above Right: 100 hp Mercedes D I drawing. [B43]

Right: The Postage stamp showing Pilot Ingold and his LVG biplane (100 hp Mercedes D I)

Below Right: 100 hp Mercedes D I aircraft engine, carburetor side. [B43]

Below: Mercedes aircraft engine DI (1914), was reproduced in England by Milnes-Daimler-Mercedes Ltd London. [A1]

JNGOLD erzielt seinen WELTREKORD mit

Flugmotorenöl der Raffinerie ZELLER & GMELIN, Eislingen-Berlin.

Aviatik Pfeil-Rumpf-Doppeldecker.
Militärtyp 1913.

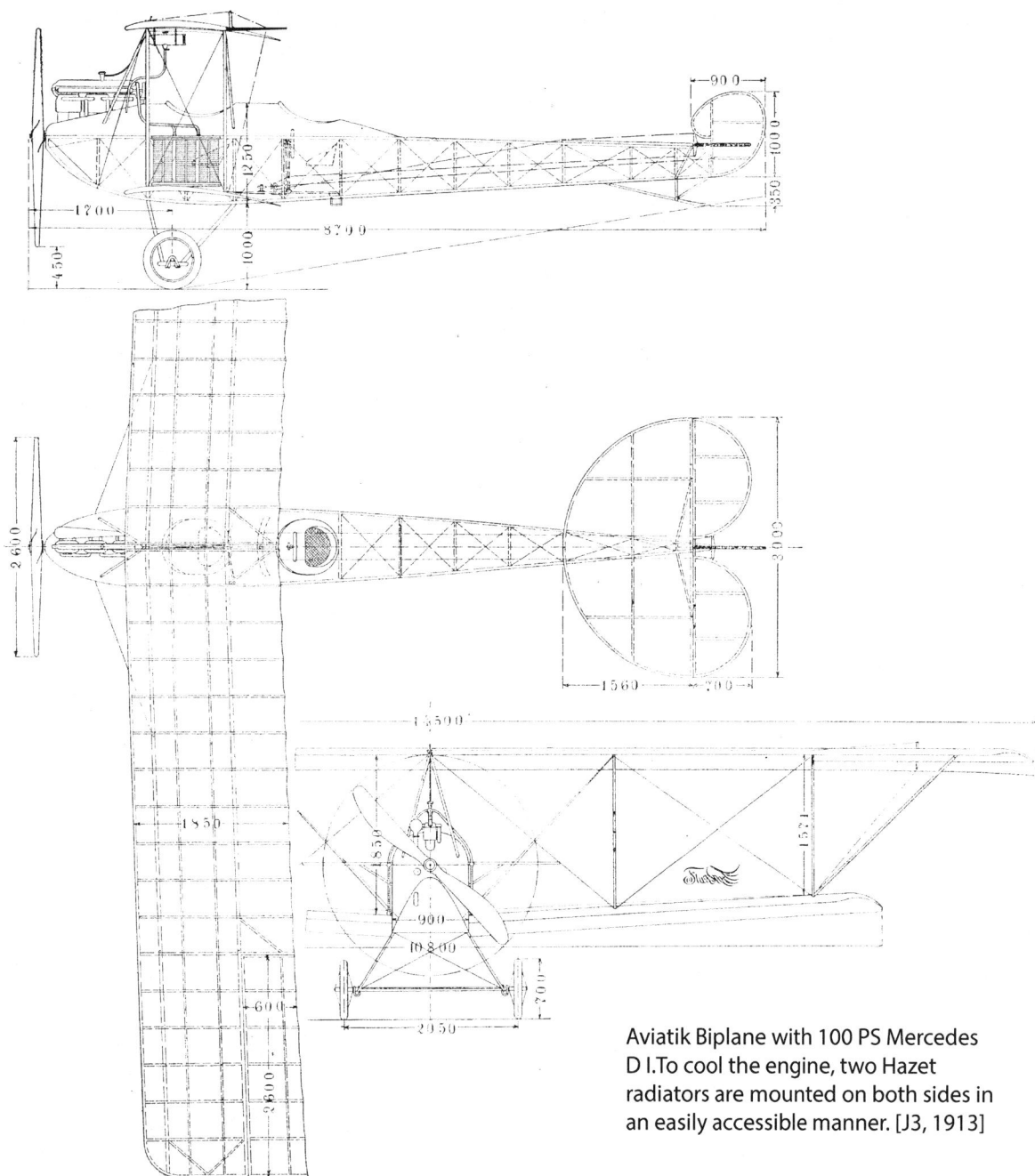

Aviatik Biplane with 100 PS Mercedes D I. To cool the engine, two Hazet radiators are mounted on both sides in an easily accessible manner. [J3, 1913]

out; for while the jointing between the jacketing of each pair of cylinders ensures a clean run-through to a pair of water outlets aft, thus getting rid of piping where it would be most in the way, the inlet pipe on the exhaust side, having a branch to each jacketing, ensures an even delivery of cold water to each pair of cylinders side, having a branch to each jacketing, ensures an even delivery of cold water to each pair of cylinders.

Engines equipped with the Mercedes DF 100 were extremely successful and thus formed the basis for Germany to catch up with the technical lead of other countries, especially France.

At the beginning of 1914 the German trade press reported among other things about the successes of Ingold and Langer, both travelling on different aircraft (the LFG's Aviation Arrow biplanes and Roland Arrow biplanes) but equipped with 100 hp

Section through
Mercedes D I. [B43]

Rear view D I
engine. [B43]

Vergaserseite   *Auspuffseite*

100 hp Mercedes D I,
View of the rear units,
including the king shaft.
[J10, 1915]

Above: Rear view of 100 hp Mercedes D I on a test stand.

Engine Datasheet	
Daimler Motoren Gesellschaft, Stuttgart-Untertürkheim	
Designation	**Mercedes 105/95 hp 6 cylinder in-line (F 1246, D I, DF 100)**
Year:	1913
Purpose:	Aircraft engine
Number of Cylinders:	6
Arrangement of Cylinders:	Inline piston engine
Bore [mm]:	120
Stroke [mm]:	140
Displacement [l]:	9,5
Compression [Ratio]	4,5
RPM [min-1]: norm./max.	1300/1400
Power [hp]: norm./max.	95/105
Power per displacement [hp/l]:	10,0
Carburetor(s)	
No.:	2
Type:	
Fuel consumption per hp per hour [g]:]	
Oil Pump	
No.:	
Oil consumption per hp per hour [g/PS/h]:	
Ignition No.:	2
Type:	Bosch ZH 6 magnetos
Firing order:	1 – 5 – 3 – 6 – 2 – 4
Cooling	Water
Weight of complete engine (dry) & ext. masses	
Total [kg]:	192
Weight per displacement [kg/l]:	20,2
Weight per hp [kg/hp]:	2,0

Remarks: F1246
Applications*: A.E.G. B.I, K I, G.I; Ago E.I; Albatros B.I (L.1), B.II (L.2), B.IIa (L.30), DE, L 9; Aviatik B-P13, B-P14, B-P15; Daimler R.I, R.II; D.F.W. Taube, Mars biplane, B.I, B.II, T 28 Floh, Flying Boat; Euler B.I (LVG B.I), B.II; Fokker M 4, M 18; Friedrichshafen FF19; Gotha LE 2, LE 2 "Gotha-Taube", LE 3, LE 4, LD 1, LD 2, G.I (UKL), WD1, WD7, WD22, WD24, Gotha Büchner "See"; Halberstadt Taube I (4-wheel)s, Taube III; B.II, D.I, Bristol-Halberstadt A.I; Hansa-Brandenburg LDD, Jeannin 1912 Stahltaube, Kondor Taube Type G, Taube Type H; K.W. Type 401; LFG Stahl-Pfeil; LVG E3, B.I; Otto B.I; Pfalz E.V; Rumpler Eindecker (Taube), B.I, 4A15, 4B11, 4C, SSW Bulldog. * Listing has no claim to completeness!

Mercedes DF 100.

On February 3, 1914, Bruno Langer had broken the world record, which had long been held by Fourny in French possession, by flying continuously for 14 hours 7 minutes in a closed flight path. Four days later Ingold beat the duration of Langer's flight by flying continuously for 16 hours 20 minutes, and on February 11, Langer beat his own record again with 16 hours flying time.

Thelen took his 100 hp Mercedes-Albatros biplane with 4 passengers into the air on February 11, 1914 shortly before 11 a.m., despite the extraordinary load (330 kg net weight) after a barely 50 m run-up, with the intention of breaking the altitude record set by Garaix on February 6. He succeeded brilliantly! Garaix had only reached 2750 m, while Thelen reached 2850 m in 75 minutes and was only prevented from climbing even higher by the severe cold. After 95 minutes, he brought his apparatus back down smoothly to earth.

No sooner had the permanent world record been transferred into German possession than an extension of Ingold's extraordinary cross-country flight performance followed a few days later, when he remained aloft in his 100-hp Mercedes Aviatik Arrow biplane on February 7 from 7:35 min in the morning to 11:55 min in the evening, i.e. 16 hours and 20 minutes. Ingold took off from Mühlhausen i. E. with the intention of breaking the world record in cross-country flight without a stopover. For this purpose he had 600 litres of petrol and 55 kg of oil on board, i.e. for about 19 hours of fuel.

This small selection of events in spring 1914 shows what a great leap forward not only the German aircraft industry made, but also the contribution made by engine developers.

3.16.11 Six-Cylinder 120/105 hp In-line Aircraft Engine (F 12556, D II)

The Mercedes D II was a six-cylinder, single overhead camshaft valvetrain liquid-cooled inline aircraft engine built by DMG during the early stages of World War I. Producing about 105 to 120 hp, this engine was at the low-end of the power range of contemporary engines and was generally outperformed by rotaries whose power-to-weight ratio tended to be much better. The D II was produced only in a few numbers, but its design formed the basis for the later most built Mercedes D III and which was used by almost all German aircraft manufacturers during WWI.

The general design elements of the D II was taken over from the slightly smaller predecessor engine D I. The still paired cylinders were separately milled from steel and bolted to the top of the crankcase. Steel sleeves were fitted over the cylinders and welded on to form a cooling jacket. Much of this complexity is due to the differential rates of expansion of steel and aluminium, which precluded

Above: Mercedes .D II as exhibit (Deutsches Technikmuseum Berlin)

Above: D II engine installation on Albatros C.I biplane with side radiators. [J2, 1915]

Left: Carburetor side of Mercedes D II. [L13]

Above: This is an Albatros B.III which was visually similar to the C.III and used the Mercedes D.II 120 hp. [J2, 1915]

screwing the cylinders into the crankcase, and the alloys of the era meant that an aluminium cylinder was not possible. Both engines also used a scavenger pump to pump oil out of the crankcase to a separate

Above: D II engine details, valve springs, carburetor, camshaft, magneto. (Deutsches Technikmuseum Berlin).

Above: Mercedes D II engine details, venting tap on early engines. (Deutsches Technikmuseum Berlin)

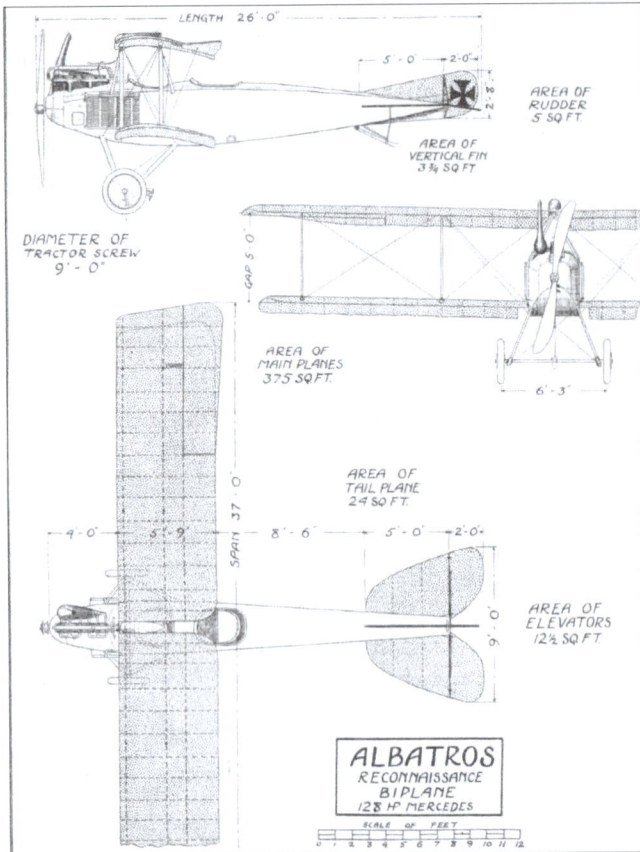

Above: Albatros B.III reconnaissance biplane with Mercedes D II. [J2, 1915]

Above: D II engine details, twin-barrel carburetor. (Deutsches Technikmuseum Berlin).

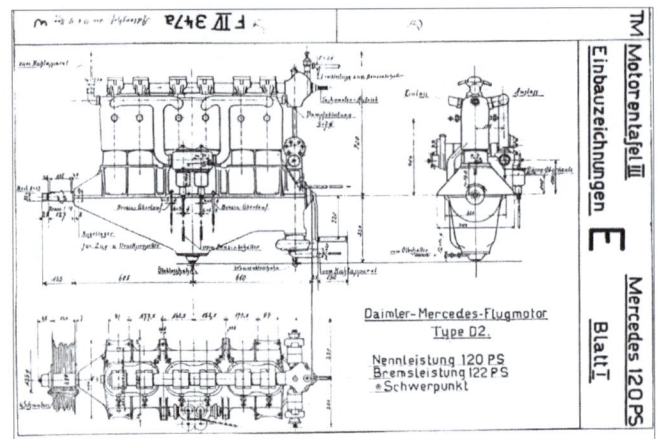

Above: D II engine drawings. [A2]

cylinder, where a second high-pressure pump supplied oil to the engine. This arrangement allowed for a much smaller "sump" on the bottom of the crankcase, reducing the overall size of the engine, although in the case of the D II it was not nearly as much as the Austro-Daimler.

To start the engine another unique feature was the ability to shift the camshaft to a half-compression position for starting. As common, the D II had one twin-barrel carburetor located together on one side of the engine, feeding the cylinders through two manifolds. The D II also used the typical cooling jacket design, with every two cylinders being covered by a single jacket.

It is to be mentioned that the carburetor is equipped with an automatic auxiliary air regulation and a special nozzle for slow running. The air heated by the engine body and the hot cooling water from the cylinder jackets are used for heating. Its design is similar to the Cudell carburetor.

The usual Bosch hand-operated starting magneto was fitted near to the pilot so that, after swinging the propeller to draw a charge into the cylinders, the mechanic can get out of the way leaving the actual starting of the engine to the pilot.

The D II was introduced in 1914. It was quickly replaced by the D III. The production ended around 1916. The D III was essentially a scaled-up D.II, although it abandoned the paired cooling jackets.

During the production in 1916, the engine itself underwent minor modifications. The derivative D IIa was equipped with an advanced oil pump and improved camshaft bearings. The operational characteristic of the D IIa was in the main points identical with the D II.

The D II engine can be found example wise in Aviatik B.II, Albatros B.I and B.II, DFW B.II, Fokker D.I, V 6, Friedrichshafen FF.29, Halberstadt D.II.

After protracted negotiations, it was finally possible in the spring of 1926 to achieve at least a partial lifting of the restrictions imposed on German aviation. In the summer of the same year, the Daimler and Benz plants merged to form Daimler-Benz Aktien-Gesellschaft.

In the course of 1926, construction of the "D II" 6-cylinder aircraft engine, which had already proved its worth during the World War, was resumed.

Engine Datasheet	
Daimler Motoren Gesellschaft, Stuttgart-Untertürkheim	
Designation	**Mercedes 120/105 hp 6 cylinder In-line (F 12556, D II)**
Year:	1913/16
Purpose:	Aircraft engine
Number of Cylinders:	6
Arrangement of Cylinders:	Inline piston engine
Bore [mm]:	125
Stroke [mm]:	150
Displacement [l]:	11,0
Compression [Ratio]	4,5
RPM [min-1]: norm./max.	1300/1400
Power [hp]: norm./max.	105/120
Power per displacement [hp/l]:	9,5
Carburetor(s)	
No.:	1
Type:	Mercedes twin barrel rotary slide carburetor with automatic auxiliary air regulation
Fuel consumption per hp per hour [g]:]:	
Oil Pump	
No.:	
Oil consumption per hp per hour [g/PS/h]:	
Ignition No.:	2
Type:	Bosch ZH 6 magnetos
Firing order:	1 – 5 – 3 – 6 – 2 – 4
Cooling	Water
Weight of complete engine (dry) & ext. masses	
Total [kg]:	204
Weight per displacement [kg/l]:	18,5
Weight per hp [kg/hp]:	1,94

Remarks:
Applications*: A.E.G. B.II, B.III, Albatros B.I (L.1), B.II (L.2), B.IIa (L.30), B.III, G.I; Aviatik B.II, D.I (Halb. D.II); D.F.W. B.II; Euler B.III (LVG B.III); Fokker M 16, M 18, D.I, W2, V2; Friedrichshafen FF29, FF29a, FF33 & FF33A; Goedecker B-Typen (1915); Gotha B.I (LD 7), WD7; Halberstadt B.III & Einsitzer, D.II, D.V; Junkers J 1; Kondor A Biplane, B.I, W 1; L.V.G. B.II, B.III, D 10, E.I; Siemens-Forssman R.
* Listing has no claim to completeness!

Its robust design and absolute reliability made it particularly suitable for training aircraft. Through design improvements it was possible to increase the power output from 125 to 150 hp.

3.16.12 Six-cylinder 160 hp aircraft engine (DF 160, F1466, D III)

The original Mercedes D III, or F1466 as it was known internally at Daimler, was introduced in 1914. While it saw widespread use in early examples of the C-series of two-seat general-purpose biplanes, the D III was too large for contemporary fighter designs and did not see use in that role. At the time, fighters were generally powered by lighter rotary engines of power output levels from 80 to about 110 hp, or by water-cooled inline engines in the 100 to 120 hp range such as the earlier Mercedes D II. Around 1917 the D III was being widely used in fighters, most notably on the Albatros D-series and Roland D.I thru D.III aircraft. Production of this version was dropping down by May 1917, with only a handful continuing to be delivered until October, since the engine was gradually replaced by D IIIa.

The initial D III engine was introduced in 1914 at 160 hp, but a series of changes improved this to 170 hp in 1917, and 180 by mid-1918. These later models D IIIa, D IIIav and D IIIavü were used on almost all German fighters until the end of WW1, and its only real competition, the BMW III, was available only in very limited numbers.

The D III was generally based on the same principles as the earlier Mercedes D II, suitably scaled up for higher power settings. Like most inlines of the era, it used a large aluminum crankcase as the main structural component, with separate cylinders made from steel. New was the technology for screwing a threaded cylinder of steel into an aluminum crankcase. This did not exist before that time. Jackets for cooling water covered the top 2/3 of the cylinder, feeding a radiator via connections at the back of the engine. The only obvious design change from the earlier D II was to use separate cooling jackets for each cylinder, whereas the D II used one jacket each for a trio of adjacent pairs of cylinders.

The engine has separately arranged steel cylinders with water cooling. Each cylinder has one inlet and one outlet valve installed inclined, but symmetrically to the cylinder axis. These are kept closed by springs. The valves are operated by a common camshaft, which was located above the cylinders, by means of an oscillating rocker arm. This camshaft was located in an oil-tight housing which supports the rocker arms. The drive

Above: Mercedes D II engine as an exhibit in the Deutschen Technikmuseum Berlin.

mechanism was located at the rear of the motor and consists of a vertical drive with bevel gears at the top and bottom.

The aluminium crankcase is divided in the middle of the crankshaft. The oil pump is installed in the lower part of the housing. The latter also forms the oil reservoir, which is located at the lowest point of the housing. Around the lower part of the crankcase runs the intake pipe of the carburetor, which ends in a wide space for the air intake. On the upper part of the crankcase there are three nozzles for the ventilation of the crankcase. A pipe connected to the middle socket opens into the carburetor intake manifold. As a result, some of the gases in the crankcase are sucked out through the carburetor.

An engine works as a four-stroke engine as follows:

1st stroke: Downward movement of the piston, intake of the fuel-air mixture;

2nd stroke: rising of the piston, compression of the mixture;

3rd stroke: downward movement of the piston, ignition and combustion of the mixture;

4th stroke: rising of the piston, expulsion of the burnt exhaust fumes.

The first downstroke of the piston causes a suction effect in the cylinder, whereby a stream of air is sucked in through the suction valve, which entrains a fine jet of fuel from the injection nozzle. The explosive mixture is formed by spraying the petrol jet.

At the following upstroke of the piston, with the suction and exhaust valves closed, the sucked-in gas mixture is compressed. Shortly before the dead point

Above: Final assembly of 160 hp D III engine with aircraft. [B45]

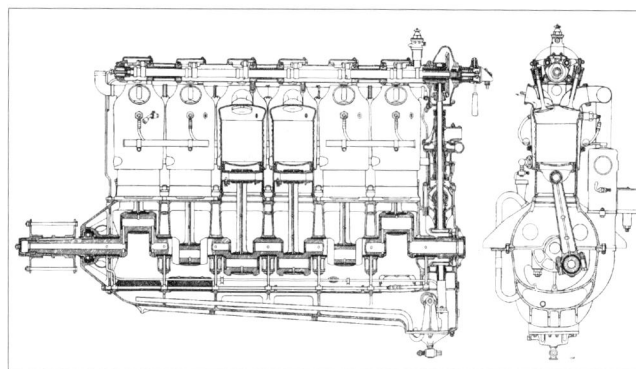

Above: 160 hp Mercedes D III Carburetor side. [M24]

Above: 6 Cylinder Mercedes D III, Exhaust side. [M24]

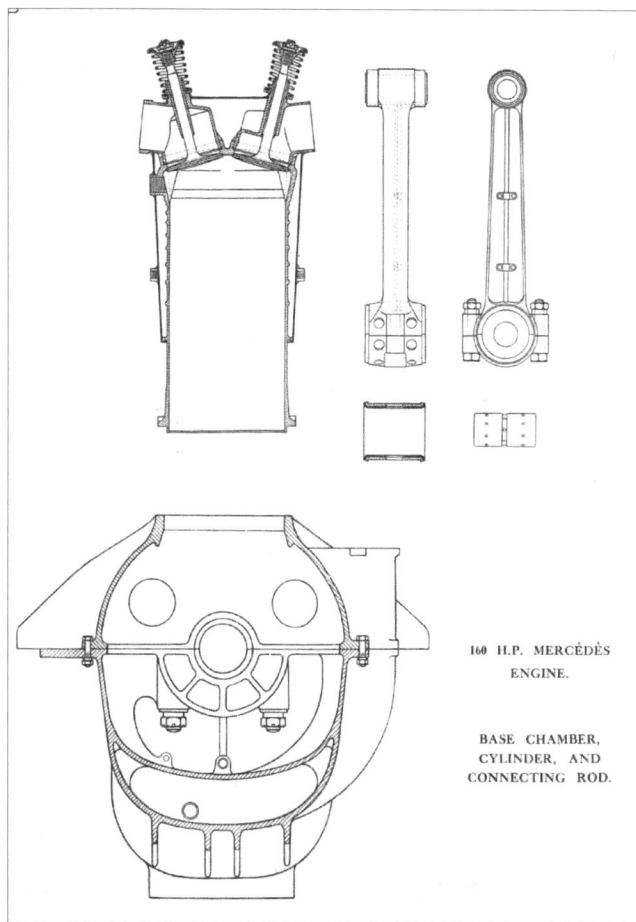

Above: D III engine drawing. [A15]

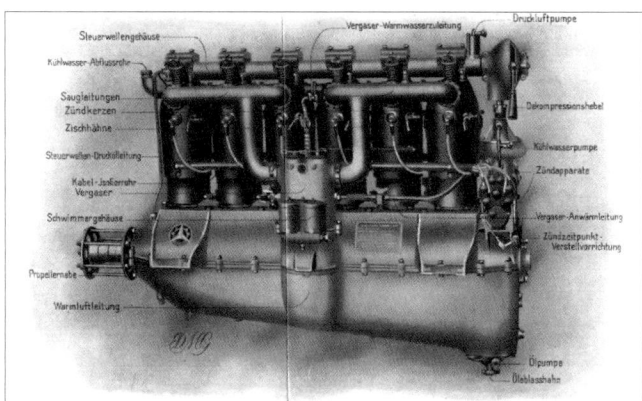

160 H.P. MERCÉDES ENGINE.

BASE CHAMBER, CYLINDER, AND CONNECTING ROD.

Above: Detail view Mercedes engine D III. [A15]

the compressed mixture is ignited. This combustion produces the driving force that pushes the piston of the engine downwards. Through the connecting rod, the force is transmitted to the crankshaft, causing it to rotate.

Through the subsequent upstroke of the piston, the burnt gases are discharged to the outside through the now open exhaust valve.

These four operations are repeated during two full rotations of the crankshaft, during which time all six cylinders ignite once.

The D III featured a rather prominent overhead cam operating the single intake and exhaust valves, powered by a shaft running up from the crankshaft at the rear of the engine. Ignition was provided by two sets of spark plugs, one located on either side of the cylinders, each powered by a separate magneto for redundancy. The ignition cables were protected in tubes running down either side of the cylinders. Fuel was fed into the cylinders via pipes on the port side of the engine, supplied from a twin-barrel carburetor located just above the crankcase. Both the fuel and

Engine Datasheet	
Daimler Motoren Gesellschaft, Stuttgart-Untertürkheim	
Designation	**Mercedes 160 hp 6 cylinder In-line (F 1466, DF 160, D III)**
Year:	1914/15
Purpose:	Aircraft engine
Number of Cylinders:	6
Arrangement of Cylinders:	Inline piston engine
Bore [mm]:	140
Stroke [mm]:	160
Displacement [l]:	9,4
Compression [Ratio]	4,8
RPM [min-1]: norm./max.	1360/1450
Power [hp]: norm./max.	140/160
Power per displacement [hp/l]:	9,5
Carburetor(s)	
No.:	1
Type:	Twin-jet dual carburetor
Fuel consumption per hp per hour [g]:]:	
Oil Pump	
No.:	
Oil consumption per hp per hour [g/PS/h]:	
Ignition No.:	2
Type:	Bosch ZH 6 magnetos
Firing order:	1 – 5 – 3 – 6 – 2 – 4
Cooling	Water
Weight of complete engine (dry) & ext. masses	
Total [kg]:	270
Weight per displacement [kg/l]:	18,3
Weight per hp [kg/hp]:	1,92

Remarks:
Applications*: A.E.G. C.IV, C.IV(Fok), C.VII, C.VIII, C.VIII Dr, D.I, Dr.I; Ago C.I, C.II, C.III, C.V; Albatros C.I, C.III (L.10), C.IV, C.VIIIN, C.IX, C.XIII, D.I (L.15), D.II (L.17), D.IV, D.V/Va (L.24), D.VI, D.XII, Dr.I, W.2, W.4; Aviatik C.I, C.III, C.VIII, D.II; BFW CL.I (Type 17, 1916); D.F.W. C.II, Dr.I (T.34-II), D.I (T.34-I); Euler C (LVG C.III), Euler Experimental-Puscher, D, Dr.II; Fokker M 16, M21, D.IV, D.VII, V6, V8, V10, V.20, V.21, V.23, V.29; Friedrichshafen FF35, FF43, FF54, FF64; Gotha G.I (UKL), WD2, WD3, UWD (WD4), WD5, WD6, WD9 (9a), WD11, WD12, WD22, WD23; Halberstadt CL.II, G.I; Hannover CL3; (continued)
* Listing has no claim to completeness!

Above & Above Right: The 160 hp Mercedes engine in a captured German Albatros C.I biplane. [J2, 1915]

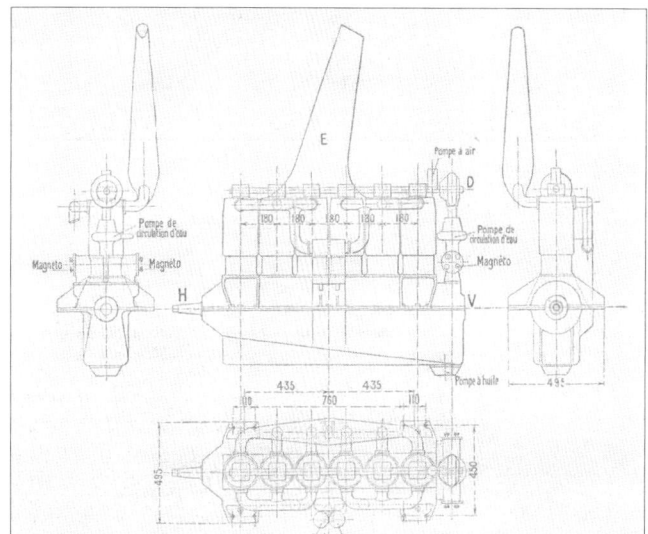

Above: Schematic of D III engine. (French Enemy Report)

Left: Mercedes aircraft engine DF 160 (1914), special version of the D III with angular gear for installation in flying boats. [A1]

Applications, continued: Hansa-Brandenburg KD/D.I, LW, NW, GNW, GW, KDW, W.12, W.23; Junkers J 2/E.I, J 7, J 8; Kondor D.VII; L.F.G. Roland C.I, Roland C.II, Roland C.V, Roland D.I, Roland D.II, Roland D.IIa, Roland D.III, Roland D.IV/Dr.I, Roland D.V, Roland D.VIa, Roland W "750"; Lübeck-Travemünde F1; L.V.G. C.I, C.II, C.III, C.VII, D.II (D 12), W.1; Naglo D.II Quadraplane; N.F.W., N.F.W. E.II; Oertz F.B.3; Otto C.II; Pfalz D.I, D.II, D.IIIa, D.XIII, D.III Triplane Conversion; Rumpler 5A4, 6A2, 6B1, 6B2, C.I/Ia, 7C1, 7D 1/2/4/7; Sablatnig SF1, SF2; Schütte-Lanz C.I, Dr.I, D.III, D.VI, G.I; Zeppelin C.I; Zeppelin Staaken V.G.O.I, V.G.O.III, R.IV, R.VI 30/16, R.VII.

Piston Design Changes from D I (1913), D II (1913/16), D III (1914/15), D IV (1915), D IVa (1915), to D IIIav/avü (1917)

The pistons used in 200 hp D IIIavü engines are of the usual Mercedes construction, being built up with steel crowns which carry the gudgeon pins. The crowns are screwed and welded into their cast iron skirts, and as shown in the sectional drawing (Fig. 2), are considerably domed as compared with the concave heads used in the standard 180 hp Mercedes D.IIIa engines, thus giving a compression ratio of 5.73: 1, i.e. an increase of 23.54 %.

Standard 180 hp Mercedes connecting rods are fitted and the distance from the gudgeon pin centre to the top of piston is the same as before.

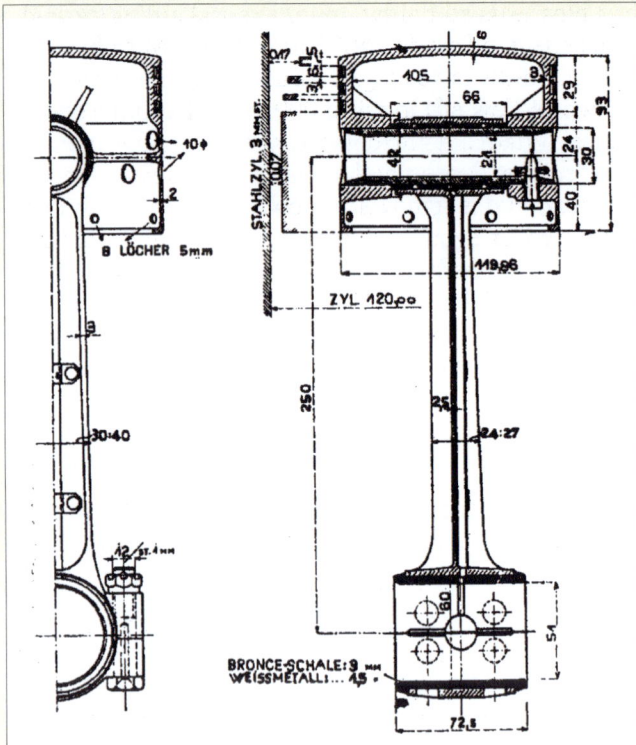

Above: Mercedes 100 hp D I. [A15]
Piston: Cast iron   Cylinder: Steel   Bore: 120 mm

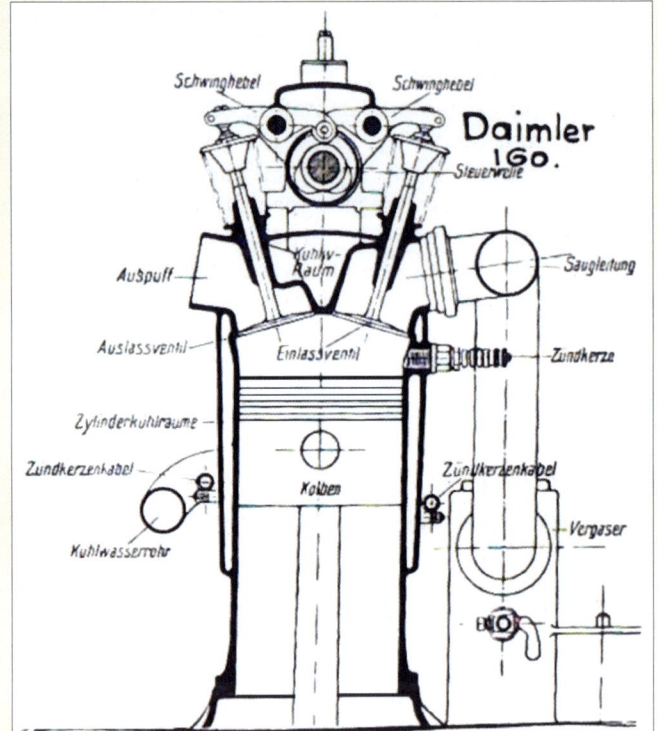

Above: Mercedes 160 hp D II. [A15]
Piston: Cast iron   Cylinder: Steel   Bore: 125 mm

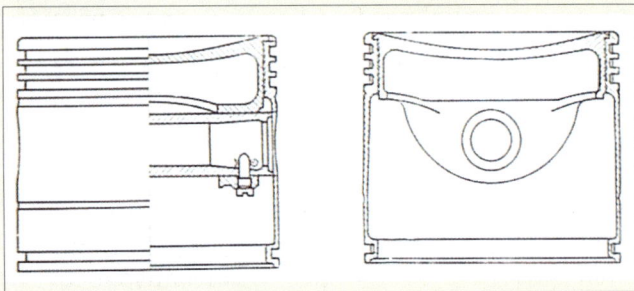

Above: Mercedes 160 hp D III. [A15]
Piston: Cast iron   Cylinder: Steel   Bore: 140 mm

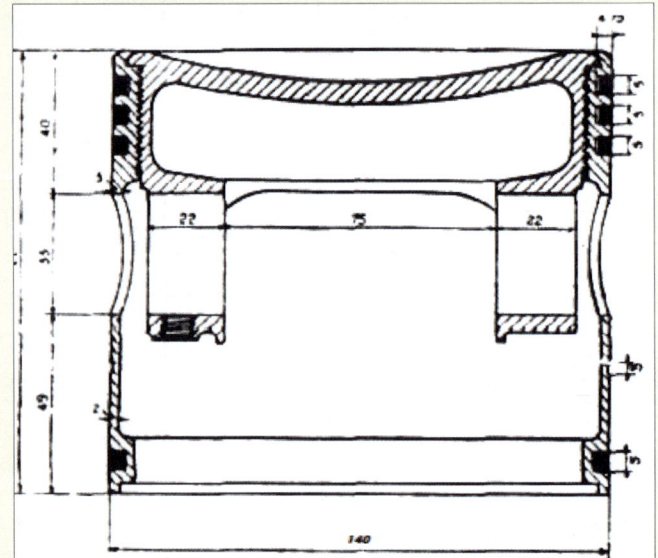

Right: Mercedes 220 hp D IV. [B4]
Piston: Cast iron   Cylinder: Steel   Bore: 140 mm

Mercedes 220 hp D IV
8-cylinder. [A15]

Mercedes D.IV

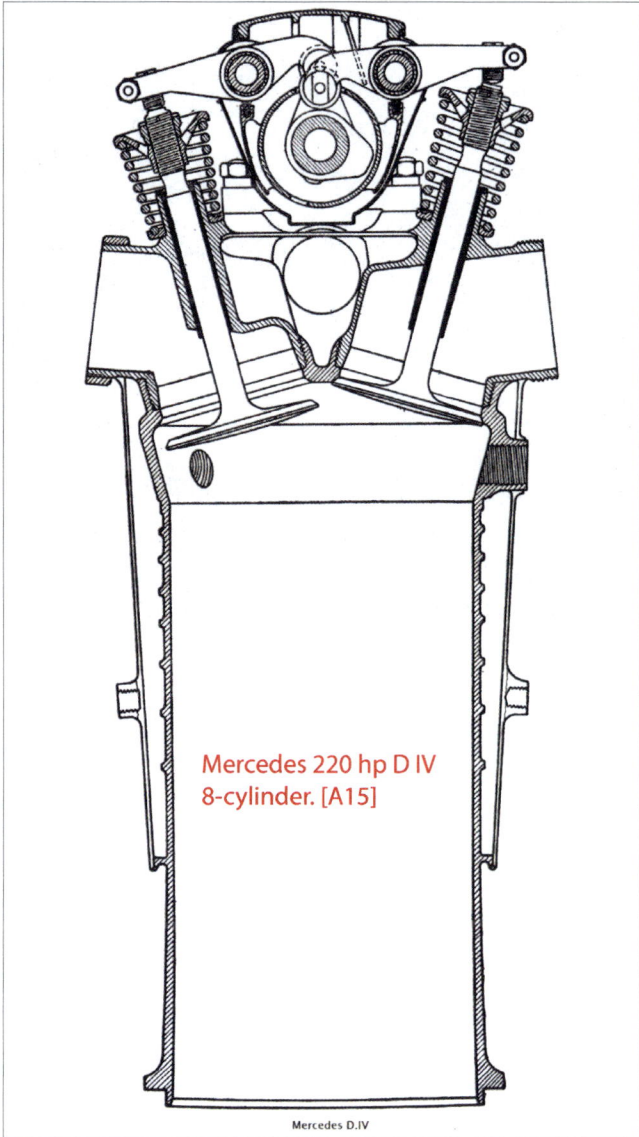

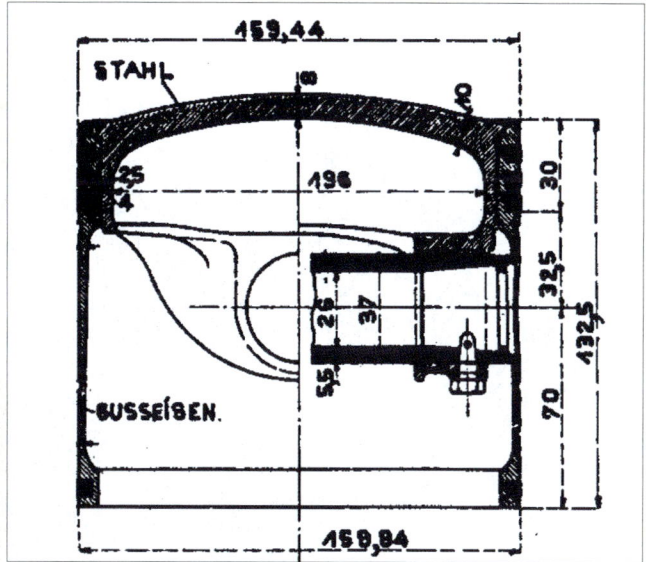

Above: Mercedes 260 hp D IVa. [B4]
Piston: Cast iron   Cylinder: Steel   Bore: 160 mm

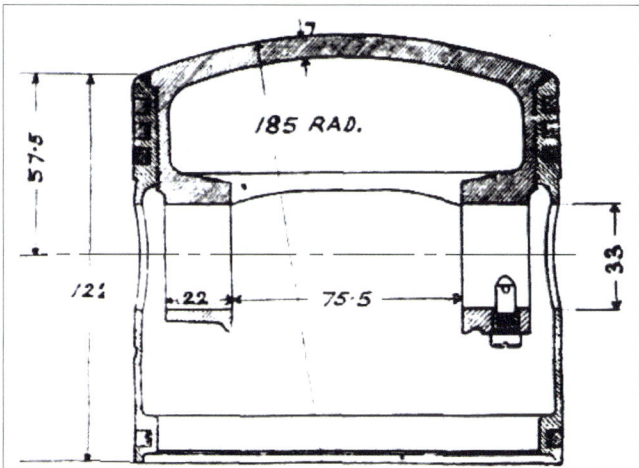

STAHL

GUSSEISEN.

Mercedes 180 hp
D IIIaüv. [J2, 1919]"

185 RAD.

Above: Mercedes 180 hp D IIIaü. [A15]
Piston: Cast iron/steel crown (later Aluminum)
Cylinder: Steel   Bore: 140 mm

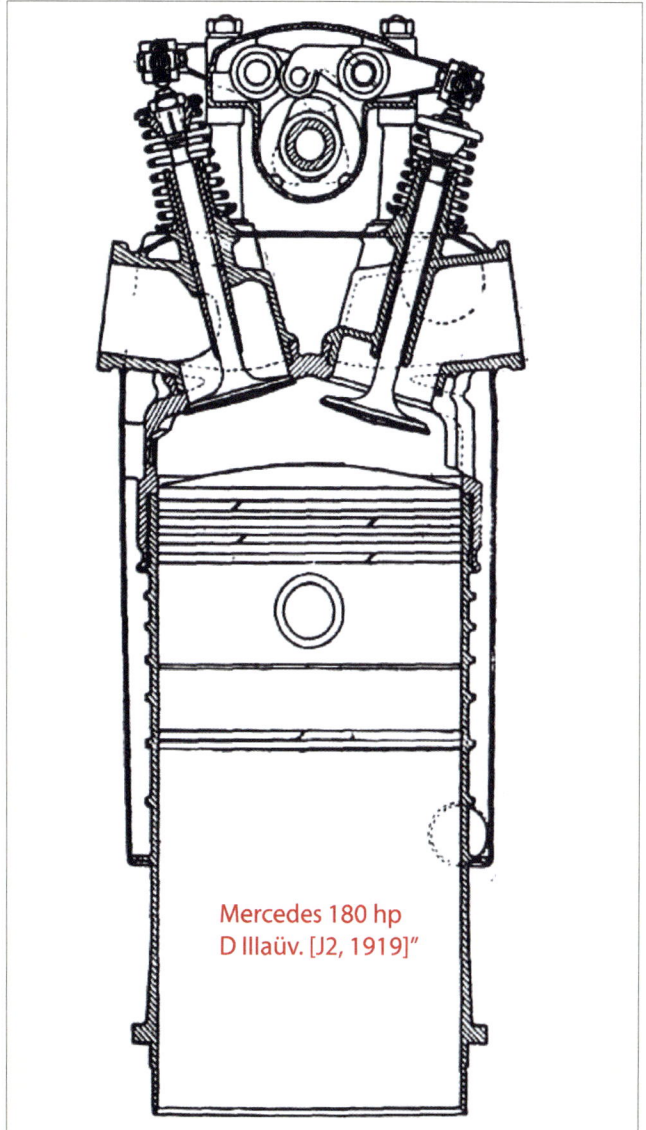

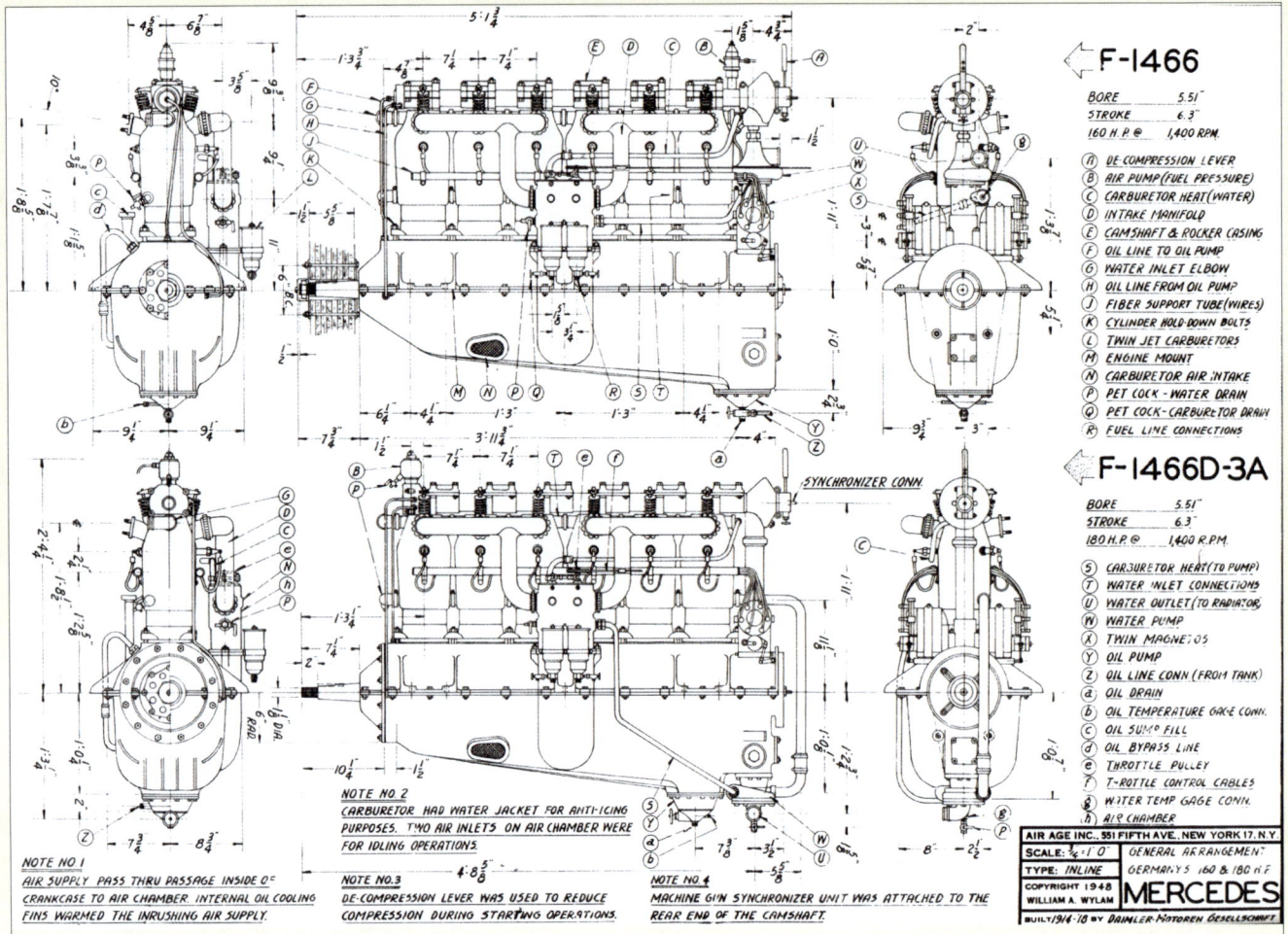

F-1466

BORE	5.51"
STROKE	6.3"
160 H.P @	1,400 RPM.

(A) DE-COMPRESSION LEVER
(B) AIR PUMP (FUEL PRESSURE)
(C) CARBURETOR HEAT (WATER)
(D) INTAKE MANIFOLD
(E) CAMSHAFT & ROCKER CASING
(F) OIL LINE TO OIL PUMP
(G) WATER INLET ELBOW
(H) OIL LINE FROM OIL PUMP
(J) FIBER SUPPORT TUBE (WIRES)
(K) CYLINDER HOLD-DOWN BOLTS
(L) TWIN JET CARBURETORS
(M) ENGINE MOUNT
(N) CARBURETOR AIR INTAKE
(P) PET COCK - WATER DRAIN
(Q) PET COCK - CARBURETOR DRAIN
(R) FUEL LINE CONNECTIONS

F-1466D-3A

BORE	5.51"
STROKE	6.3"
180 H.P @	1,400 R.P.M.

(S) CARBURETOR HEAT (TO PUMP)
(T) WATER INLET CONNECTIONS
(U) WATER OUTLET (TO RADIATOR)
(W) WATER PUMP
(X) TWIN MAGNETOS
(Y) OIL PUMP
(Z) OIL LINE CONN (FROM TANK)
(a) OIL DRAIN
(b) OIL TEMPERATURE GAGE CONN.
(c) OIL SUMP FILL
(d) OIL BYPASS LINE
(e) THROTTLE PULLEY
(f) T-ROTTLE CONTROL CABLES
(g) WATER TEMP GAGE CONN.
(h) AIR CHAMBER

SYNCHRONIZER CONN.

NOTE NO 1
AIR SUPPLY PASS THRU PASSAGE INSIDE OF
CRANKCASE TO AIR CHAMBER. INTERNAL OIL COOLING
FINS WARMED THE INRUSHING AIR SUPPLY.

NOTE NO.2
CARBURETOR HAD WATER JACKET FOR ANTI-ICING
PURPOSES. TWO AIR INLETS ON AIR CHAMBER WERE
FOR IDLING OPERATIONS.

NOTE NO.3
DE-COMPRESSION LEVER WAS USED TO REDUCE
COMPRESSION DURING STARTING OPERATIONS.

NOTE NO 4
MACHINE GUN SYNCHRONIZER UNIT WAS ATTACHED TO THE
REAR END OF THE CAMSHAFT.

AIR AGE INC., 551 FIFTH AVE., NEW YORK 17, N.Y.

SCALE: ⅜=1'0"	GENERAL ARRANGEMENT
TYPE: INLINE	GERMANY'S 160 & 180 H.P
COPYRIGHT 1948	**MERCEDES**
WILLIAM A. WYLAM	

BUILT 1914-18 BY DAIMLER-MOTOREN GESELLSCHAFT

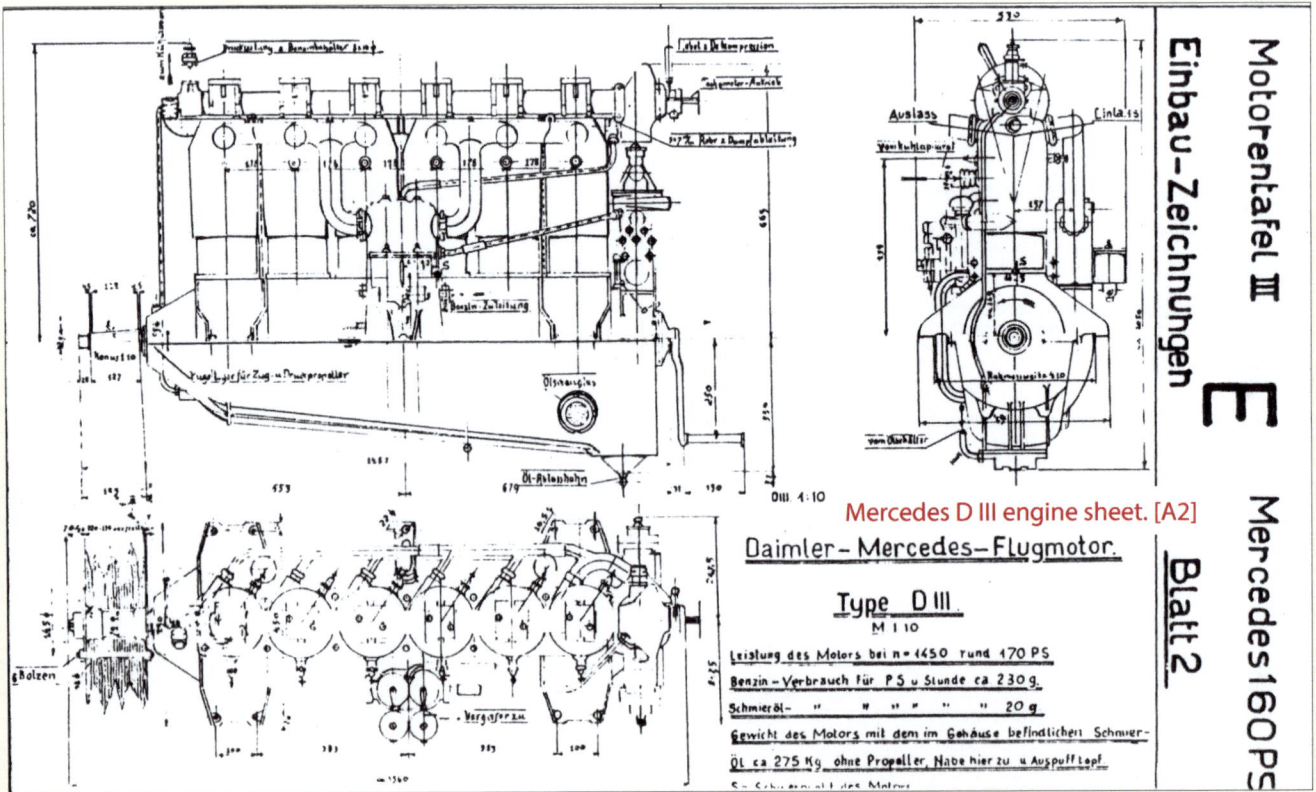

Mercedes D III engine sheet. [A2]

Motorentafel III
Einbau-Zeichnungen
E
Mercedes160PS
Blatt 2

Auslass   Einlass

Daimler - Mercedes - Flugmotor.

Type D III
M 110

Leistung des Motors bei n = 1450 rund 170 PS

Benzin - Verbrauch für PS u Stunde ca 230 g.

Schmieröl - " " " " " 20 g.

Gewicht des Motors mit dem im Gehäuse befindlichen Schmier-
Öl ca 275 Kg ohne Propeller, Nabe hier zu u Auspufftopf.

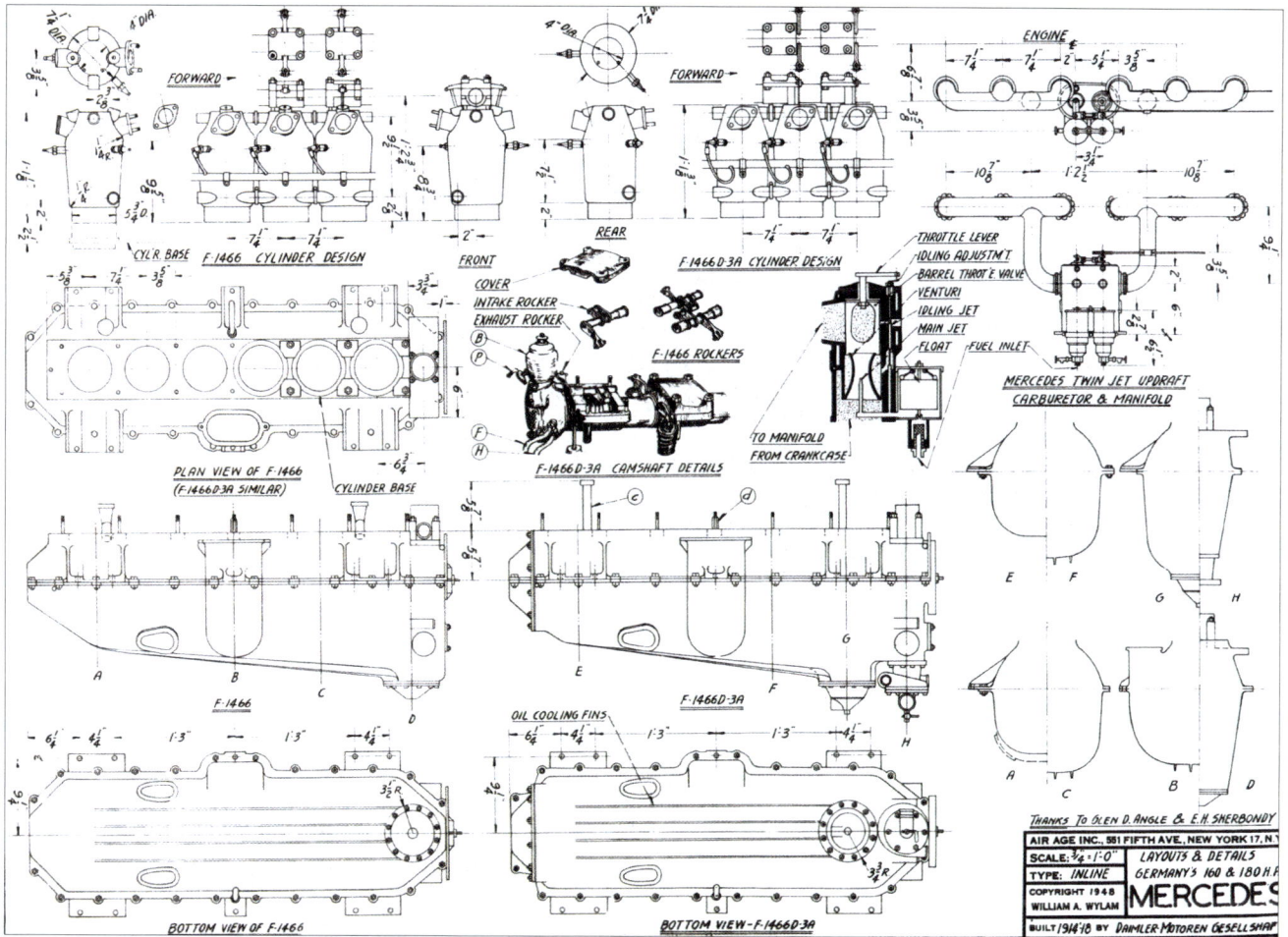

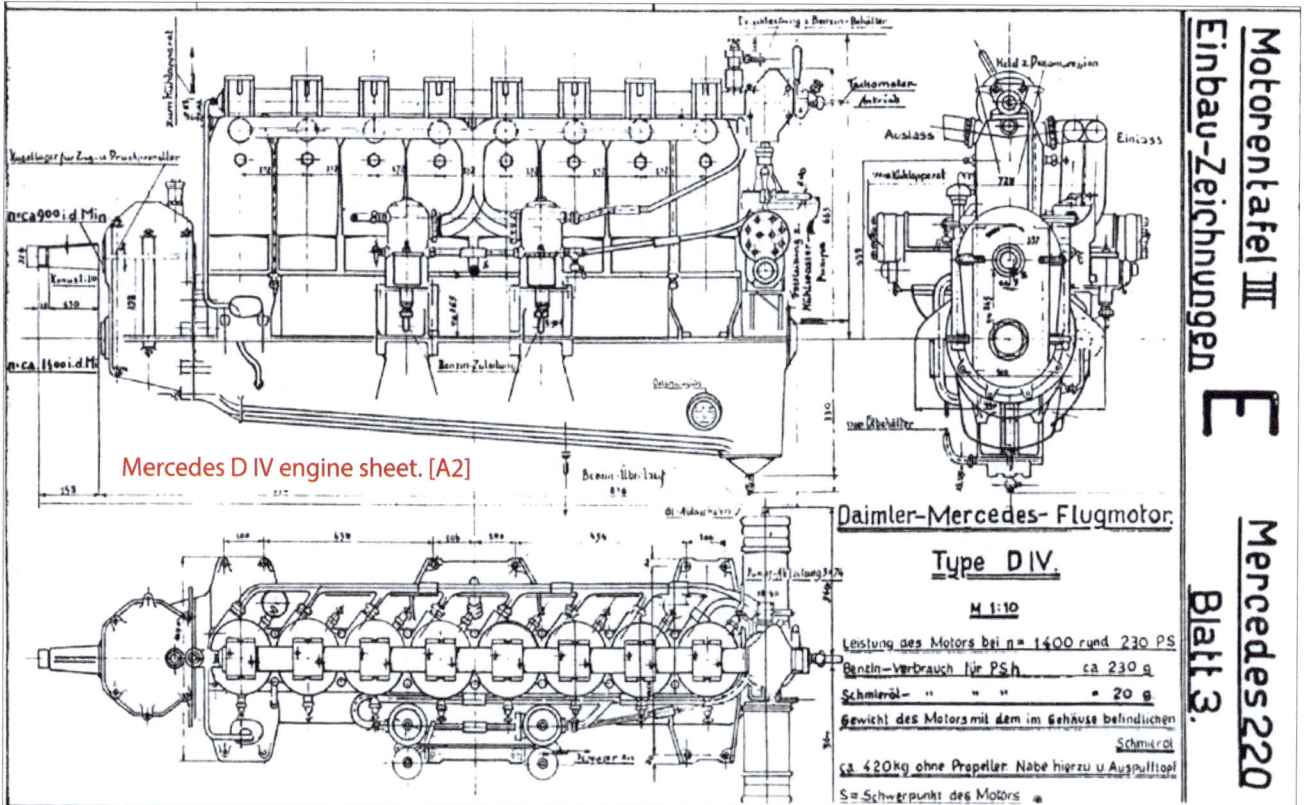

Mercedes D IV engine sheet. [A2]

80

Above: Mercedes D III with 160 hp, 1 twin-barrel carburetors, 2 magnetos, carburetor side. [A1]

Above: Mercedes D IIIa, exhaust side of engine but without an exhaust manifold/muffler fitted. [A15]

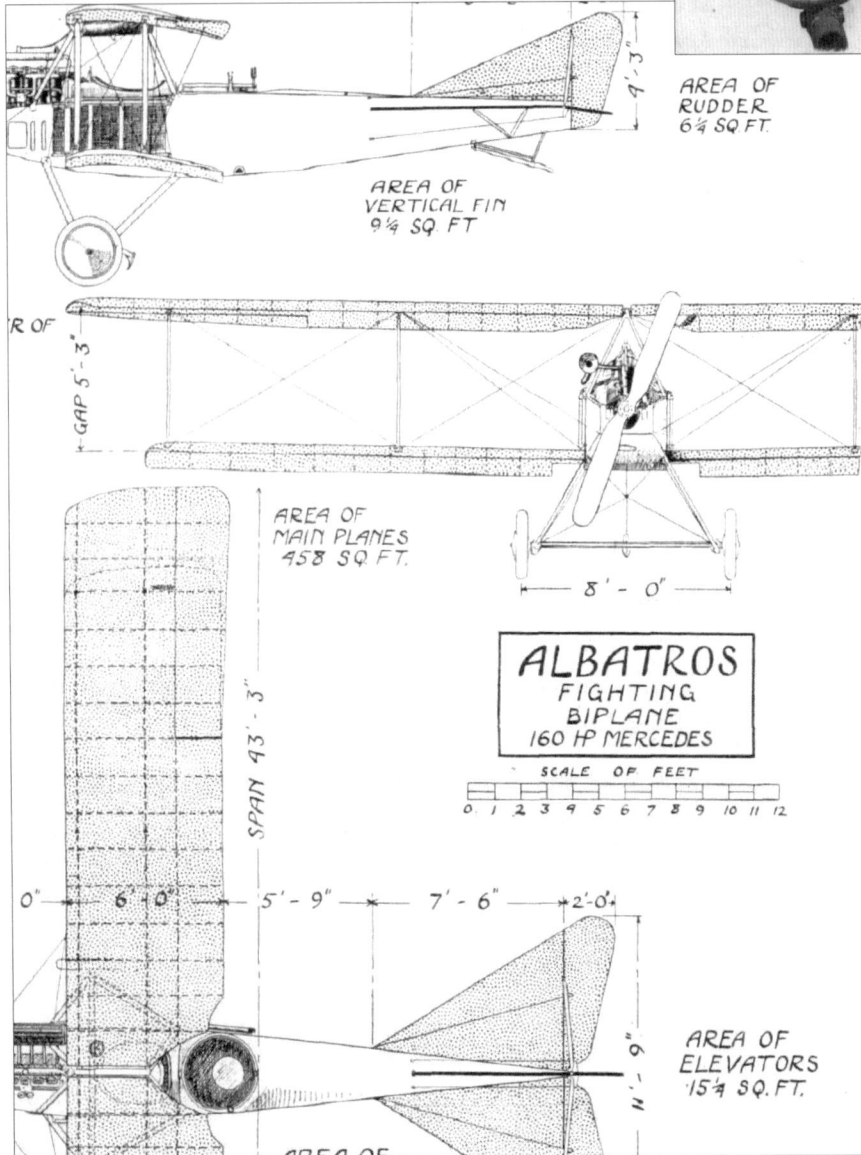

AREA OF RUDDER 6¼ SQ.FT.

AREA OF VERTICAL FIN 9¼ SQ. FT.

GAP 5'-3"

AREA OF MAIN PLANES 458 SQ.FT.

8'-0"

SPAN 43'-3"

ALBATROS
FIGHTING
BIPLANE
160 HP MERCEDES

SCALE OF FEET
0 1 2 3 4 5 6 7 8 9 10 11 12

0" 6'-0" 5'-9" 7'-6" 2'-0"

AREA OF ELEVATORS 15¼ SQ.FT.

AREA OF

Left: Plan, front, and side elevations to scale of an Albatros C.I Biplane. Side radiators were used with the Mercedes D III engine. [J2, 1915]

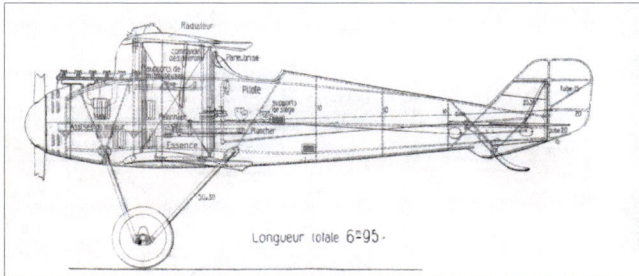

Above: 160hp Mercedes in Roland D.II. J12, 1918]

oil reservoirs were pressurized by an air compressor run off the crank.

3.16.13 Six-Cylinder 180 hp In-line Aircraft Engine (DF 170, F14566, D IIIa)

Above: Carburator side of D IIIa. [A1]

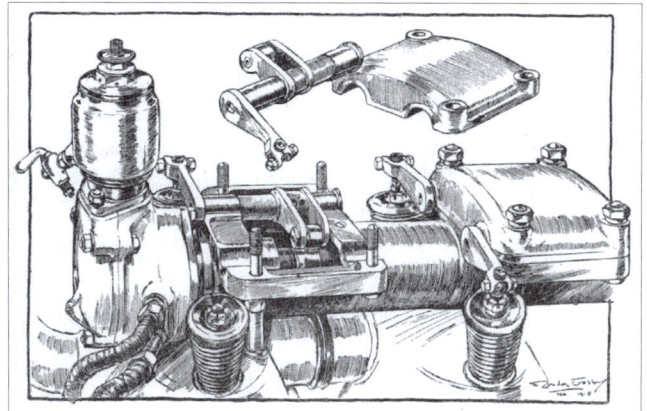

Development of the basic design of the Mercedes D III engine led to the slightly modified 170 hp D IIIa, which took over on the production lines in June 1917.

Briefly described, the 180 hp Mercedes was a combination of the 160 hp D III and the 260 hp Mercedes D IVa engines. In comparison with the standard type D III Mercedes, the new engine showed a marked improvement, both in the design as a whole and in its general performance during power and consumption tests, and as a comparison between the two engines the following comparative table of the leading particulars of the engines is herewith given:

In addition to the development of the D IVa engine, the weaknesses that had become apparent in the 160 hp D III engine were eliminated on the basis of the experience gained in front-mounted operation:

The aluminum-alloy cam housing, which was prone to breakage in the D III, was made of steel in the D IIIa, the rocker arm bearings were improved, the water pump was moved from the center of the main shaft to the lower end to prevent wetting of the ignition devices in the event of leaks, and the cylinders were mounted in the manner proven in the D IVa. Furthermore, the changes refer to changing the camshaft to match the design of the 260 hp D IVa engine, and installing an oil level pump and increasing the size of the air pump.

The single inlet and exhaust valves of each cylinder, which work at an angle of 15° to the central axis of the cylinder, are interchangeable as in the 160 hp engines and are of similar design; the valve operating gear is, however, of new design, and follows more the construction of the valve gear on the 260 hp Mercedes engines (D IVa). General details of this construction and working of the valve gear shown in the shown sketch.

It has to be noticed that the rocker arms and their

Above: Overhead Camshaft and new valve gear showing detachable valve rockers and new new design of air pump. [A15]

spindles are integral, being machined from steel forgings. The camshaft casing is constructed entirely from malleable-iron castings, and the valve rocker spindles work in direct contact with the malleable-iron, no bronze bushes being provided as bearings

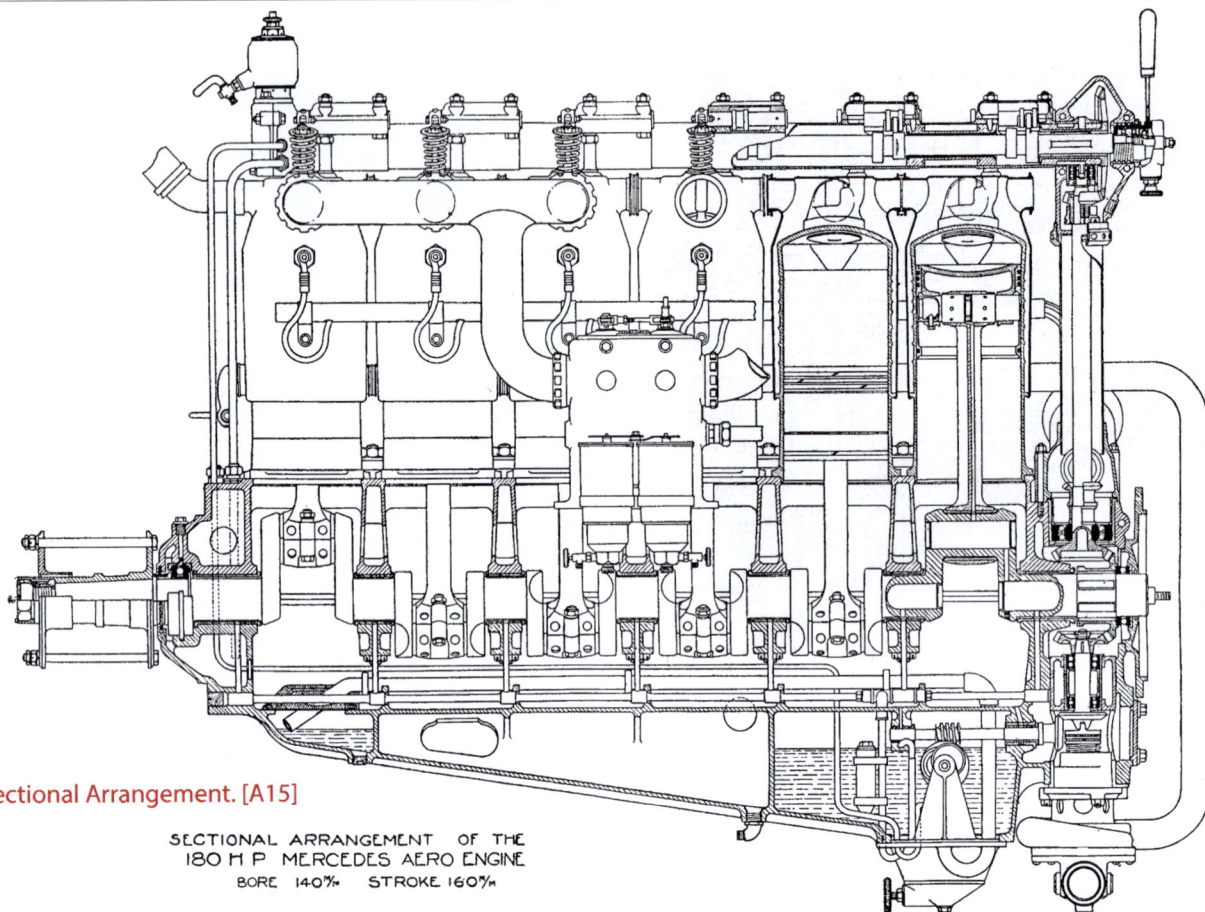

Sectional Arrangement. [A15]

SECTIONAL ARRANGEMENT OF THE
180 H P MERCEDES AERO ENGINE
BORE 140ᵐ/ STROKE 160ᵐ/

for the rocker arm spindles, and the covers of the camshaft casing form the top portion of the rocker spindle bearings.

The rocker spindles are hollow, and are lubricated through two holes drilled radially in the spindles by oil thrown off the revolving cams into the two holes drilled in the rocker arm carrying the cam roller. This design of valve gear is undoubtedly a great improvement on the arrangement adopted in the 160 hp Mercedes, the construction of which is well

Comparison of Mercedes D III & D IIIa		
Specification	**D III (160 hp)**	**D IIIa (180 hp)**
Bore [mm]	140	140
Stroke [mm]	160	160
Compression ratio	4.5 : 1	4.64 : 1
Average B.H.P. and speed	162 @ 1400	174 @ 1400
B.M.E.P. [lbs. per sq. inch]	102.0 @ 1400	109.1 @ 1400
Total weight (dry)* [lbs]	618	635
Weight per B.H.P. [lbs]	3.80	3.65
Fuel Consumption per hour [pints]	94.2	94.83
Fuel consumption per B.H.P. hour [pints]	0.58	0.545
Oil consumption per hour [pints]	5.0	7.3
Oil consumption per B.H.P. hour [pints]	0.031	0.042
* This weight is the weight of engine (dry), excluding propeller hub and exhaust manifold.		

Engine Datasheet			
Daimler Motoren Gesellschaft, Stuttgart-Untertürkheim			
Designation	**Mercedes 160/180 hp 6 cylinder In-line (D IIIa, a(ü), av(ü))**		
Type	D IIIa	D IIIa(ü)	D IIIav(ü)
Year:	1916	1917	1917
Purpose:	Aircraft engine		
Number of Cylinders:	6	6	6
Arrangement of Cylinders:	Inline piston engine		
Bore [mm]:	140	140	145
Stroke [mm]:	160	160	160
Displacement [l]:	14,8	14,8	15,8
Compression [Ratio]:	4,5	4,64	5,73
Power [hp]: norm./max.	160	180	200
RPM [min-1]: norm./max.	1450	1400	1400
Full pressure altitude [m]	3000	1800	3000
Power per displacement [hp/l]	12,2	10,8	11,4
Carburetor(s)			
No.:	1	1	1
Type:	One Mercedes twin-barrel carburetor		
Fuel consumption per hp per hour [g]:]:	220	200	200
Oil Pump No.:	1	1	1
Oil consumption per hp per hour [g/PS/h]:	15	17	17
Ignition No.:	2	2	2
Type:	Bosch ZH 6 magnetos		
Firing order:	1 – 5 – 3 – 6 – 2 – 4		
Cooling	Water		
Weight of complete engine (dry) & ext. masses			
Total [kg]:	268	298	310
Weight per displacement [kg/l]:	18,1	20,0	19,6
Weight per hp [kg/hp]:	1,48	1,86	1,72

Remarks: Type Certification: D IIIa – February 1915, D IIIav(ü) – June 1918.
Applications*: D.IIIa: Albatros D.III (L.20), D.V/Va (L.24), D.IX, D.XIII; D.F.W. D.II; Euler Dr. 5; Fokker D.VII, V11, Friedrichshafen FF60; Gotha WD27; Halberstadt CL.IV; Hannover CL5, Cls.I; Hansa-Brandenburg W.12, W.32, KD/D.I; Junkers J 10/CL.I; L.F.G. Roland D.XV; Pfalz D.III, D.XII; Rumpler D.I; Schütte-Lanz D.VII; Zeppelin-Lindau (Dornier) CL.II, D.I.
D.IIIa(ü): Fokker D.VII; Fokker V18; Halberstadt CLS.I.   **D.IIIav(ü):** Fokker D.VII
* Listing has no claim to completeness!

Above: Mercedes DIIIa last version, exhaust view. [A1]

Above: Mercedes aircraft engine D IIIa, last version with oil level pump, improved control housing and FT-drive (generator). [A15]

known, having the rocker arms working through slots in the camshaft casing, which are provided with felt-packing strips and baffle plates for retaining the oil in the camshaft casing.

The old 160 hp D III type multiple-plunger oil-pump had been replaced by the larger pump, similar in design to the Mercedes 260 hp D IVa pump. The oil pump was attached to the bottom of the rear oil sump or reservoir, at the rear end of the base chamber. This visible detail is very well suited to distinguish a D IIIa engine from its D III predecessor.

Mercedes D IIIa(ü)

The more powerful derivative was unofficially called "D IIIaü, whereby the "ü" stands for "über". D IIIaü engines had domed pistons and operated "over-compressed", means at a higher compression ratio. These engines, which had been designed as high-altitude engines were not able to operate at full throttle at sea level. For that reason, such engine has been (manually) de-rated up to a dedicated altitude. In case of the improved D IIIa(ü) the compression was regulated through a self-compensating carburetor.

This 180/200 hp D IIIa(ü) was introduced in late 1917. The D IIIa(ü) represented a substantial improvement in the design of the D III and D IIIa in order to meet the increased military demands.

This engine changed the pistons again, this time to a domed profile that further increased the maximum compression. Additionally, a new altitude-compensating carburetor was added, which

Above: Mercedes D IIIa 6-cylinder exhaust side.

Facing Page, Below Right: Mercedes D IIIa front view.

Right: 200 hp high compression Mercedes engine D IIIa(ü). [ER]

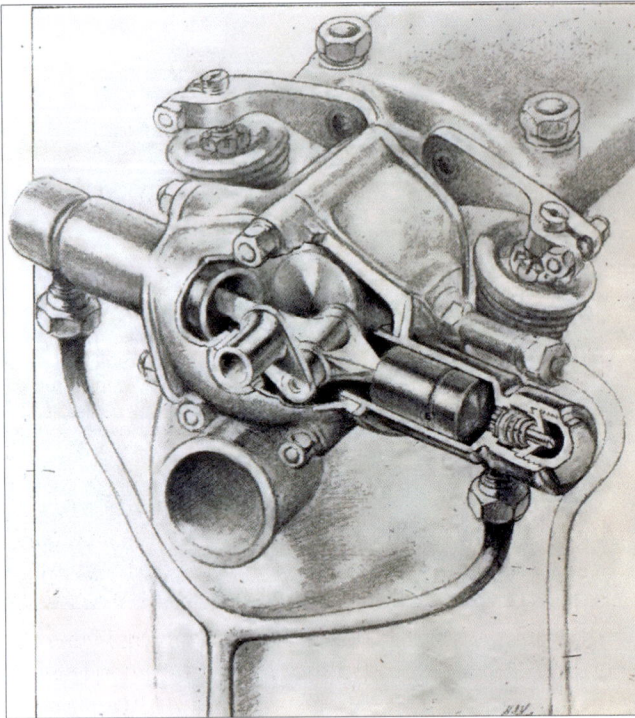

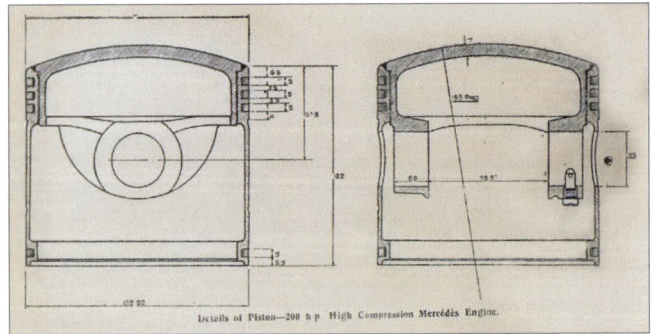

Details of Piston—200 h p High Compression Mercédès Engine.

Above: Details of the piston D IIIa(ü). [A15]

Left: Air pump of the high compression Mercedes engine. [A15]

Right: Sketch of throttle barrel and automatic air valve of the piston D IIIa(ü). [A15]

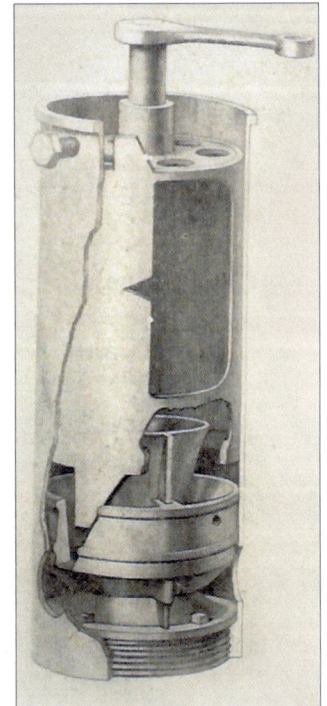

improved performance at higher altitudes. To support operations at these altitudes, water from the radiator was used to heat the air intake and prevent icing in the carburetor. The "aü" model with improved D III and D IIIa engine blocks was the most produced German fighter engine in 1918 and was installed in most fighter designs from the end of 1917. In total 12.000 Mercedes D IIIa have been produced over the last two years of the war.

Mercedes D IIIav(ü)
Nevertheless, the final version attempting to keep the D III block competitive was the 200 hp (200–217 hp) D IIIav (or avü), introduced

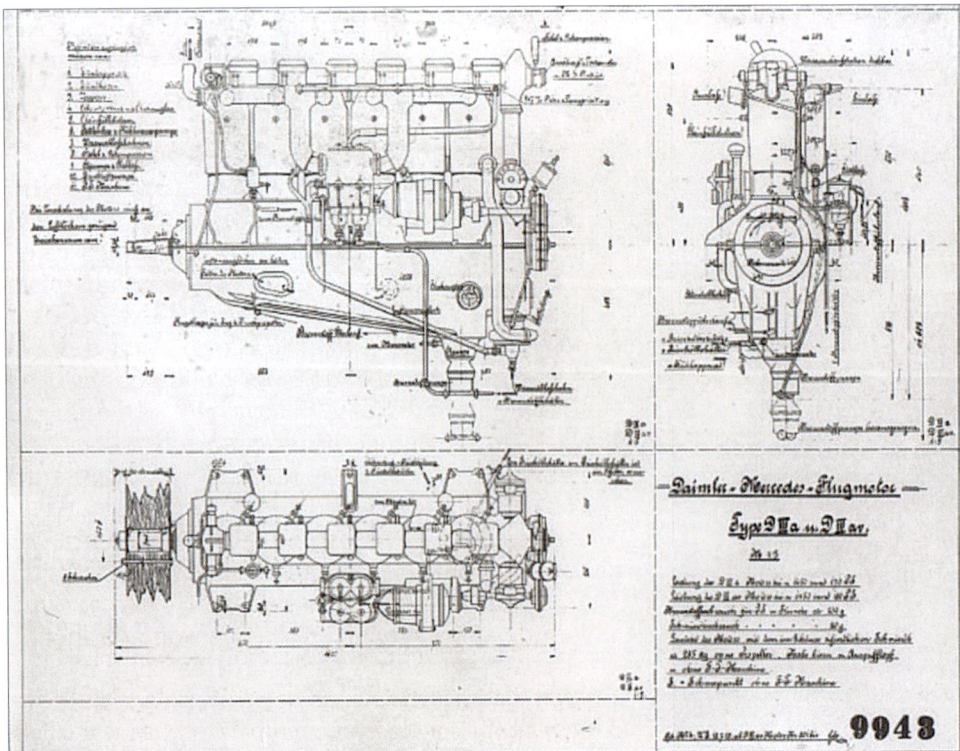

Facing Page, Lower Left: Test setup of the Wittig compressor on the test bench with D IIIa. [A1]

Left: 200 hp high compression Mercedes engine D IIIa(ü). [A1]

Above: D IIIa carburetor side.

Right: D IIIa aft view.

mid-October 1918. The "av" used slightly longer pistons, increasing the compression yet again, while at the same time allowing them to move faster due to the reduced weight. In addition, the cylinders had a modified bore of 145 mm, instead of the previous 140 mm. The maximum allowable rotation increased from 1,400 in the earlier models to 1,600 in the "av", accounting for most of the gains in power. The D IIIav engine obtained military type certification in June 1918, but it is questionable whether this engine was built in series and used in aircraft. The increased use of benzene in German aviation fuel may have supported this final upgrade of power, because its higher octane rating was better suited for the higher compression ratio.

The engine numbers of the 160 hp D IIIa engines (new design with closed cast iron control shaft housing and bottom-mounted water pump) started with 32700. Engine numbers 33200–34999 were still provided for the Mercedes D.III (old design).

D IIIa applications:

AEG C.IV, Ago C.I, Albatros C.I, C.III, C.XIII, D.II, D.III, D.V/D.Va, W.4, Aviatik C.I, C.III, Fokker D.IV, D.VII, Halberstadt CL.II, CL.IV, Hannover CL.III, Hansa-Brandenburg C.I, Junkers CL.I, D.I, LFG Roland C.II, D.II, D.VI, D.XV, Rumpler C.I, Rumpler 6B, Pfalz D.III, D.XII, Schütte-Lanz G.I and several of Germany's giant aircraft (Riesenflugzeug) of World War I.

3.16.14 Eight-Cylinder 185 hp V-type Engine (FV 10678, DF 3b, D IIIb)

Already in 1916 the German authorities examined captured aircraft engines on their test benches, among them for example the Hispano V8 engine. It turned out that the Hispano was designed for speeds above 2000 rpm and for operation with transmission. In October 1916, the Idflieg felt obliged by the results of the tests to develop a high-speed engine that was as similar as possible to the Hispano. These engines were supposed to deliver up to 200 hp at 2000 to 2200 rpm, especially for the D fighters. In addition, a reduction gear should be able to reduce the output speed by half.

Another big advantage of this V-engine principle should be the shorter length, because the arrangement of the cylinders resulted in an engine length which was a bit longer than that of a normal 4-cylinder engine. This detail was desirable especially for the fast, but smaller fighter planes, because the center of gravity of the plane did not move forward significantly.

Around the middle of 1918, DMG brought out

Above, Below, & Bottom: Mercedes 185 hp 8-cylinder V-type (D IIIb, FV 10). [A1]

Engine Datasheet	
Daimler Motoren Gesellschaft, Stuttgart-Untertürkheim	
Designation	**Mercedes 200/185 hp 8-cylinder V-type (FV 10678, DF 3b, D IIIb)**
Year:	1917/18
Purpose:	Aircraft engine
Number of Cylinders:	8
Arrangement of Cylinders:	V-type piston engine, 90°
Bore [mm]:	106
Stroke [mm]:	170
Displacement [l]:	12,0
Compression [Ratio]	6,0
RPM [min-1]: norm./max.	1800/1950
Power [hp]: norm./max.	185/200
Power per displacement [hp/l]:	15,4
Carburetor(s)	
No.:	
Type:	
Fuel consumption per hp per hour [g]:]:	
Oil Pump	
No.:	
Oil consumption per hp per hour [g/PS/h]:	
Ignition No.:	
Type:	
Firing order:	
Cooling	Water
Weight of complete engine (dry) & ext. masses	
Total [kg]:	260
Weight per displacement [kg/l]:	21,7
Weight per hp [kg/hp]:	1,41

Remarks: With reduction gear (2 : 1).
Applications*: Daimler CL.I (L8), D.I (L6), D.II (L9), L.11, L.14
* Listing has no claim to completeness!

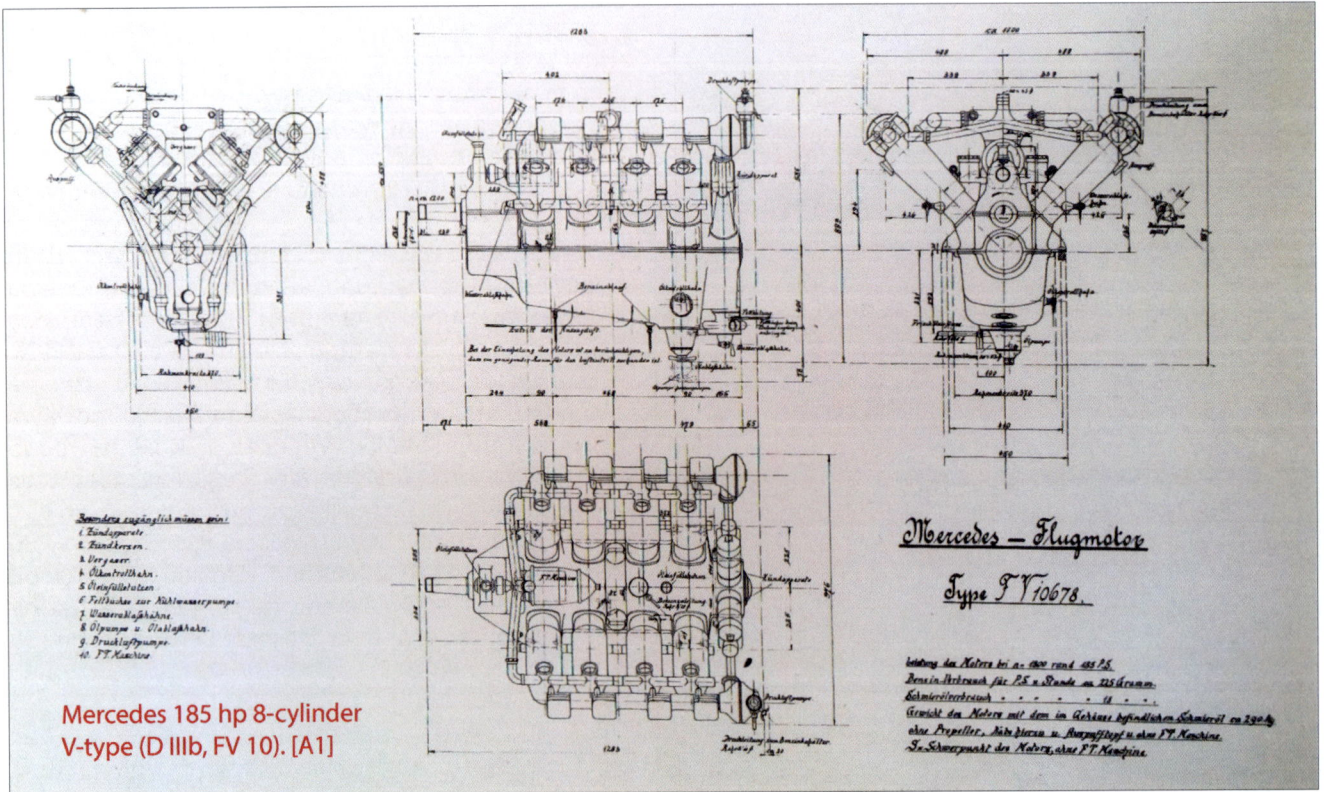

Mercedes 185 hp 8-cylinder V-type (D IIIb, FV 10). [A1]

an 8-cylinder V-engine in power class III (150–200 hp) for the first time. This new engine type was designated D IIIb in accordance with military specifications.

The development of this new aircraft engine did not run smoothly. Several times the stroke and bore were changed or modifications to the gearbox were necessary. By the end of the war, this engine was no longer ready for production, and therefore no type approval was obtained. Few engines were tested in

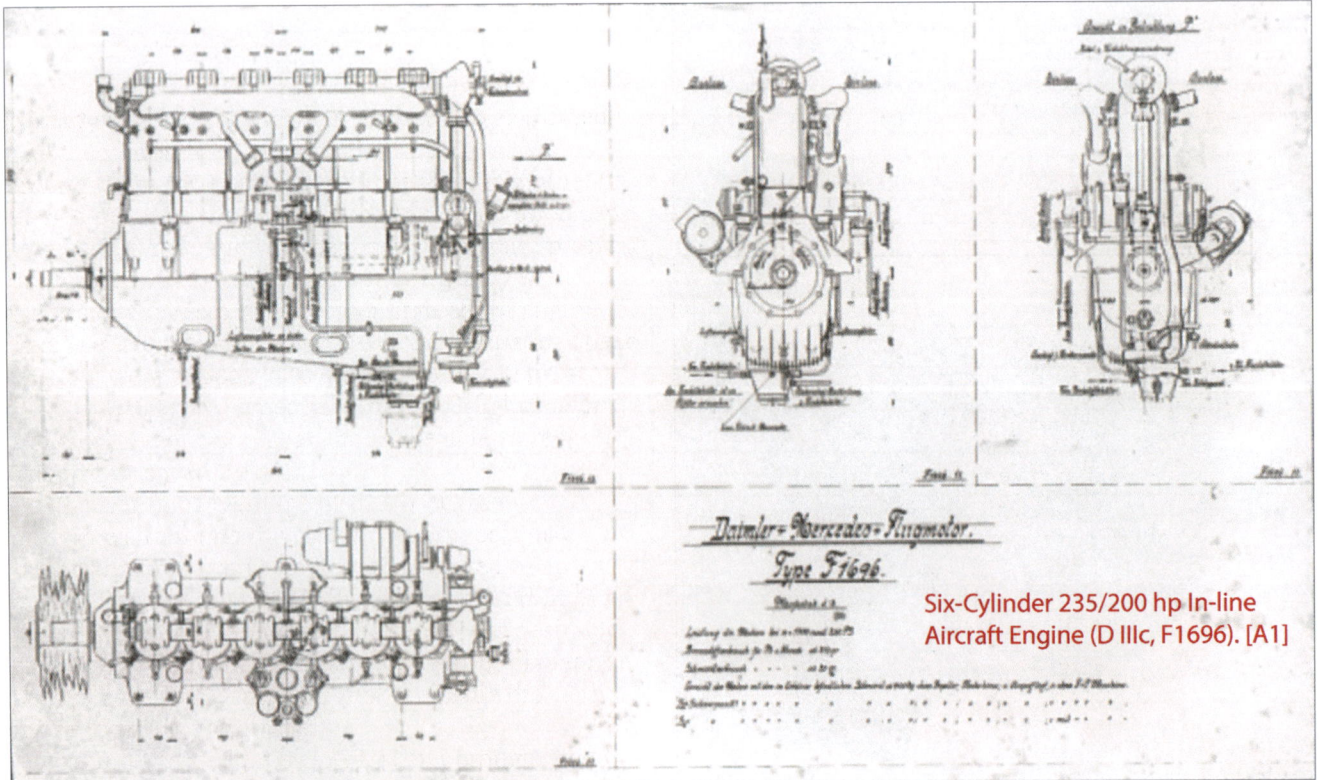

Six-Cylinder 235/200 hp In-line Aircraft Engine (D IIIc, F1696). [A1]

practice. Well known are test flights in a Daimler-Jagdeinsitzer D.I. According to official factory specifications the power output was 200 hp at 1950 rpm.

3.16.15 Six-Cylinder 235/200 hp In-line Aircraft Engine (D IIIc, F1696)

Based on the D IIIa, DMG developed a further 6-cylinder engine in the 150 to 200 hp power class under the company's internal designation F1696, which was to be used as the D IIIc once it had been approved. For this engine, which was designed to deliver up to 235 hp, the 160 mm cylinders were again used, with a piston stroke of 190 mm. Development was not completed due to the end of the war.

3.16.16 Eight-cylinder 230/220 hp In-line Engine (D IV, F1468, DF220)

With the Mercedes D IV, Daimler Motoren Gesellschaft offered a powerful 220 hp aircraft engine as early as 1915/16. The type testing of this engine took place in December 1915 and was finished in June 1916.

While retaining the bore and stroke, the addition of two more cylinders to the D III resulted in the eight-cylinder Mercedes D IV engine, which completed acceptance testing at the end of 1915. The engine with a displacement of 19.7 litres and a power output of 220 hp was the first German series-production aircraft engine with a propeller reduction gearbox, but was also delivered without it. Due to the long overall length of 2 m, problems arose with both the casing stiffness and the vibration resistance of the crankshaft. As the engineers were not able to improve the reliability of the engine, further testing was stopped and it was replaced in production by the unrelated six-cylinder Mercedes D IVa. The production was discontinued after the delivery of 429 units.

The general design was based on the pistons of the well-known D.III 6-cylinder design and developed around 220 hp, making it a Class IV motor under the Idflieg classification system then in use in Imperial Germany. The D IV existed with or without reduction gear. Different firing orders allowed the drive shaft of the motor to be run on the right or left side as required.

Applications:
AEG C.V, G.III, R.I, AGO C.II, C.VIII, Albatros C.V, DFW R.I, Gotha G.II, LVG C.IV, different R-planes (Riesenflugzeuge).

Extract from Investigation Report, taken from *The Aeroplane* 1918:
The following detailed report on the design of the 8-cylinder Mercedes engine is based on an investigation of the engine (No. 23,003) taken from the German two-seater Albatros Biplane (G.37) which was brought down by anti-aircraft guns near Armentieres on the 12th of May, 1917.

This engine has been tested at the Royal Aircraft Factory and results of B.H.P. developed, petrol and oil consumption, etc., during tests are given herewith, together with details of the engine design and the leading particulars of the engine. Although this engine, according to reports, is now obsolete, the design having been abandoned in favour of the German standard six-cylinder vertical type, details and illustrations of the engine will no doubt prove of considerable interest, more particularly to those interested in the design of the special engines used for airship work.

In its general details this engine follows closely the design of the 160 H.P. Mercedes engines as regards the construction of the cylinders, pistons, valve gear, etc., and also in the lubrication system. It is therefore very similar to the 160 H.P. engine, with an extra pair of standard cylinders and a massive propeller shaft reduction gear, and the necessary alterations to the design of the crankshaft and the induction system, and in consequence of this similarity in detail to the 160 H.P. Mercedes, it will

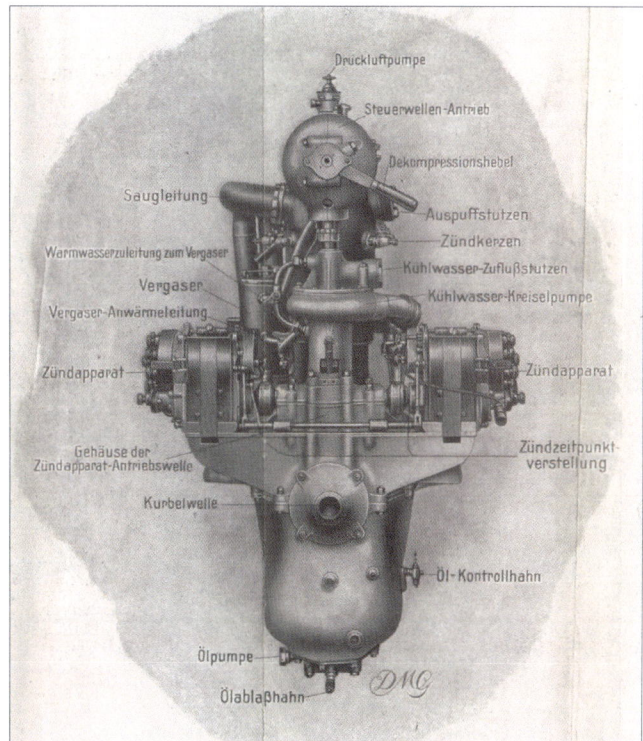

Above: Front view 220hp DIV Mercedes 8-cylinder 1918. [M31]

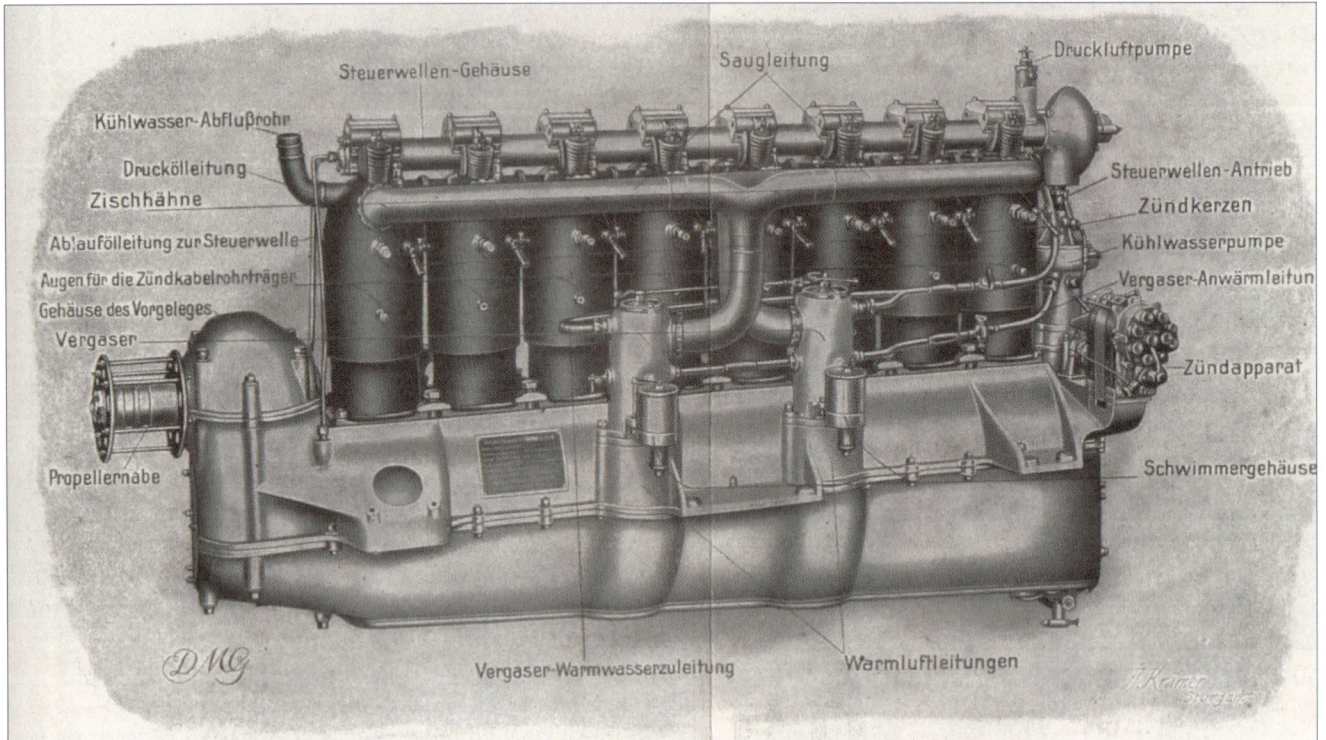

Above & Facing Page, Above: Carburetor side of the 220hp D IV Mercedes 8-cylinder 1918. [M31]

Below & Facing Page, Below: Exhaust side of the 220hp D IV Mercedes 8-cylinder 1918. [M31]

be unnecessary to deal at any length in this report with the design of those parts of the engine which are identical, a report on the former having already been issued, and the design being now well known in this country.

During calibration tests at the Royal Aircraft Factory, the engine showed a very good general performance, developing a maximum of 286 B.H.P. at 1,750 r.p.m. and an average of 242 B.H.P. at a normal crankshaft speed of 1,350 r.p.m.

Summary of Test

Average petrol consumption   141.3 pints

Figs. 1 & 2.—Inlet and Exhaust Sides of the 8-cylinder 240-h.p. Mercédès Engine. Built up of 8 Cylinders of the 160-180-h.p. Size.

Engine Datasheet	
Daimler Motoren Gesellschaft, Stuttgart-Untertürkheim	
Designation	**Mercedes 235/220 hp 8-cylinder in-line (D IV, F 1468, DF 220)**
Year:	1915
Purpose:	Aircraft engine
Number of Cylinders:	8
Arrangement of Cylinders:	In-line piston engine
Bore [mm]:	140
Stroke [mm]:	160
Displacement [l]:	19,7
Compression [Ratio]	1 : 4,8
RPM [min-1]: norm./max.	1400/1300
Power [hp]: norm./max.	235/220
Power per displacement [hp/l]:	11,9
Carburetor(s)	
No.:	2
Type:	Mercedes rotary valve carburetor
Fuel consumption per hp per hour [g]:]	230
Oil Pump	
No.:	
Oil consumption per hp per hour [g/PS/h]:	20
Ignition No.:	2
Type:	Bosch HL 8 or MEA ignitors
Firing order:	Right turn: 1–3–2–4–8–6–7–5
	Left turn: 1–3–4–2–6–8–7–5
Cooling	Water
Weight of complete engine (dry) & ext. masses	
Total [kg]:	410
Weight per displacement [kg/l]:	20,5
Weight per hp [kg/hp]:	1,74

Remarks: Variant with or without reduction gear; turned left or right.
Applications*: A.E.G. C.V, G.III; Albatros C.V/16 (L.14), C.V/17 (L.14a); OAW (Alb.) C.II; Daimler G.II; D.F.W. R.I; Euler Experimental triplane; Gotha G.II ; Kondor W 2 C; K.W. Type 947, K.W. Type 1650; Lübeck-Travemünde F2; L.V.G. C.IV; Siemens-Forssman R
* Listing has no claim to completeness!

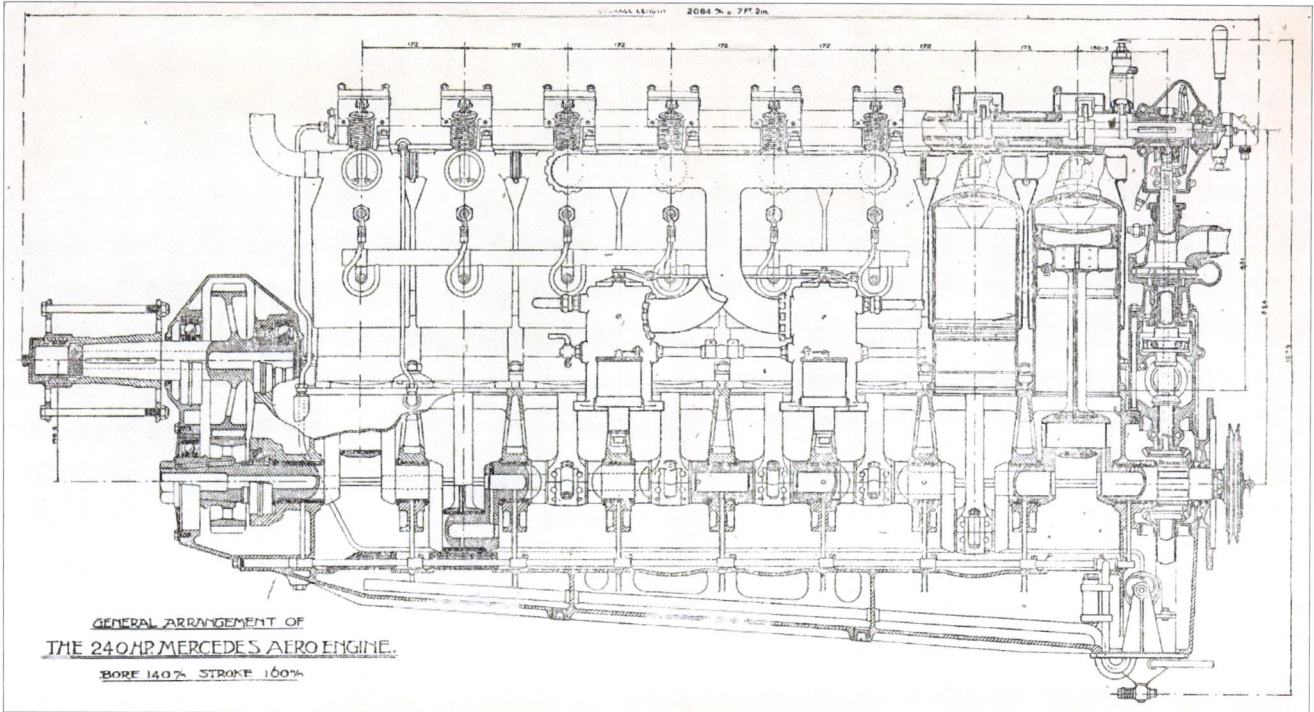

GENERAL ARRANGEMENT OF
THE 240 HP MERCEDES AERO ENGINE.
BORE 140% STROKE 160%

Above: Sectional drawing of the 220hp D IV Mercedes 8-cylinder 1918. [J10, 1918]

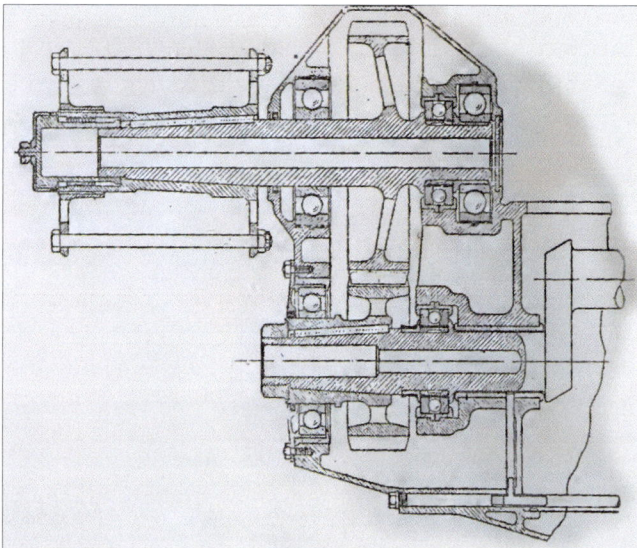

Above: Reduction gearing of the D IV 240hp. [M31]

Average petrol consumption	0.582 pints per B.H.P. hour
Average oil consumption	0.042 pints/B.H.P./hr
Oil temperature	37,5 °C
Max. B.M.E.P. at 1,100 r.p.m.	120 lbs./sq. in.
Average B.M.E.P. at 1,350 rpm	118 lbs./sq. in.

The total weight of complete engine, dry including propeller hub and exhaust manifold = 900 lbs., equivalent to 3.72 lbs per B.H.P.

An attempt was made to throttle the engine below 900 r.p.m., but the running was irregular.

During a power and consumption run of 1 hour's

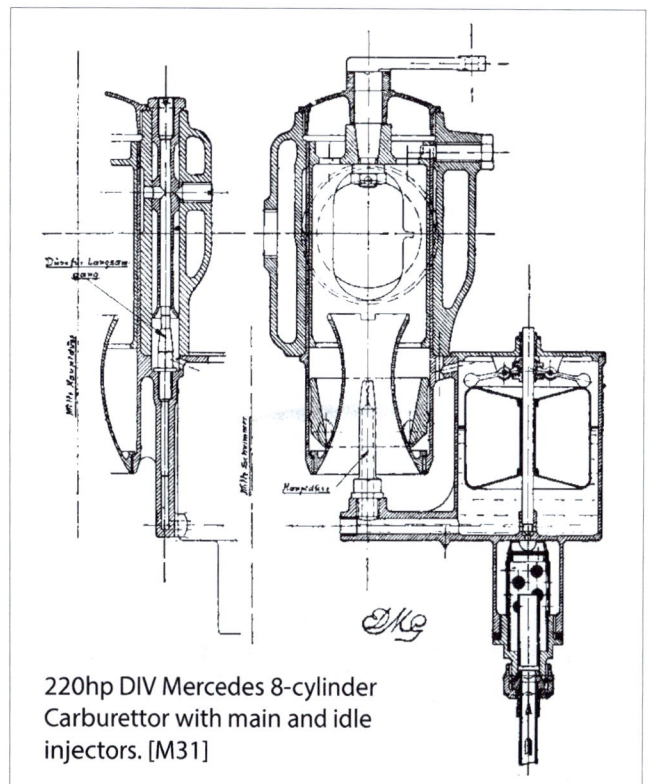

220hp DIV Mercedes 8-cylinder Carburettor with main and idle injectors. [M31]

duration an average of 267 B.H.P. was developed, at an average speed of 1,550 r.p.m., and at an average petrol consumption of 155 pints per hour = 0.582 pints per B.H.P. hour.

Oil consumption = 10.10 pints per hour= 0.042 pints per B.H.P hour.

Above: Mercedes Daimler Flugmotor 1915, in-line 8-cylinder D IV with 238 hp, carburetor side. [A1]

Above: Mercedes D IV installed in an Albatros C.V. [J12, 1918]

Left: Mercedes Daimler Flugmotor 1915, in-line 8-cylinder D IV with 238 hp, exhaust side. [A1]

Water temperature, inlet = 65°C; outlet = 78°C.

This test should not, however, be taken as representing the normal performance of the engine, as the average speed at which it was run, namely 1,550 r.p.m., is higher than that which would be obtained for any length of time in the air.

Details of Construction.

Cylinders: These, as already stated, are of the standard 160 H.P. type, and are made entirely of steel, being built up of machined steel forgings with the valve pockets screwed and welded into the cylinder head. The water jackets are of sheet steel, 1.5 mm. gauge, all joints being acetylene-welded in position.

The single inlet and exhaust valves are operated by the usual Mercedes type overhead camshaft and valve gear, which is fitted with the well-known half compression gear at the rear end of the camshaft casing. This design of half compression gear is used on all types of Mercedes engines, including the 260 H.P , and the latest 180 H.P. Mercedes engines. Note: The sectional view of the connecting rod is shown at right angles to its correct position in the cylinder.

Pistons: Standard 160 H.P. pistons are used with concave steel crowns, screwed and welded into the cast iron skirts, which are fitted with three rings above the gudgeon pin, and one at the bottom of the skirt.

Connecting Rods: The H. section connecting rods and floating small-end bushes are similar to those used on the 160 H.P. engines except that the big-end bearings are 3.5 mm. shorter in the 8-cylinder engines. This reduction in the length of the big-end bearings has been affected by turning off the outer faces of the connecting rod big-end brasses, evidently with the idea of reducing as much as possible the overall length of the engine.

Crankshaft: The exceptional length of crankshaft and the disposition of the cranks is shown in Fig. 8. The crankshaft runs in 9 plain white metal bearings, and is fitted with a thrust ball-race at the front, at which end the driving pinion is supported by a large ball-bearing, mounted on an extension of the driving pinion.

Reduction Gear. In view of the fact that this engine is apparently the first attempt to introduce an indirect airscrew drive on any enemy aero engine in service, the construction of the reduction gear, as fitted to the 8-cylinder Mercedes engine, is of considerable interest. The general lay-out is shown in Fig 3, and most of the details of construction in Fig. 9. The smaller, or driving, pinion of the reduction gear is keyed to the tapered extension of

Above: Forsmann R with Mercedes D IV inboard engines. [A1]

Above: Forssmann R taking off. [A1]

the crankshaft, the key being fitted parallel to the taper on the crankshaft. The driving gear is held in position on the shaft by a large locking nut, fixed by a grub screw.

As already stated, the front end of the driving pinion is supported on a large ball race, 148 mm. dia., carried on an extension of the boss in front of the pinion. The larger, or driven, pinion is integral with the airscrew shaft, and is machined from a solid forging, the gear wheel having holes drilled through the dished webs of the wheel to save weight. The number of teeth on the driving pinion is 26, and on the driven pinion 40, giving a speed ratio of 1.54:1. The diameter of the crankshaft pinion is 168 mm.,

and that of the airscrew shaft pinion is 250 mm.

The airscrew shaft is mounted on two large ball bearings, and is provided with a thrust ball-race, which is located by a double flanged ring, registering with a groove cut in the bearing housing.

3.16.17 Six-Cylinder 260 hp In-line Aero-Engine (D IVa, F1686, DF260)

The research on the 260 hp 6 cylinder D IVa, which replaced the failed Mercedes D IV inline eight-cylinder engine, started in 1915 and was initially intended mainly for use in bomber aircraft. The military type design approval for this engine was

Exhaust side of Daimler 260 hp D IVa. [M28]

Carbureattor side of Daimler 260 hp D IVa. [M28]

Above & Left: Mercedes D IV on display. (Deutsches Museum München)

granted in June 1916.

As early as 1916, Daimler-Werke began systematic trials to "supercharge" its aircraft engines with the aid of a blower or compressor as the world's first aircraft engine factory. Series production of blower aircraft engines could have started in the fall of 1918, but this was prevented by the end of the war.

Nevertheless, the D IVa represented an over-compressed high-altitude engine with 260 hp at 1370 rpm (275 hp at 1450 rpm). It had single steel cylinders, an overhead camshaft and four valves per cylinder (two intake and two exhaust valves). The carburetor was located behind cylinder 6, which required a very long intake line, which in turn resulted in an uneven cylinder filling and led to a less favourable fuel consumption.

In 1917 and 1918 a Mercedes D IVa with petrol injection pump was tested at the Junkers company, whereby ldflieg intended to have this engine equipped as standard in order to eliminate the irregular mixture distribution by means of the fuel pump.

This Page: Mercedes 260hp D IVa on display. [B43; J2, 1918]

The D IVa was also installed in G and R aircraft and for this purpose was also supplied as a "mirror engine", i.e. exhaust pipes were arranged on the left or right side as required. In addition, the engines could be ordered clockwise or counter clockwise. A total of 4555 units were built.

To further increase altitude performance, the D IVa was tested with a Roots blower, with the compressor driven by gears from the front end of the crankshaft. Among other things, Schwade-Werke tested this engine with a two-stage Schwade rotary charger, driven at the rear end of the crankshaft by a centrifugal clutch at 10500 rpm. Other aircraft

This Page: Mercedes 260hp D IVa exhaust side (above) and intake side (below). [A15, A2]

Above: Mercedes 260hp D IVa rear view. [A2]
Right: Mercedes 260hp D IVa front view. [A2]

Below: Mercedes 275hp D IVa engine sheet.

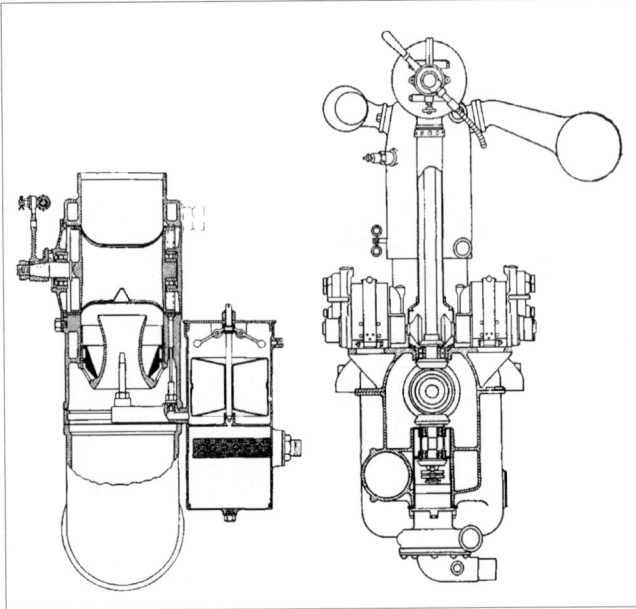

Above: Vertical carburetor drive of Mercedes 260hp D IVa. [J2, 1918]

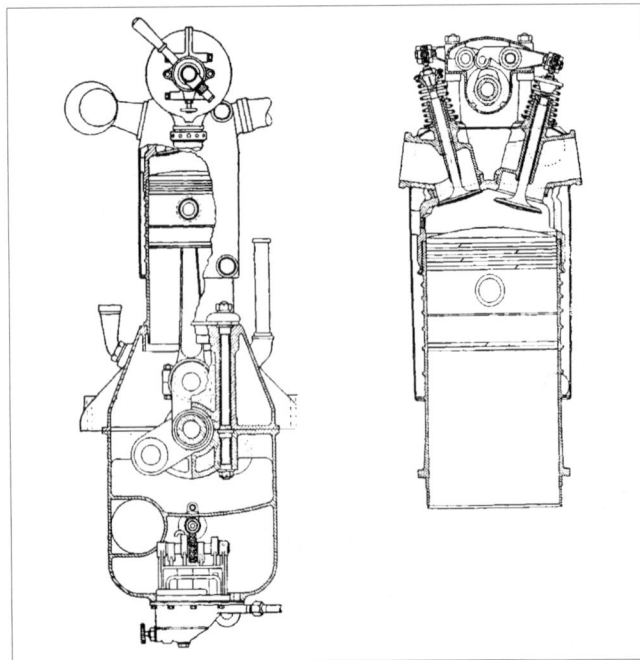

Above: Cross section of Mercedes 260hp D IVa. [J2, 1918]

Above: Front end of camshaft of Mercedes 260hp D IVa with experimental Schwade supercharger. [J2, 1918]

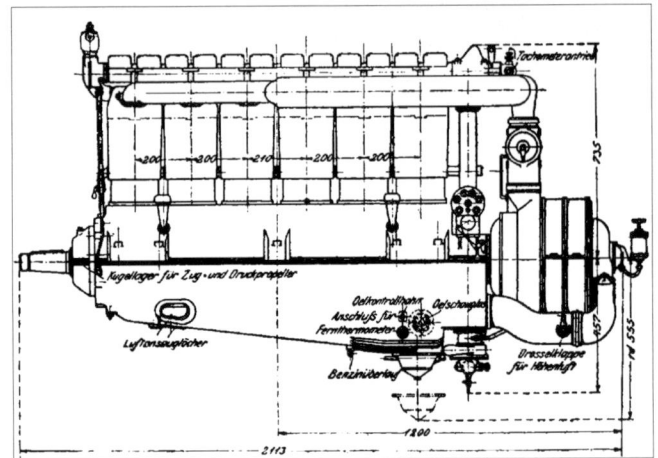

Above: Mercedes 260hp D IVa with experimental Schwade supercharger. [L11]

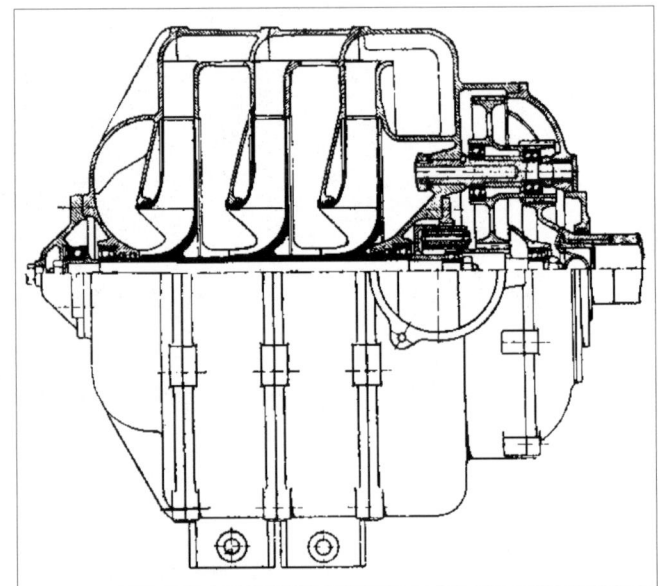

Above: Experimental Schwade supercharger used with Mercedes 260hp D IVa. [L11]

manufacturers, such as AEG and Siemens-Werke each equipped one engine with compressors.

The figure below shows the assembly of a 260 hp aircraft engine with a fan from Schwade & Co. The blower is directly coupled to the engine and is designed for an average of approx. 1000 kg/st at a maximum pressure ratio of $b_0/b=1.52$. It consists of four consecutive chambers (Fig. 4). The first chamber contains the gearbox, while the others each contain an impeller with the associated guide vane ring. The

Engine Datasheet	
Daimler Motoren Gesellschaft, Stuttgart-Untertürkheim	
Designation	**Mercedes 275/260 hp 6-Cylinder In-line (F1686, DF260, D IVa)**
Year:	1915/18
Purpose:	Aircraft engine
Number of Cylinders:	6
Arrangement of Cylinders:	In-line piston engine
Bore [mm]:	160
Stroke [mm]:	180
Displacement [l]:	21,7
Compression [Ratio]:	5,6
Power [hp]: norm./max.	1370/1450
RPM [min-1]: norm./max.	260/275
Full pressure altitude [m]	3500
Power per displacement [hp/l]:	12,7
Carburetor(s)	
No.:	1
Type:	Twin jet Mercedes carburetor with automatic mixture control
Fuel consumption per hp per hour [g]:]:	230
Oil Pump	
No.:	
Oil consumption per hp per hour [g/PS/h]:	20
Ignition No.:	2
Type:	Bosch ZH 6
Firing order:	1–5–3–6–2–4
Cooling	Water
Weight of complete engine (dry) & ext. masses	
Total [kg]:	405
Weight per displacement [kg/l]:	18,7
Weight per hp [kg/hp]:	1,47

Remarks: Variants with or without reduction gear; turned left or right. Critical altitude: 3500 m.
Applications*: A.E.G. G.IV/IVa/IVb/IVb-lang, A.E.G. G.IVk, G.V, J.III, AR.I; Ago C.VIII, C.IX; Albatros C.X (L.25), C.XII (L.27); BFW N.I (1916); Daimler G.III, L.12; D.F.W. R.II; Friedrichshafen FF45 (G.III/G. IIIa), FF53, FF61 (G.IV), FF62 (G.V) FF67, N.I; Gotha G.III, G.IV , G.V/Va/Vb, G.VI, GL.VII, GL.VIII, WD15, WD20, WD28; Hansa-Brandenburg W.26, W.33; L.F.G. Roland C.VIII; Linke Hofmann R.I, R.II; Pfalz C.I; Rumpler C.IV, C.VI, 8C12, G.III; SSW R.II, R.VII; Zeppelin Staaken R.VI, R.VIII, R.IX, Type L, Type 8301, Type 8303. * Listing has no claim to completeness!

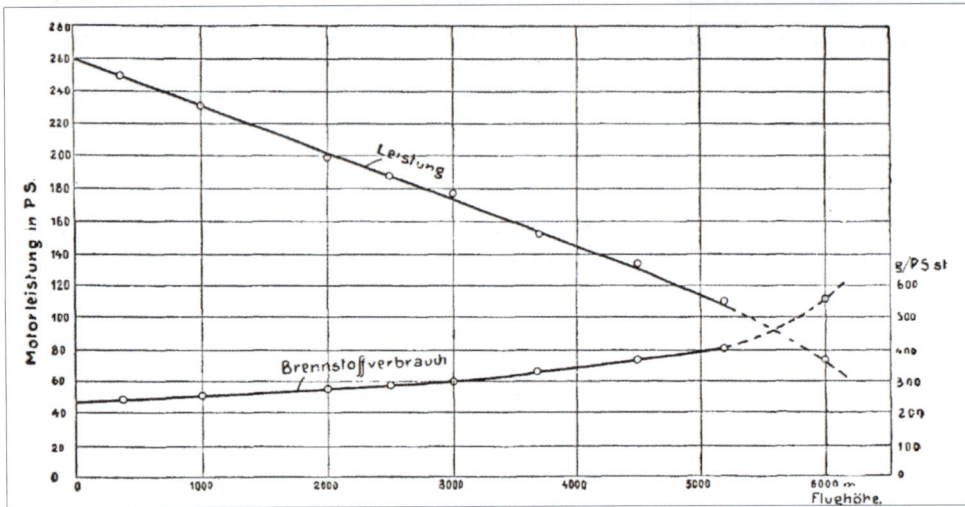

Above & Above Left:
Mercedes aircraft engine experimental version of D IVa with Roots blower for supercharging. [A1]

Left: Mercedes D IVa power curve. [A1]

chambers are made of cast aluminium, the impellers of special steel. The gearbox has two opposite intermediate wheels running on fixed bolts with ball bearings. The air flows to the fan through the lower housing of the motor to cool it. The blower weighs 47.5 kg. If the weight of the 260 hp aircraft engine is assumed to be 420 kg and one considers that the engine without fan only produces 170 hp at an altitude of 3.5 km, but the drive of the fan requires about 20 hp, then the engine without a blower at this altitude has a unit weight of 2.5 kg/hp against 1.95 kg/hp with fan.

The engine has generally performed well. Frequent complaints arose at the beginning due to overheating and seizing of the cams and rocker arms on the 5th and 6th cylinders, when the bronze rods had to be replaced by cast iron bearings due to shortage of material. By modifying the oil drain line and widening the connecting channels at the rocker arm pits, this defect, which mostly occurred when the engine was climbing, i.e. when the engine was at an inclined position, was rectified.

Applications:
AEG G.IV, AEG G.V, AEG R.I, AGO C.VIII, Albatros C.X, C.XII, C.XV, Friedrichshafen G.III, G.IV, N.I, Gotha G.III, G.IV, G.V, G.VI, G.VII, Linke-Hofmann R.I, R.II, Rumpler C.IV, Zeppelin Staaken R.VI. Some more developments have been carried out in parallel to the D III and D IV aeroengines, e.g.

Mercedes D IVb (F182206)
The D IVb was by design a typical 6 cylinder in-line petrol engine, which developed 325/285 hp at 1550/1450 rpm. The internal designation F182206 indicates a bore of 182 mm and a stroke of 200 mm.

At the end of 1918, after Germany's surrender, the first experimental engine was completed and tested on the company's own test stand in December. Delivery of this engine was scheduled for April 1918. The compression ratio was 6 : 1.

A small number of pieces have been built in 1928/29 and tested as tank engine.

Mercedes D IVh
A further water-cooled 8-cylinder in line

Above: Two views of D IVa in a Gotha G.V. [J12, 1918]
Left: Experimental D IVa with supercharger.
Left: D IVa powered the Rumpler C.IV and some of its versions. [J12, 1918]

Above: Drawing of D IVa powered Rumpler C.IV. [J12, 1918]

Above & Below: Left and right views of D IVa engine module from a Gotha G.V. [A15]

experimental engine was built in 1916, called D IVh. This 230/200 hp engine was tested with a suspended cylinder arrangement and reduction gear (Bore/stroke 140/160 mm, total displacement 19.7 litres).

Above: Zeppelin-Staaken R VI R27/16 powered by four Mercedes D IVa. [A1]

Left: Drawing of D IVa-powered Gotha G.III installation. [J12, 1918]

Below & Below Left: High-altitude Mercedes D IVa for G-types with 260 hp. [A1]

Above: Drawing of D IVh straight-8 engine. [A1]

Above: D IVh straight-8 engine at Krakow Museum, Poland.

Right: AEG G.IV powered by two Mercedes D IVa engines. [A1]

Above: Mercedes D IVa aircraft engine with ZF collective gearbox on the test bench for an AEG giant aircraft; with air brake propeller. [A1]

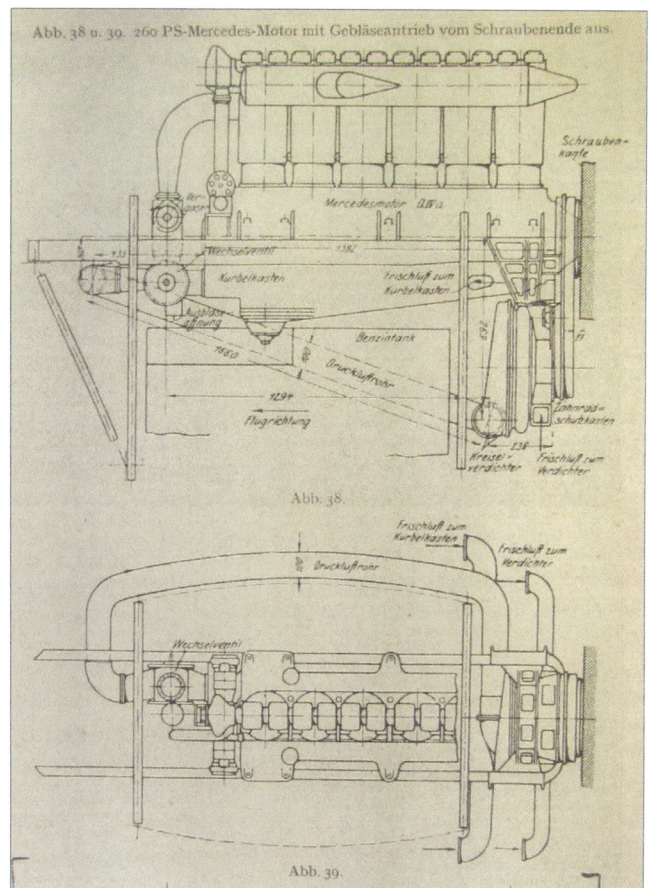

Above: D IVa with fan drive from the screw end. [J13, 1919]

3.16.18 Eighteen Cylinder 500 hp W-type Engine (D VI)

From 1915 onwards, Germany had begun to experiment with very large aircraft, known as giant planes. These planes had been developed from the G-Class bombers and were also known as R type planes. The practical implementation began in 1916, and the military potential of such an aircraft was recognized quickly. Transporting large bomb loads into enemy territory became a new strategy for the German military, especially since the inadequacies of airships designed for this task had been recognised. Enormous efforts were made to increase the production of G and R aircraft and at the same time to withdraw the airships from long-range bombing missions.

To encourage the development of larger and more powerful R-planes, larger and more high-performance aircraft engines were needed. As early as 1915, the Idflieg (Inspection of the Air Force) had encouraged various German engine manufacturers to develop large aircraft engines with a power output of 500 hp (375 kW). These engines were known as class VI engines and were to be used to power R-planes. Daimler Motoren Gesellschaft (DMG) was one of the companies working on the construction of such a large Class VI aircraft engine.

The circumstances which led to the fact that the focus on large engines was only placed at such a late stage in the war have already been dealt with in section 2. The fact is, however, that the technical lead of the Allied Forces could no longer be recovered.

The D VI engine was based on the Mercedes-typical cylinders of the 180 hp D IIIa engine and adopted proven modules from the 260 hp D IVa engine. Both these engines were originally six-cylinder in-line water-cooled engines. The D VI, however, had three rows of six-cylinder engines, resulting in a W-18 power unit. The middle row of cylinders was vertical, and the left and right rows were at an angle of 40 degrees to the middle row.

The D VI engine used individual steel cylinders with one intake and one exhaust valve. The valves of each cylinder row were actuated by a single overhead camshaft driven from the rear of the engine via a vertical shaft. The camshaft acted upon rocker arms that protruded from the camshaft housing above each cylinder to the exposed cylinder valves. A water jacket made of pressed steel was welded to the cylinder. Each piston was made of a forged-steel head screwed and welded onto a cast iron skirt. The cylinder's compression ratio was 4.7 to 1.

Each individual cylinder was attached to the

Above: Mercedes D VI W-18 engine of 500 hp.

two-part steel crankcase by four stud bolts. The crankshaft was supported by seven main bearings and was directly connected to the propeller. A water pump was driven by the crankshaft at the front of the engine. At the rear of the engine, a vertical shaft extending from the crankshaft drove a magneto for each cylinder bank and an oil pump. Each of the cylinders had two spark plugs (dual ignition).

Induction air was drawn into an air chamber inside the crankcase where it was warmed. The air then passed through two water-jacketed pipes cast

Above & Below: The massive Mercedes D VI W-18 engine of 500 hp.

integral with the lower crankcase half at the rear of the engine. The two pipes split into three inline carburetors, each feeding one cylinder bank via an intake manifold. The intake manifold was made of copper and was water-jacketed. The left cylinder bank had its intake manifold positioned on the right side. The centre and right cylinder banks had their intake manifolds positioned on the left side. The exhaust was expelled from each cylinder via an individual stack on the side opposite the intake. The

Engine Datasheet	
Daimler Motoren Gesellschaft, Stuttgart-Untertürkheim	
Designation	**Mercedes 500 hp 18-Cylinder W-type Engine (D VI)**
Year:	1915
Purpose:	Aircraft engine
Number of Cylinders:	18
Arrangement of Cylinders:	W-type piston engine
Bore [mm]:	140
Stroke [mm]:	160
Displacement [l]:	44,3
Compression [Ratio]:	6,4
Power [hp]: norm./max.	520
RPM [min-1]: norm./max.	1440
Full pressure altitude [m]	11,7
Carburetor(s)	
No.:	3
Type:	In-line Daimler
Fuel consumption per hp per hour [g]:]:	395
Oil Pump	
No.:	
Oil consumption per hp per hour [g/PS/h]:	
Ignition No.:	
Type:	
Firing order:	
Cooling	Water
Weight of complete engine (dry) & ext. masses	
Total [kg]:	742
Weight per displacement [kg/l]:	16,7
Weight per hp [kg/hp]:	1,43

Remarks: 5 engines delivered; series production suspended.

Above & Right: The massive Mercedes D VI W-18 engine of 500 hp.

End view: W-type D.VI [A1]

Above: Mercedes D VI vertical drive.

D VI had a 140 mm bore and a 160 mm stroke. The engine's total displacement was 44,3 litres. The D VI produced at the test bench 513 hp at 1440 rpm for take-off and had a maximum continuous output of 493 hp at 1400 rpm. Specific fuel consumption was 395 g/hp/h. The engine weighed 742 kg.

The Daimler D VI engine was tested from 1916. The Idflieg ordered 12 engines in March 1917 (deliveries: XII/17 - 4, I/18 - 4, II/18 - 4). A second order for 20 engines was received in July 1917 (delivery by March 1918). The D VI engine passed the certification test in December 1918, but World War I was already over at that time and such an engine was therefore no longer used in war.

A total of 5 D.VI engines were still delivered (July, August, September 1918 1 each, October 1918 - 2 engines).

The sole surviving D VI engine has been preserved and is on display at the Flugausstellung L.+ P. Junior Museum in Hermeskeil, Germany.

3.16.19   Other developments

F 10656: 90 hp 6-Cylinder In-line Engine

This engine took part in the Kaiser-Prize competition 1912 without being rated. Nevertheless, DMG tested this engine in a combination of 3 engines mounted in a common chassis and working on a central collective gear to drive in parallel 2 propellers via remote shaft.

FR Engines

Under the internal company designations FR 10549, FR 11279, and FR 11689 were built and tested replicas of the well-known French rotary Le Rhône engine.

The idea to test such engines was born by Idflieg in 1914/15.

F 235256, Water-Cooled 6-Cylinder In-line Engine (1916/17)

This engine developed 650/550 hp at 1300/1250 rpm. The cylinder dimensions (bore 235 mm/stroke 250 mm/displacement 65,1 l) were too large in relation to the state of development at that time. The development to an aircraft engine was stopped. This engine was used later in German tanks instead.

Endnotes

1. Already in 1887 Wölfert installed an electrical engine in this airship. However, it appeared that

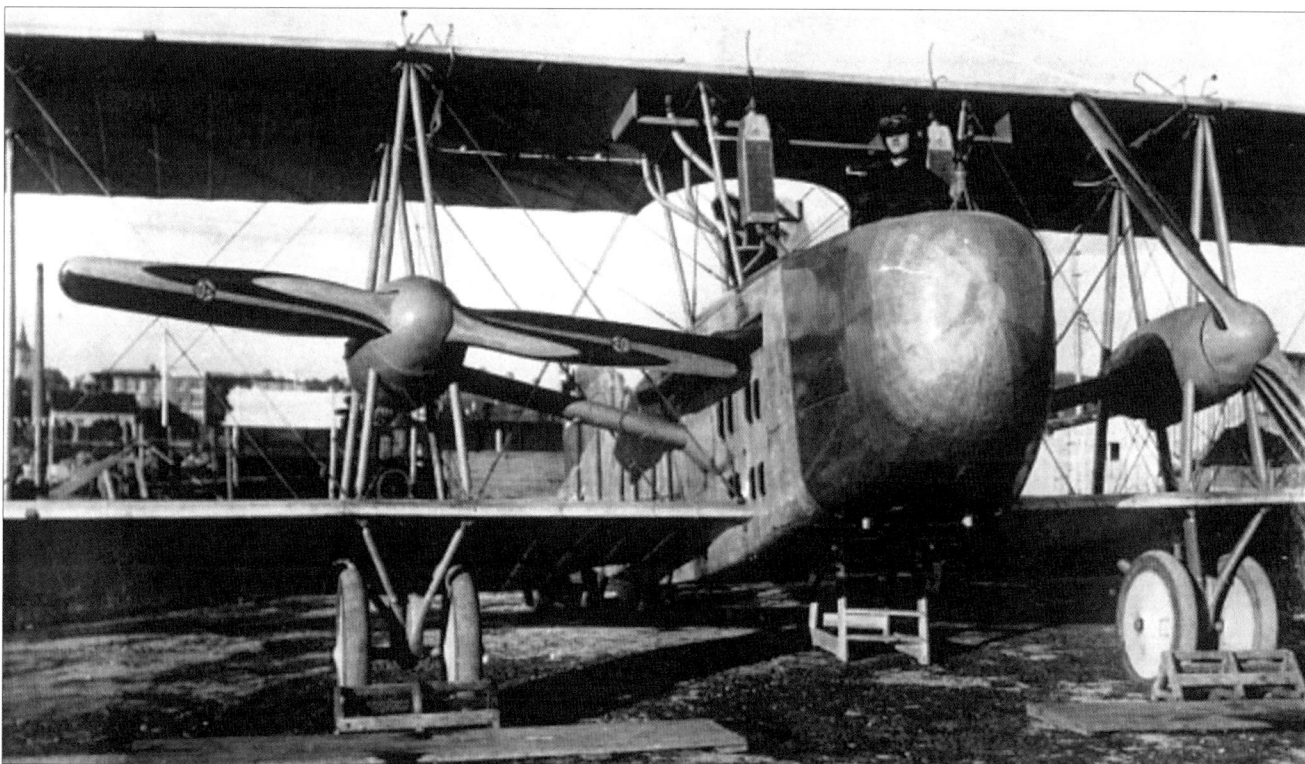

Top: Mercedes 90hp 3x F10656. [A1]

Above: Daimler F10656 G III with 3 x 95 PS Daimler F 10656 and Axial propellers. [A1]

Right: Mercedes 1914–15, aircraft engine power unit for large aircraft with cone clutches and central gearbox with 3x F 10656 of 90 hp each. [A1]

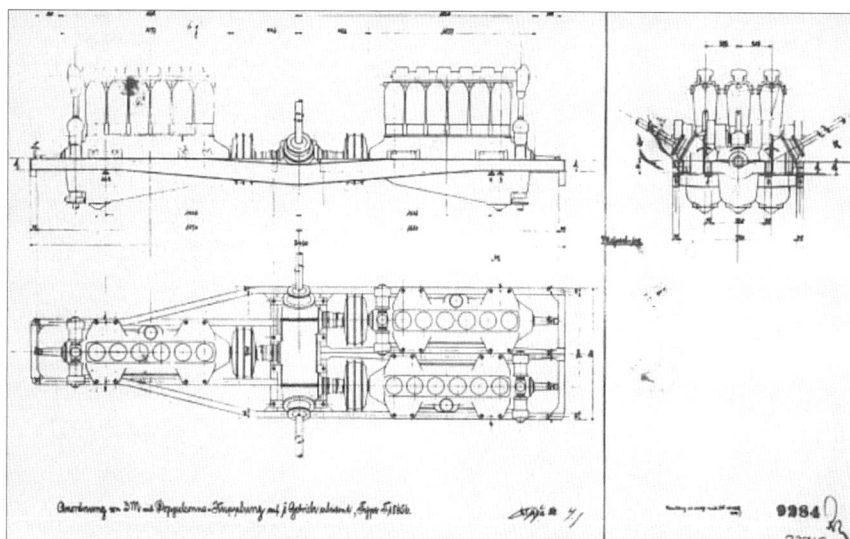

114

Mercedes 90 hp 6-cylinder in-line F 10656

Year:	1914
Purpose:	Aircraft engine
Number of Cylinders:	6
Arrangement of Cylinders	In-line piston engine, water cooled
Bore [mm]:	106
Stroke [mm]:	150
Displacement [l]	7,9
Compression [Ratio]	4,6
Power [hp]: norm./max.	90
RPM [min-1]: norm./max.	1400
Weight [kg]	145

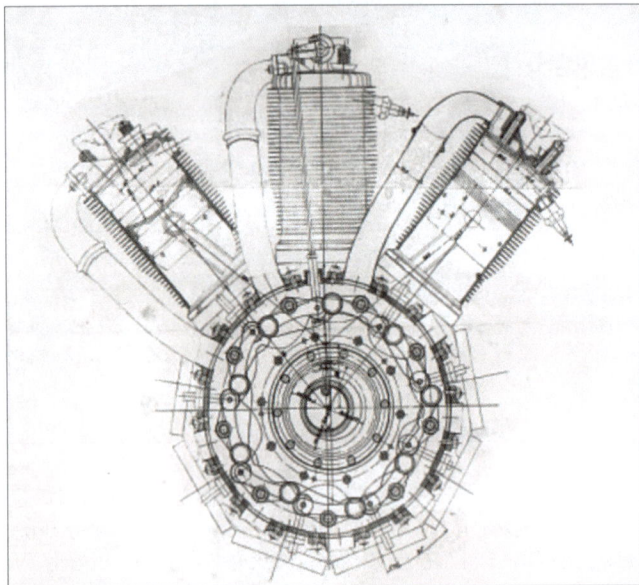

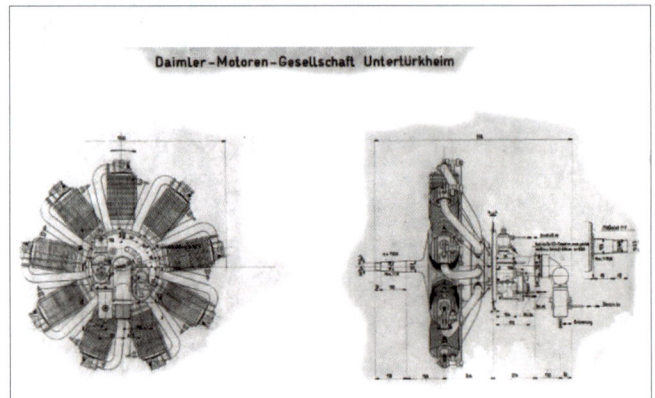

Above: Daimler aeroengine 1916, FR 11689, 9-cylinder rotary. [A1]

Left: Mercedes Flugmotor 1916, FR 11279 with 110 PS Le Rhone copy. [A1]

this 9 hp motor together with the accumulator had too heavy a mass (300 kg).
2. These engines were the world's first four-cylinder in-line engines.

3. See "*Illustrierte Aeronautische Mitteilungen*" 1903.
4. Sometimes found in elder dictionaries as "Make and break ignition".

Mercedes 9-cylinder Rotary FR Experimental Engines

Purpose:	Aircraft engine		
Year:	1914/15	1916	
	FR 10549	FR 11279	FR 11689
Number of Cylinders:	9	9	9
Arrangement of Cylinders	Rotary piston, air-cooled		
Bore [mm]:	105	112	116
Stroke [mm]:	140	170	180
Displacement [l]		13,4	17,1
Power [hp]: norm./max.	80	110	125
RPM [min-1]: norm./max.	1200	1200	1200

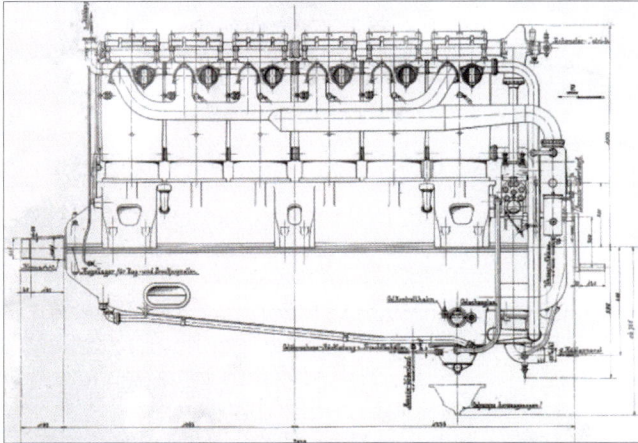

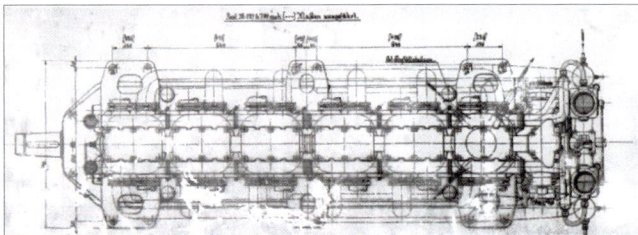

Above, Above Right, & Right: Mercedes aircraft engine 1917–18, aircraft engine F 235 256 an inline six cylinder with 650 hp was too heavy as an aircraft engine and was used as a tank engine. [A1]

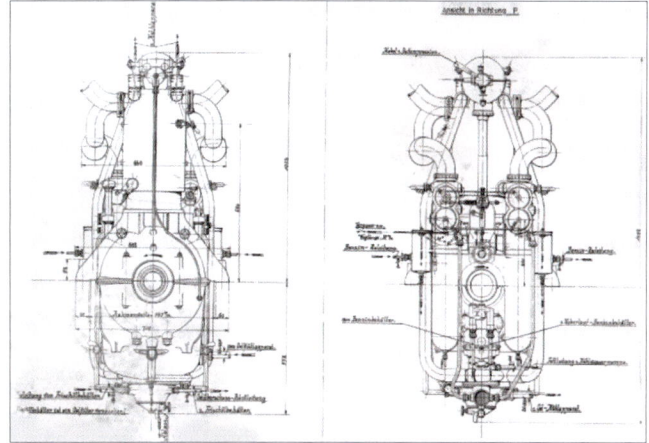

5. Bruno Lange, *Typenhand der deutschen Luftfahrttechnik*, Bernhard & Graefe Verlag, 1986.
6. It should not be forgotten that the DMG main business was the production of automobiles, and engines for cars, trucks, boats, submarines, ships etc.
7. Since the beginning of the 20th century, Wilhelm Maybach has been striving to develop improved successors to the first generation of Mercedes models for motor vehicles. The new models were characterised by somewhat larger and more powerful engines as well as a number of detailed improvements, which above all made them easier to operate. They were given the designation "Mercedes-Simplex", whereby the suffix to the name was intended to refer to the simplified operability.
8. The second Kaiserpreis competition was announced, but was not held due to the outbreak of war.
9. This data are taken from a Ministry of Munitions Report H.B. on The 180 H.P. Mercedes Aero Engine, March 1918.
10. Daily order (Tagesbefehl) Marine-Flug-Chef dated April 11, 1918.

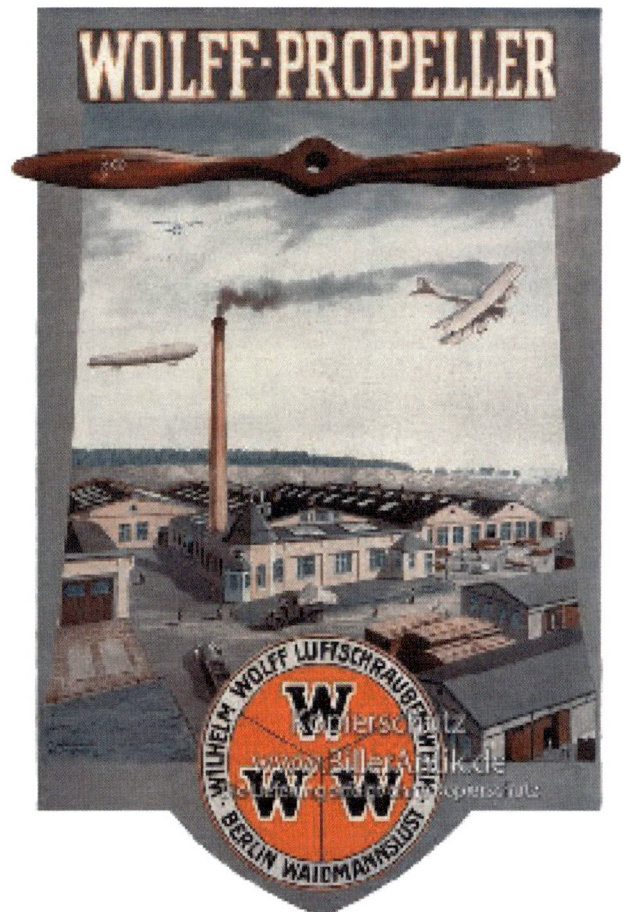

| Type | T/O Power | RPM | Cylinder | | | | Wt. [kg] | Year | Remarks & Information |
			No.	Bore, mm	Stroke, mm	Displ. [L.]			
B4F (B4L)	30	1400	4	90	140	3,6	130	1909	Identical with B4L
J4F	160	1600	4	175	165	16,1	290	1908/09	
D4F (F 1144)	59	1400	4	110	140	5,35	126	1909/12	Monoplane Fiedler, Otto, (first) Heinkel; Biplane Albatros, Dorner III, Loytzkoy, Widmann
E4F (F 1244)	64	1200	4	120	140	6,35	130	1910/12	Militär-Rumpler-Tauben Kathreiner-Preis-Motor. Price: 7.500 Mark
E4uF (Fh 1244)	72,3	1412	4	120	140	6,3	133	1911/12	Inverted cylinders, 4th place at Kaiser-Price-comp.
E4uF (Fh 1244)	72,3	1412	4	120	140	6,3	144	1912	Experimental engine, Inverted cylinders, with gear box
C4F (F 1034)	49	1400	4	100	130	4,1	100	1911	For the first time with overhead camshaft. Price: 5.000 Mark
G4F (F 1454)	100,6	1373	4	140	150	9,25	183	1912/13	Militär-Mars Biplane, overhead camshaft, vertical drive (Königswelle). Price: 10.000 Mark
E6F (F 1246)	100 (108)	1350 (1400)	6	120	140	9,5	200	1911 (1912)	Overhead camshaft, double carburetor, H. Hirth won the flight on the Upper Rhine and the Berlin-Vienna race in 1912. 2 kg/hp. Price: 11.500 Mark
DF 80 Dd6F (Da6F) F 10546	90,5	1400	6	105	140	7,2	150	1912/13	Militär-Rumpler-Taube, First German steel cylinder aircraft engine; Steel cylinders and sheet metal cooling jacket welded together in pairs, overhead camshaft, 2 valves per cylinder, twin carburetors; 2nd prize at the Kaiserpreis competition in 1912. Price: 9.500 Mark
Fh 1256	118	1400	6	120	150	10,2		1913/15	*Compression: 4,5; Inverted Cylinders*

Summary of Daimler/Mercedes Airplane Engines (Source: Daimler-Benz-Museum, Stuttgart)

Type	T/O Power	RPM	Cylinder				Wt. [kg]	Year	Remarks & Information
			No.	Bore, mm	Stroke, mm	Displ. [L.]			
DF 100 (DF 110) F 1246 D I	110	1400	6	120	140	9,5	192	1913/16	Compression: 4,5; All military aircraft with in-line engines; Reproduction at Milnes-Daimler-Limited, England.
F 12556 D II	135	1400	6	125	150	11	204	1913/16	Compression: 4,5; All military aircraft with in-line engines. Later also as D IIa.
FR 10549	80	1200	9	105	140	10,9	112	1914	rotary test engine, replica of the "Le Rhône" engine
F 10656	90	1400	6	106	150	7,9	145	1914	Compression: 4,6; Experimental engine for Kaiser-Price competition 1912; Variant with 3 engines mounted in a common chassis and working on the central collective gear for the driving of 2 propellers via remote shaft.
F 1466 DF 160 D III	170	1450	6	140	160	14,78	265	1914/16	Compression: 4,8; In most German WWI aircraft. 11,5 hp/l.
DF 220 F 1468 D IV	238	1400/910	8	140	160	19,7	420	1915	Compression: 4,6–4,8; Without and with reduction gear (1,54); Albatros C V und LVG C IV, R-Planes; Tests with Wittig compressor.
D IVh	238	1400/910	8	140	160	19,7		1915	Compression: 4,8; Inverted cylinders; Without and with reduction gear (1,54)
D VI	520	1440	18 W-type	140	160	44,3	742	1915	Compression: 4,7; Experimental engine; W-Type
FR 11279	110	1200	9	112	170	13,4		1916	Rotary test engine; Turbine of the French "Le Rhone" engine
FR 11689	125	1200	9	116	180	17,1	150	1916	Rotary test engine; Copy of the French "Le Rhone" engine

Summary of Daimler/Mercedes Airplane Engines (Source: Daimler-Benz-Museum, Stuttgart)

			Cylinder				Wt. [kg]	Year	Remarks & Information
Type	**T/O Power**	**RPM**	**No.**	**Bore, mm**	**Stroke, mm**	**Displ. [L.]**			
F 1466 D IIIa	180	1450	6	140	160	14,8	286 (345)	1916/17	Compression: 4,6; also with reduction gear; Albatros D V, Rumpler D I and other; tests with both Wittig and Roots compressors. In total built 12.000 D IIIa-engines.
DF 260 F 1686 D IVa	260/ 275	1450-1500	6	160	180	21,7	400/ 432	1915/18	Compression: 4,7; Also with superchargers from Siemens, Roots or Schwade, AEG radial compressor; Also with reduction gear (1,54); Albatros C XII, FFH G III, Rumpler C IV and other. In total 4.580 engines built.
DF 170 F 14566 D IIIavü	177 (until 3000 m)	1450	6	145	160	15,8	315	1918	Compression: 5,8; Oversized, over-compressed. Fokker D VII and other fighters. In total built 3.100 engines.
DF 160 F 1466 D IIIaü	170 (until 1800m, to be de-rated at low altitude)	1450	6	140	160	14,8	298	1918	Compression: 5,8; Over-compressed. Fokker D VII and other fighters
DF 3b FV 10678 D IIIb	186-201	1800-1950	8 V-type	106	170	12,0	260	1917	Compression: 6,0; With or without reduction gear; Albatros Biplane, Dr II, Daimler Monoplane L 11; from 1918 with Roots supercharger.
F 182206 D IVb	285 (until 4000 m)	1450	6	182	200	31,2	440	1918	Compression: 6,0; Over-compressed
F 1696 D IIIc	235	1450	6	160	190	22,9	400	1918	No serial production because of the end of the war.

Summary of Daimler/Mercedes Airplane Engines (Source: Daimler-Benz-Museum, Stuttgart)

3.17 Delfosse Motorenfabrik GmbH, Köln

3.17. 0 General

The technically skilled August Arthur Delfosse built his first motorcycle at the age of 15. It is well known that he made his first gliding tests with a self-built gliding apparatus in 1902 on the Mülheimer Heide in Cologne.

In 1909 Delfosse built a monoplane which he demonstrated at the Cologne Flight Week and the Brussels Motor Show. He then founded the first aircraft engine factory in Germany in Riehl. While the frames and wings of the previously used flying machines were usually made of wood and bamboo cane, Delfosse already used seamless steel tubing, which was joined together using the autogenous welding process. The advantages of this innovation were that, despite the significant weight reduction, the frame and wings were more durable, and repairs could be carried out more easily. A further reduction in weight was achieved by using the three-cylinder 24 hp Delfosse engine specially designed for this aircraft.

The Delfosse monoplane had a total weight of only 145 kg. The engine was in front, the propeller had a diameter of 2.10 m and was mounted directly on the engine axle.

The company Aug. Arthur Delfosse Motorenfabrik GmbH was founded with the aim of supplying engines and accessories for the growing aircraft industry.

The first advertisements of the Delfosse company appeared in 1910 in the magazine "Flugsport":

Below: The monoplane of Ing. Aug. Arthur Delfosse, equipped with 23 hp 3-cylinder fan-shaped engine. [J6, 1910]

"Complete flying machines, guaranteed to fly". These flying machines were of course equipped with engines from the company's own production.

3.17.1 Fan-Type Engines
Three-Cylinder 30/24 hp Fan-Type Aircraft Engine (Type I)

For his first monoplane, Delfosse first developed a fan-shaped 3-cylinder engine in 1908/09. This engine was purely air-cooled and designed in the way it was common at that time. The valves were controlled via push rods.

Above: 23 hp Delfosse 3-cylinder engine 1910. [J6, 1910]

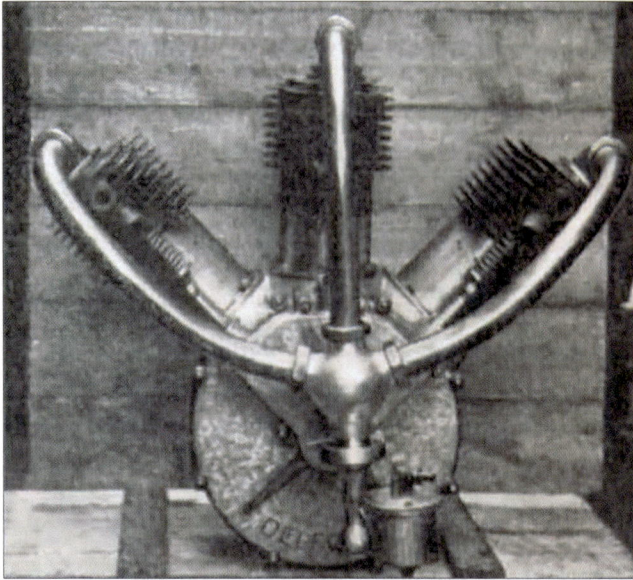

Above & Right: 23 hp Delfosse 3-cylinder engine 1910. [J6, 1910]

Below: 23 hp Delfosse 3-cylinder engine drawing 1910. [J6, 1910]

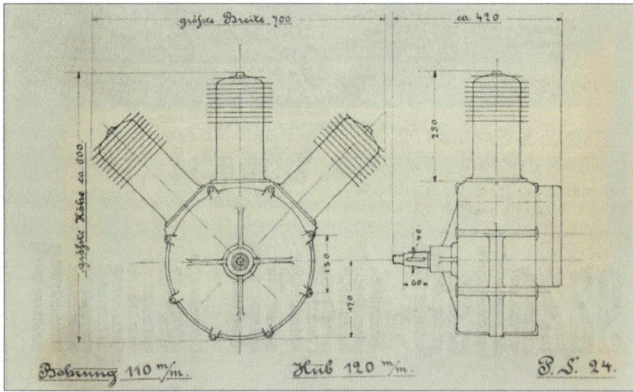

3 Cylinder Delfosse

Flugmotor 24/30 HP mit **Bosch-magnet**-Zündung fast neu, zum Spottpreis von Mark **1050.—** abzugeben.

Offerten: **1507** an die Exped. erb.

Above: 23 hp Delfosse 3-cylinder engine. [J3, 1911]

The engine was equipped with a H.T. magneto, but also a version with a 6 volt accumulator is known.

The fan-shaped cylinders of this engine are offset by 72 degrees, so that magneto ignition could be used. The bore was 110 mm with 120 mm stroke, speed 1200-1500. 24/30 hp, minimum power 24 hp with 110 kg traction.

Other features were: Special metal cylinders, very large valve chambers and chrome nickel crankshaft.

This engine was practically tested together with the flying machine of Lieutenant Lanyi. The built-in Delfosse engine (stroke 120 mm, bore 110 mm) produced 30 hp at 1400 revolutions. The whole apparatus weighed 205 kg without pilot.

The flight tests carried out were satisfactory, but longer flights could not be undertaken due to unreliability of the engine.

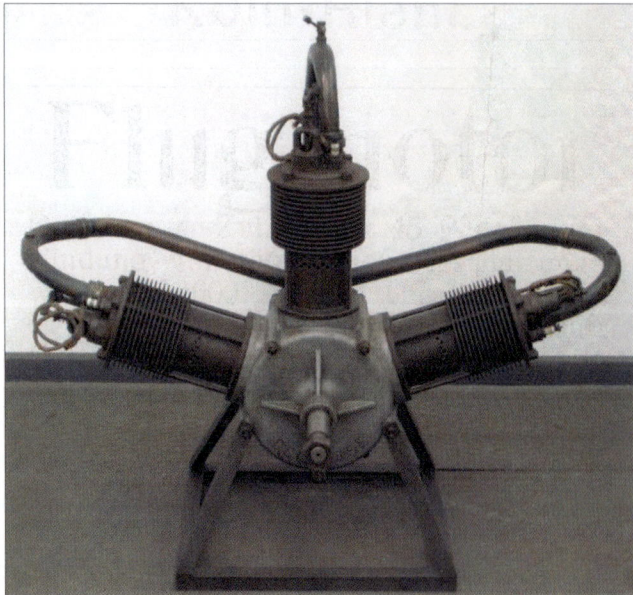

Above: Original Delfosse 3-cylinder fan-type 40/30 hp engine (1909), Type II, exhibit of the Deutsche Technikmuseum Berlin.

Right: Biplane of Lieutenant Lanyi (Hungary, 1911). The built-in Delfosse engine (stroke 120 mm, bore 110 mm) produced 30 hp at 1400 revolutions. [J6, 1910]

Right: View of the engine installation, spark plug cables, control rods, gas-air mixture supply lines. [J6, 1910]

Three-Cylinder 40/30 hp Fan-Type Aircraft Engine (Type II)

Also, in 1909 Delfosse Motorenfabrik GmbH launched an improved 3-cylinder engine. The bore of this engine was now 120 mm and the stroke was extended to 140 mm.

In the manner of pacing engines, its cylinders are bored at the end of the stroke to allow part of the exhaust to escape immediately through this circle of holes. These engines thus become less hot than if the exhaust were forced to escape completely through the exhaust valve. The suction valves on this engine, like those on the Wright and Kersten engines, are automatic.

Otherwise the principles of the overall design of the engine were retained. The spark plugs were now located directly on the cylinder top and no longer on the side.

Four-Cylinder 45/35 hp Fan-Type Aircraft Engine (Type III)

The Delfosse four-cylinder engines were designed in a similar way to the 3-cylinder engines. The cylinders of this air-cooled, 45/35 hp engine were arranged 51,43 degrees apart. Delfosse promised a guaranteed power output of the engine of 130 kg. No series production took place.

It seems that more and more often it happened that the engines supplied by Delfosse were unreliable or did not reach their guaranteed performance. The announcement on the right from the magazine "*Flugsport*" of 1911 clearly proves this.

Four-Cylinder 70/50 hp Fan-Type Aircraft Engine (Type IV)

The basic design of this engine is similar to all its predecessors. On the photo you can see the rear

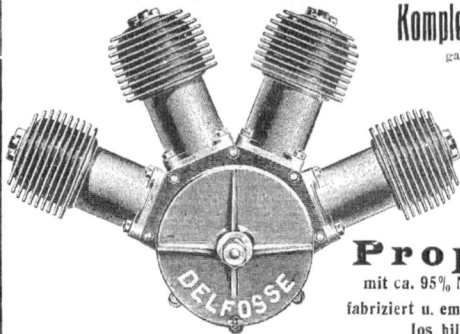

Aviator Heitmann´s monoplane, powered by a 4-cylinder Delfosse power unit. [J3, 1910]

mounted control of the exhaust valves and the exhaust flanges. The spark plugs are not wired.

Six-Cylinder 60/50 hp Fan-Type Aircraft Engine (Type V)

In 1911 Delfosse presented its first air-cooled 6-cylinder motor with double fan shaped design. This engine produced 60/50 hp at 1300/1200 rpm.

The crankshaft was double cranked. Bore/stroke 110/140 mm. Nothing has become known about a serial production of this type.

Six-Cylinder 100/80 hp Fan-Type Aircraft Engine (Type VI)

The construction of this model is like the type V air-cooled 6-cylinder engine: double fan shape, With the larger Bore of 120 mm this engine delivered 100/80 hp at 1300/1200 rpm. On request the type VI motors were also delivered with water cooling.

Both the type V and type VI engines were built as experimental engines. There is no evidence so far that these engines were tested on an aircraft.

It is very likely that Delfosse did not meet the expectations of its customers with its radial engines. The dissatisfied customers were asked with the enclosed advertisement (*Flugsport* 1910) to join forces to "take joint action against the companies mentioned". This may have been the reason why Delfosse stopped building the fan-shaped radial engines and now turned exclusively to the rotary

Above: The picture shows two rotary engines plus a 4-cylinder fan-type model. [J3, 1912]

engines already established among aircraft builders.

3.17.2 Rotary Engines

The Delfosse rotary engine also follows the design of the well-known Gnôme engine. Here, too, the intake valve is arranged in pistons, but has a different design from the Gnome in that there is not a double counterweight, but only a single one. The valve closing spring acts on the counterweight. The spring can be precisely adjusted by means of a screw. (see drawings below).

In the case of the exhaust valve, the valve tappet acts as a counterweight. To control the valves, there are as many special control shafts as there are cylinders. Here, the control cam and the drive gear form one piece. Like the housing, the control shafts are mounted in ball bearings on the stationary crankshaft.

Three-Cylinder 28/24 hp Rotary Aircraft Engine

At the General Aircraft Exhibition (ALA) held in Berlin in 1912, Delfosse Motorenfabrik presented three of its rotary engines: a 3-, 5- and 7-cylinder engines. These engines came onto the market under the name "Rotativ" at prices between 1,800 and 7,000 Marks.

The 3-cylinder engine was, with a few exceptions, like all other Delfosse engines, air-cooled. The valves were located in the upper part of the steel cylinders. This engine was also equipped with a H.T. magneto from Bosch. The crankshaft was mounted on ball bearings.

Five-Cylinder 45/45 hp Rotary Aircraft Engine

An important point in the construction of rotary engines is the correct dimensioning of the individual parts and the most careful selection of the material used for their manufacture. While the crankcase of this Delfosse engine was made of an aluminum alloy, the cylinders, the most important and most exposed to wear, were made of special cylinder cast iron. A large number of very thin fins dissipated the heat generated by combustion in the cylinder, so that even after running for four hours, there was no critical temperature rise. Just like the cylinders, the pistons were made of special gray cast iron. In order to allow the cylinders to run evenly, the hardness of the piston alloy was reduced by a small amount.

In the 5- and 7-cylinder rotary engines, as in the 3- and 4-cylinder engines, the cylinders were either screwed onto the housing or clamped into a

Above: Delfosse 50hp rotary from *Jane's All The World's Aircraft 1913*.

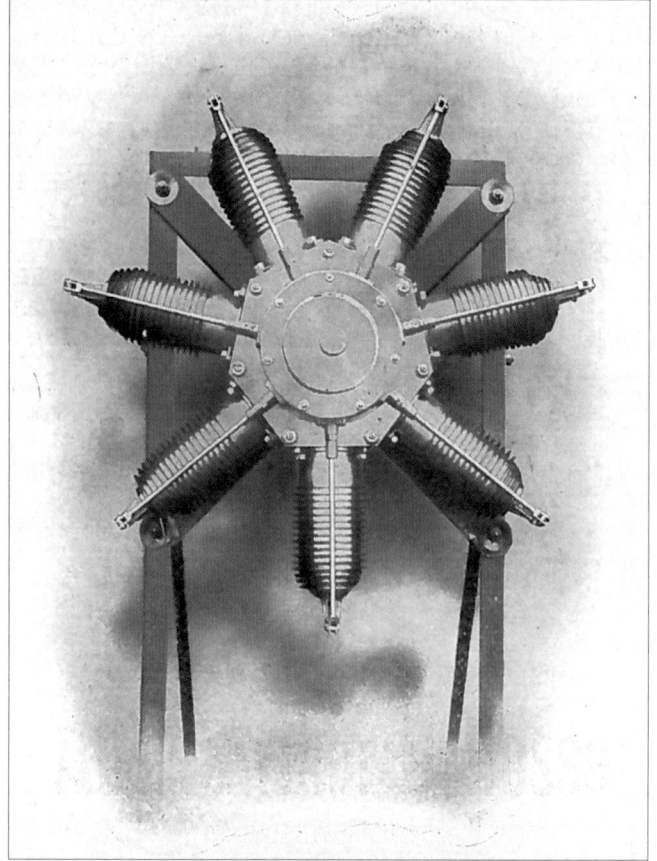

Above: 7-cylinder Delfosse rotary engine. [J3, 1912]

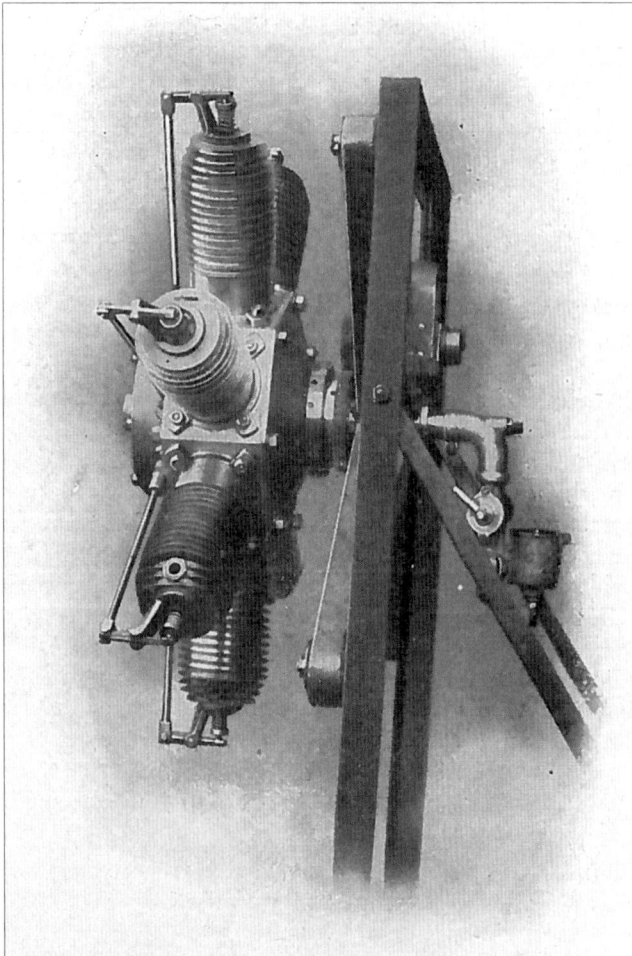

Above: Delfosse 7-cylinder rotary. [J3, 1912]

corresponding groove with a collar located at the lower edge of the cylinder. The propeller mounting and front bearing were located on a shaft stub, which was forged from a single piece of steel together with the front housing cover. The rear cover was made of cast meteor steel and accommodated the distributor ring for ignition distribution and the magnetic drive gear rim on the outside of its extended hub. Particular care was taken in the choice of material for the crankshaft, as well as in its machining. The crankshaft was forged from the best chromium-nickel steel, which, in addition to being very hard, is also very tough. All rotating parts of the engine, such as the housing, push rods and cam wheels, were equipped with ball ring bearings. The crankpin bearing was a clever design. A bronze bushing encloses two double-row ball bearings, which were mounted on the crankpin. On the outer perimeter of this bronze bushing, the pushrods were joined together and held together by bronze bells. This construction had the advantage of simplicity, reliability and above all long life. A ball bearing, which was placed on the crank axle immediately behind the crank arm and supported on the former, absorbed the axial displacements caused by the pulling action of the propeller.

			Cylinder			Wt,		
Type	T/O Hp	Rev., RPM	No.	Bore, mm	Stroke, mm	kg	Year	Notes
1	30/24	1200	3	110	120		1909	Fan type
2	40/30	1400	3	120	140		1909	Fan type
3	45/35	1300/1200	4	110	140	85	1910	Fan type, experim.
4	70/50	1300/1200	4	120	140		1910	Fan type
5	60/50	1300/1200	6	110	140		1910	double fan type, experimental
6	100/80	1300/1200	6	120	140		1911	double fan type, experimental
	28/24	1000	3			35	1911	Rotating, experimental
	45/35	1100/1200	5	110	130	55	1911	Rotating, experimental
	60/50	1100/1000	7	110	140	75	1911	rotating
	75/65	1000	7	140	120	85	1911	rotating
	80/70	1100/1000	10	110	130		1912	Rotating, Doppelstern, experimental
	100/90	1100/1000	14	110	140		1912	Rotating, Doppelstern, experimental

Summary of Delfosse Aircraft Engines

Sufficient lubrication was also ensured. The Delfosse rotary engines operated in four-stroke mode. The automatic intake valve was located in the piston crown and the centrifugal force in the valve cone was counterbalanced by precisely measured counterweights. The controlled exhaust valve and the associated control linkage were also very carefully designed. The valve cones of both the exhaust valve and the intake valve were made of the best steel, thus avoiding burning or the most feared warping. A special cam wheel was provided for each cylinder, ensuring that the exhaust period was at the right moment.

Seven-Cylinder 60/50 and 75/65 hp Rotary Aircraft Engines

The Rotativ-Delfosse rotary motors were characterized by a simple design; every single part was easily accessible. Assembly and disassembly took only a few minutes. Removal of the front cover exposed the valve control system, while removal of the rear cover allowed the crank pin to be freely removed; connecting rods and pistons could be removed without having to disassemble a cylinder. The removal of a cylinder was done in the simplest way by loosening four screws. The low weight of the engine made it possible to carry a larger quantity of operating fluid. The performance of the 7-cylinder rotary Delfosse engine, even in continuous operation, was satisfactory.

Nevertheless, the company Delfosse Motorenwerke GmbH did not succeed in setting real accents in the fields of German and foreign aircraft construction. The fan motors were altogether too fragile and in the field of rotary motors the French competition, especially Gnôme, could not be beat.

Nevertheless, Delfosse attempted to develop more powerful rotary engines in 1912 (see table), but these did not get beyond the test phase. By the end of 1912, no new information had reached the engineering press. The production of engines and aircraft was discontinued.

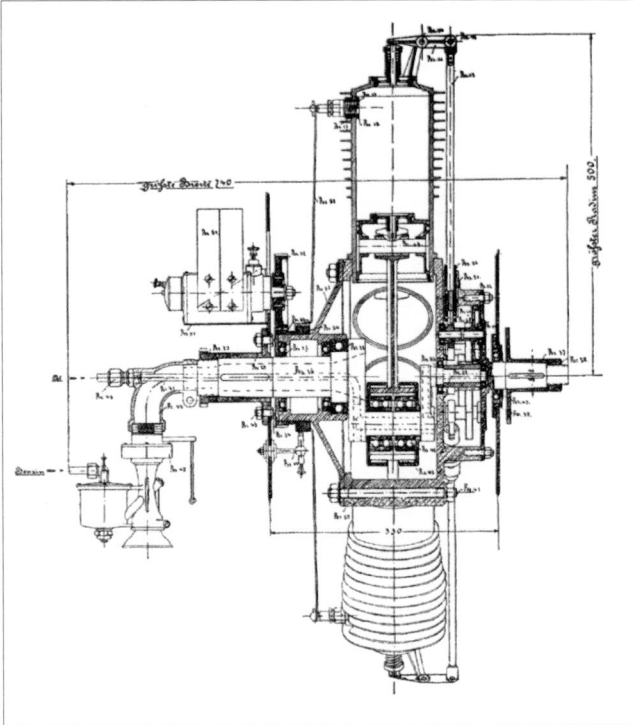

Above & Above Right: Delfosse 7-cylinder rotary. [J8, 1912]

Right: Delfosse 7-cylinder rotary. [J3, 1912]

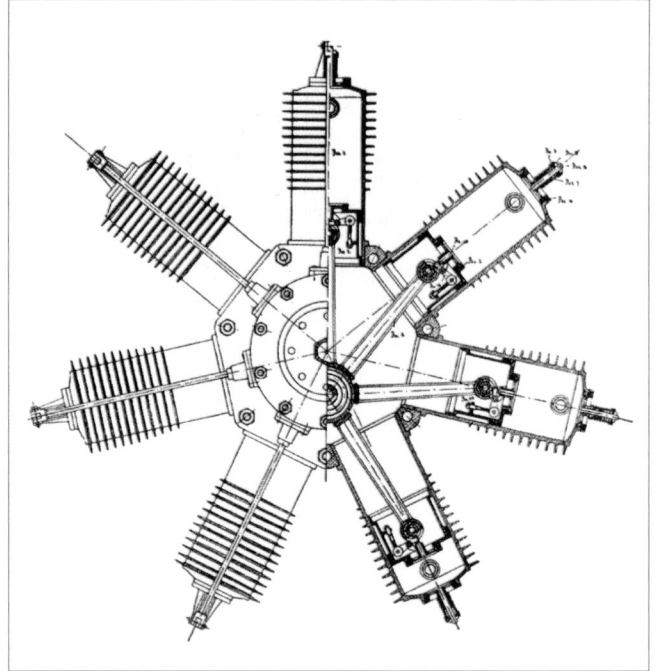

Above: Delfosse 7-cylinder rotary.

Above: Mercedes D IVa in Gotha G.IV.

Above: Mercedes D IVa in Friedrichshafen G.III.

Above: Mercedes D IVa in Gotha G.V.

Above: Mercedes D IVa in AEG G.V, a G.IV with extended span.

Above: Mercedes D IVa in AEG G.IV.

The powerful 260 hp Mercedes D IVa engine was in great demand to power twin-engine night bombers as seen here. It also powered the elegant Albatros C.XII at right and the Rumpler C.IV. The Albatros was a failure but the Rumpler was Germany's leading long-range reconnaissance airplane until the end of the war and was very hard for Allied fighters to intercept.

3.18 Deutsche Motorenbau GmbH, Berlin-Marienfelde

3.18.0 General

In the summer of 1913, the "Deutsche Motorenbau-Gesellschaft mit beschränkter Haftung" was founded with headquarters in Berlin-Marienfelde and a branch office in Berlin-Wilmersdorf. The object of the company was the production of engines, engine parts and accessories. The managing directors were Kommerzienrat Bernhard Meyer from Leipzig and the civil engineer Robert Conrad (owner of another company in Leipzig).

Robert Conrad initially developed two water-cooled in-line engines for aircraft, which were registered in 1912 under the company name "Conrad & Meyer" for the Kaiserpreis 1913 for the best German aircraft engine.

Conrad's own developments were protected by the shareholders' agreement, which stated that the engines produced on the basis of his inventions were to be sold under the name "Conrad-Motore".

For the engine production a new factory was built in Mariendorf in the size of approx. 500 sqm. However, no significant production was achieved. Despite initial failures, work continued on aircraft engines. The 6-cylinder engine launched in 1916 was manufactured under license by NAG (see section 3.52).

At the end of 1917, Siemens took over the plant with the intention of building its Sh III here.

In 1918, the development of a piston compressor for the Daimler D IIIa was started.

3.18.1 Four-Cylinder 95 hp Aero-Engine C 1 (1912)

The Conrad C I was a water-cooled 4-cylinder four-stroke aircraft engine that developed 95 hp at 1400 rpm.

In order to increase the cylinder performance and to protect the exhaust valves, which are quite heavily stressed in aircraft engines, the engine of Conrad & Meyer, Berlin was equipped with a controlled pre-exhaust, which allows most of the combustion gases to escape towards the end of the working stroke at the moment of bottom dead centre.

This engine, quite interesting also because of other details, e.g. an overhead camshaft, could

95 hp C 1, as registered for the Kaiserpreis competition 1913. [J8, 1912]

Above: Engine C 1 of the Deutsche Motorenbau GmbH, side view. Water pump, magneto, overhead camshaft, oil sump. [J8, 1912]

unfortunately not be tested because it had been heavily damaged during transport to the Deutsche Versuchsanstalt für Luftfahrt in Berlin-Adlershof, the intended engine inspection location, and therefore had to be withdrawn.

3.18.2 Six-Cylinder 65 hp 6 Two-Stroke Aero-Engine C 2 (1912)

One of the few two-stroke engines for aircraft was this water-cooled, vertical 6-cylinder aircraft engine with 65 hp at 1400 rpm. This engine was also entered for the Kaiserpreis competition in 1913, but was finally not delivered.

3.18.3 Six-Cylinder 185 hp In-line Aircraft Engine C III (1916)

Deutsche Motorenbau GmbH did not have the capacity to produce significant quantities of engines during the war. Above all there was a lack of qualified skilled workers for production. A water-cooled 6 cylinder aircraft engine developed by Conrad with 185/150 hp at 1400/1300 rpm passed the type test in February 1916. The aircraft engine had 6 individual cylinders with four valves each, an overhead camshaft with bevel gear drive behind cylinder 6. The reproduction of this engine and its further technical improvement was carried out by the Neue Automobil Gesellschaft (NAG). There the series C III Nag a and C III Nag b were built. For further information see New Automobile Company.

Above: Conrad C III, type certified in 1916. This engine was built under licence by Neue Automobil-Gesellschaft (NAG) with some modifications as C III NAG a and C III NAB b. [L12]

Bore/Stroke 135/190 mm, Total displacement 16,32 Litre.

Robert Conrad and Bernhard Meyer brought a whole series of innovations to patent maturity, e.g. "Arrangement of cooling water pump, oil pump and igniters in aircraft engines" (DRP 273496; 46c) and "Control system for four-cylinder four-stroke explosion engines (DRP 274057; 46b)". The company also cooperated with other Berlin engine manufacturers. For example, there existed a joint patent with the industrialist Julius Kruk (see also section 3.43): "Fastening the cylinders to the crankcase in rotary explosion engines" (DRP 285784).

Early production Rumpler C.IV 6820/17 was powered by the Mercedes D IVa which gave it excellent performance at high altitude. The D IVa was very reliable for the time.

3.19 Dorner Flugzeug-Gesellschaft, Berlin-Johannisthal

3.19.0 General

Hermann Dorner was a well-known German aviation pioneer of the early days. He studied shipbuilding in Berlin and became a graduate engineer in 1909.

As early as 1907, he had begun developing a glider to which an engine could be attached at the front. Dorner made his first practical gliding flights in the summer of 1908, and in September 1909 he was the only German to take part in the 1st International Flight Week in Johannisthal. He had entered the competition with his self-designed monoplane and thus for the first time presented a German powered flying machine at a major event. However, he could only show a few short jumps with his monoplane. On July 11, 1910, he won the third Lanz-Preis der Lüfte, worth 3,000 marks, with his T II monoplane, and in August he won another prize at the aviation show in Johannisthal. In the summer of 1910, he acquired pilot's license No. 18 from the German Aeronautical Association. With the money from the prizes, Dorner founded his Dorner Flugzeug GmbH in 1910. However, the great success failed to materialize; neither his aircraft nor the engines he developed brought any financial success. He closed his company in 1912 and went to work as a flight instructor at the Adlershof Aviation School. In 1913, he successfully applied for the position of technical director at the German Experimental Station for Aviation (DVL) in Berlin-Adlershof, which had been founded shortly before.

Hermann Dorner was one of the "Alten Adler".

3.19.1 Four-Cylinder 22/24 hp Aeroengine

The water-cooled engine of the airplane with which Dorner wanted to compete for the 3rd Lanz Prize was originally intended for air cooling. Later, it received larger bore cylinders and was set up for water cooling. It has about 24 hp at 1400 rpm and weighed 280 kg including the radiator.

Overall, Dorner's engines did not produce positive results to achieve economic success. From mid-1912, Dorner therefore used mainly 50 hp Dixi and Mercedes engines, but also 55 hp Körting engines.

Endnotes

1. See also in „Deutsche Zeitschrift für Luftschiffahrt" 1910, Heft 2.

Above: Dorner hang glider 1910. [J4, 1910]

Above: Early Dorner monoplane with four-cylinder engine. Radiator in front of the engine. [J3, 1912]

Above: Dorner engine. [J3, 1912]

2. The aviation pioneers who, before the outbreak of the First World War on August 1, 1914, had passed the examination to become an airplane pilot in accordance with the regulations of the German Aeronautical Association in Germany and joined the community of the same name, founded in 1927, referred to themselves as Alte Adler (Old Eagles).

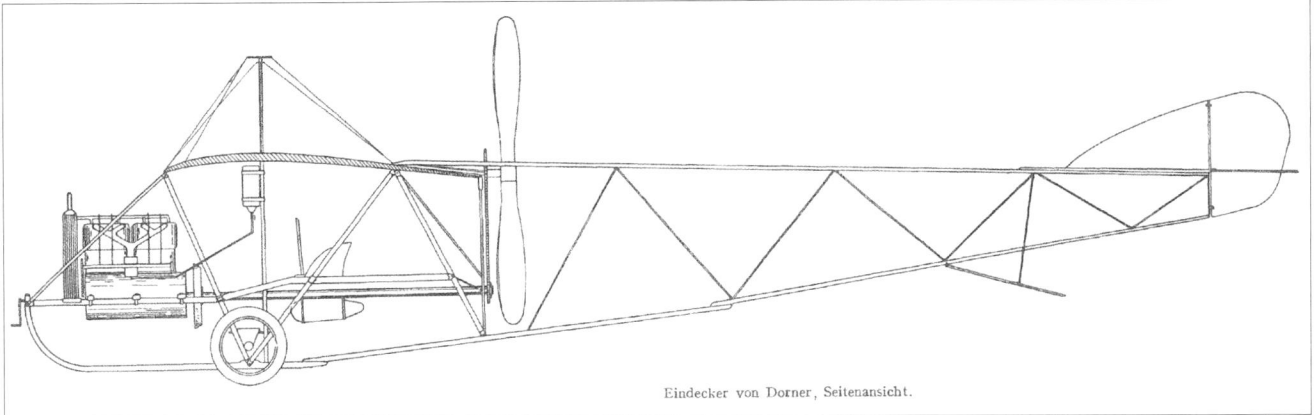

Eindecker von Dorner, Seitenansicht.

Above: Dorner hang glider 1910. [B26]

Right: Dorner monoplane seats, controls, and engine. [J4, 1912]

Above & Above Right: Front view of Dorner monoplane seats, controls, and engine. [J4, 1912]

3.20 Bernhard Escher, Sächsische

3.20.0 Bernhard Escher, Sächsische Werkzeugmaschinenfabrik AG, Chemnitz

The Sächsische Werkzeugmaschinenfabrik Escher AG in Chemnitz built various "System Schneeweis" aircraft and airship engines, which engineer Johann Emil Friedrich Schneeweis developed in 1909 and 1910.

When J. Schneeweis left the Sächsische Werkzeugmaschinenfabrik in November 1910 to found his own aircraft engine company in Chemnitz (see separate section on Schneeweis and his special factory for aircraft engines, which he marketed under the trademark "WODAN"), engine development at Escher also came to an end. The engines described here found only limited practical usage in aviation.

In 1910, the International Motorboat and Engine Exhibition was held in Berlin, at which, among other innovations, the company Escher AG exhibited a two-cylinder aircraft engine. The cylinders were arranged horizontally on the housing, facing each other. With this boxer arrangement, a good mass balance was already achieved with two cylinders, and the distance from one explosion to another was the same.

Depending on the customer's request, Escher also supplied these engines with 4 or 8 cylinders, with the option of air or water cooling. With the water-cooled cylinders, the cylinder forms a unit with the water jacket and the cylinder head. In the air-cooled cylinders, the cylinder head is mounted separately and is connected to the cylinder or crankcase by four bolts.

Inlet and outlet valves were controlled. In the cylinders with water cooling, the valve seats were removable. In the cylinders with air cooling this was not necessary, because the cylinder head could be

Above: 20 hp two-cylinder horizontally opposed air-cooled Escher type. [B25]

Above: Advertisement for 2-cylinder Escher engine. [J3, 1910]

Oskar Ursinus in his aircraft powered by a 2-cylinder (Boxer) Escher engine.

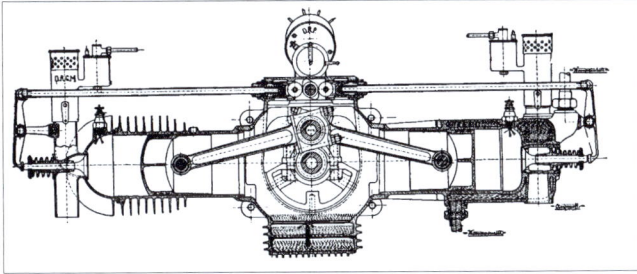

Above: Schematic of 2-cylinder Escher engine. [B25]

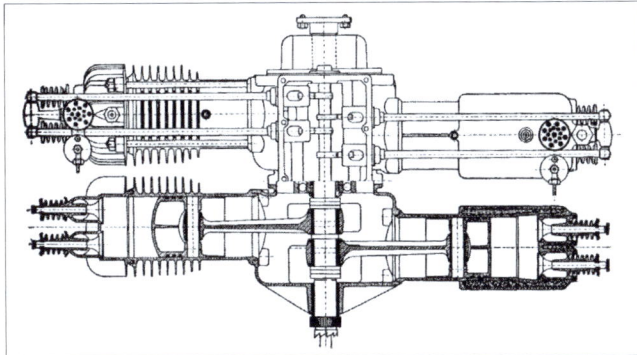

Above: 35 hp four-cylinder horizontally opposed Escher type, air- or watercooled. [B25]

Right: Advertisment for 4-cylinder in-line engine made by Escher, Chemnitz. [J3, 1910]

easily removed.

As shown in the pictures, each cylinder was equipped with a separate carburetor. The carburetor was mounted directly on the cylinder head, so that pipes for the fresh gas mixture were not necessary.

Ignition was effected by a magnetic inductor with high-voltage spark plug ignition. The magnet was mounted above the control shaft, from which it was driven by spur gears.

On the drive side of the crankshaft a light flywheel was mounted, which was constructed in the same way as wheels for bicycles, in that wire spokes running tangentially from a hub with two rings were guided to a steel ring that served as a flywheel.

In addition to these boxer engines, the Escher company also built airship and aircraft engines with four vertical cylinders. The cylinders themselves are the same as in the horizontal engines. Moreover, the construction of the stationary engines was the same, apart from the changes caused by the changed arrangement of the cylinders. In both types of engines, lubrication was provided by a gear pump installed at the bottom of the crankcase, which took oil from an oil tank located under the crankcase to press it through special piping to the cylinders, the

Right: Escher 36 hp engine in Suwelak's first monoplane (1910). [A1]

three bearings of the crankshaft and the control shaft mounted in the ball bearings.

So much is known about the airship engine built by the Escher company that in 1911 one unit was installed together with a 100 hp engine from the N.A.G. company in the airship "Suchard" which belonged to the Kiel branch of the Verein zur Förderung der Motorluftschiffahrt der Nordmark. Both 100 hp engines were placed one behind the other with the flywheels against each other and should be used only alternately during the voyage. With the help of a gearbox, they directly drove two double-bladed wood propellers of 3 m diameter supplied by Zeise-Altona via chains. The motors ran with 1000–1200 revolutions, the propellers 800–950

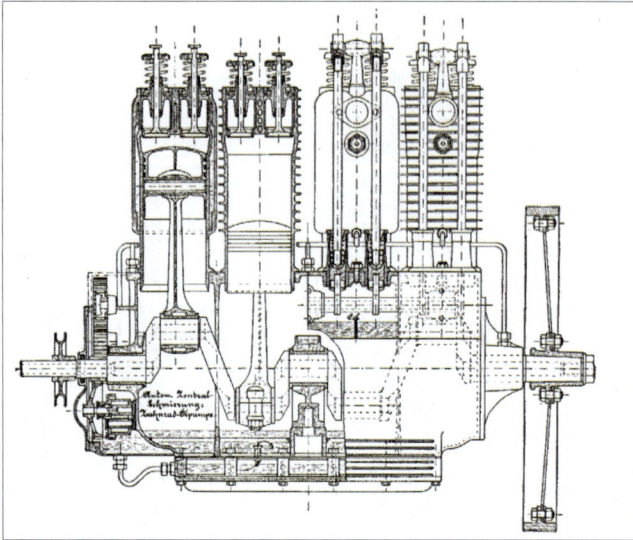

Above: Drawing of the Escher aircraft engine with vertical cylinders; 4 or 6 cylinders in line, intake and exhaust valves controlled, air or water cooling. [B25]

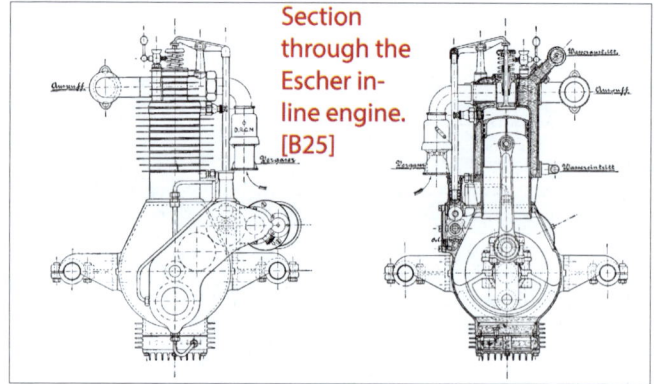

Section through the Escher in-line engine. [B25]

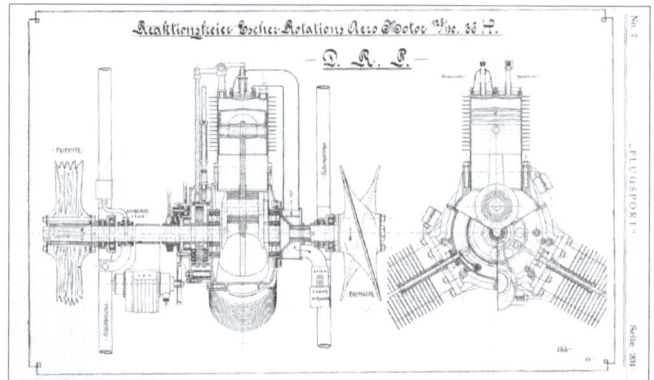

Above: Reaction free 3-cylinder rotary engine developed by Sächsische Werkzeugmaschinenfabrik AG, Chemnitz. [J3, 1910]

Sächsische Werkzeug-Maschinen-Fabrik
Bernhard Escher Akt.-Ges., Chemnitz.

Gegründet 1874   Telephon No. 468
Arbeiterzahl ca. 600   Telegr.: Bernhard Escher

liefert als Spezialität:

Escher-Motore

Flieger- u. Luftschiffmotoren D. R. G. M.

in bekannter, bestbewährter und In- und Ausland eingeführter Konstruktion in Größen von 20–200 PS, m. 1,5–3,5 kg p. PS, m. zwei, vier, sechs und acht Zylindern in stehender, liegender und V-förmiger Anordnung, welche gelegentlich der Ausstellung f. Sport u Spiel in Chemnitz mit der höchsten Auszeichnung dem Sächs. Staatspreis, prämiiert wurden.

Reaktionsfreie Rotations-Motoren

von größter Vollkommenheit und Zuverlässigkeit mit drei, fünf und sieben Zylindern in Leistung von **25, 36** und **60 PS**, eingerichtet für **zwei gegenläufige** Schrauben.

Kleine Stationär-Motoren
D. R. G. M.

billigste u. zuverlässigste Betriebskraft für mech. Werkstätten, Flieger- und Autohallen, Kleinindustrie Landwirtschaft u. Fesselballonantrieb etc. etc. in **Leistung von 2–7 PS.**

Escher - Vergaser, D. R. P. D.R.G.M.

mit **automatischer** Luftregulierung, einzige Spezialkonstruktion für Flieger- und Luftschiffmotoren, mit Vorwärmung und Drosselklappenregulierung.

Wo nicht vertreten, für **Wiederverkäufer und Exporteure vorteilhafte Bezugsquelle.**

Above: Advertisement 1910, 2- and 3-cylinder Escher engines (Boxer type & rotary engine). [J3, 1910]

rpm. The aim of the efforts was to carry out a transatlantic flight expedition.

Reaction-free rotary motor: The various advantages of engines with rotating cylinders and the good reputation they have gained in aviation circles have prompted Sächsische Werkzeugmaschinen Fabrik Bernhard Escher to pay more attention to this issue and to design a non-reactive rotary engine in addition to its existing types of flying machine engines. As a designer, Schneeweis was not satisfied with the previous designs, but rather tried to create something better and at the same time eliminate various disadvantages of these motors.

The fact that the housing rotates in the opposite direction to the motor shaft should completely eliminate the reaction torque.

The rotary engine was a four stroke engine and was normally built with 3 cylinders. Engines for higher powers with 5 and 7 cylinders were also planned.

The motor axis is in two parts. One part of the axle is the crankshaft, which, in contrast to other designs, was supported 3 times. The other part is the extension of the crankcase, which is designed as an axle and is supported by two ball bearings. Due to the low mass in the housing, the two parts of the axle, each of which had a screw mounted on it, were supposed to rotate in

The crankcase was made of a high-quality bronze alloy, the three cylinders were made of chrome-nickel steel, which in turn were made of one piece from the solid and were fixed to the case in a solid manner by means of stud bolts. The intake and exhaust valves are mounted in the bottom of the cylinder, which was worked from one piece with the cylinder.

The control of the valves is forced and is done by a peculiarly combined planetary gear, which made it possible to control all 3 cylinders with one and the same cam.

The gas supply in this new reaction-free rotary aero engine, as the company called it, is not, as usual, through the housing and the hollow shaft, but from above. through the cylinders, as in any other automobile engine at that time.

The central lubrication of the motor was designed in such a way that it could be operated and regulated during normal operation. The oil automatically reached all parts that needed lubrication.

The magneto ignition device rotated with the motor housing, with sparks being generated by a special breakaway distributor device.

The fact that all cylinders worked on one crank gave the engine a small width and thus a low weight of 1.5 kg per hp.

Due to the opposite rotation of the screws, the already intensive cooling of the rotation motor was significantly increased.

Summary of the Engines Made by Sächsische Werkzeugmaschinenfabrik AG, Escher								
Type	Cyl.	Kind	Power [hp]	RPM	Bore [mm]	Hub [mm]	Mass [kg]	Remarks
4L125	4	Boxer	50/40	1450/1350	125	120*	110	Standard design, valves controlled by pushrods, supplied with air or water cooling as required; exhibited at the ILA in 1909
2L125	2	Boxer	24/20	1450/1350	125	130	60	Aircraft engine, same dimensions as 4L125.
4L110	4	Boxer	36/30	1450/1300	110	120*	95	Aircraft engine; design as before with head-controlled valves and air or water cooled as desired. 1910
4S90	4	In-line	20/18	1550/1450	90	100	55	Aircraft engine in usual design with cast cylinder block
4S195	4	In-line	50/40	1450/1350	125	120*	130	Water-cooled aircraft engine. 1909
4S160	4	In-line	105/85	1300/1200	160	180	160	Water-cooled aircraft engine in usual design.
Versuch	3	rotary	36		125	130		1909/1910, non-reactive motor, one-off piece
„Wodan"	6 u. 8	In-line	100 & 200					License construction, See further in section Schweeweis
* Iaw. Moedebeck, Taschenbuch für Flugtechniker: 130 mm								

3.21 Fahrzeugfabrik Eisenach (Dixi)

Airship Engines

In 1911, reports about the "Dixi" aircraft engines appeared in the aviation trade press for the first time. "Dixi" was a brand name of Fahrzeugfabrik Eisenach. The name Dixi replaced the previously known car brand "Wartburg". Under the name "Dixi", automobiles, trucks, bicycles and buses were produced until 1928, but also, for a short period of 4 years, engines for airships and aeroplanes. The most famous car model was the Dixi 3/15, a licensed construction of the English small car Austin 7.

The Dixi aircraft engines of the renowned Eisenach car factory were quickly known in aviation circles thanks to the good reputation of the car company. This was due in particular to the fact that the Eisenach-based company succeeded in establishing a cooperation with the aircraft manufacturer Goedecker for the supply of engines.

However, the first Dixi aircraft engines were introduced on the Jla in 1909 as small airship engines, but with moderate success. Since then, these engines were continuously improved in the following years, but could not prevail against the competition.

The engine that emerged from the automotive sector was a four-stroke engine with 4 cylinders cast together in pairs; intake and exhaust valves arranged on one side and operated by a common control shaft. As a result, the pipes for intake of the mixture and exhaust gases were also arranged on one side above each other.

Nevertheless, there was easy access to the valves and carburetor parts.

The crankshaft ran in shell bearings in the upper part of the housing, while the lower part served only as an oil sump and to close the engine downwards.

The ignition was magneto-electric combination ignition of the Bosch company, using plugs, to which battery ignition is also connected.

The carburetor, which originated in the automotive industry, was equipped with a combined air supply, which was regulated automatically during start-up, but mechanically at higher speeds. The latter control was simultaneous with the throttling of the engine, and this resulted in a throttling of the measured fuel. The latter regulation is achieved by a conical needle that can be moved up and down in the conical nozzle.

Particular care has been taken to ensure that the water supply is kept to a minimum, while still providing intensive cooling under continuous

This Page: Airship engine of Fahrzeugfabrik Eisenach as presented at the Internationale Luftschiffahrt-Ausstellung in Frankfurt/Main in 1909, power not defined. [J4, 1909]

maximum load. This has been achieved by rapid water circulation through a centrifugal pump driven by the crankshaft and a specially designed fan, which increases the air flow rate by means of a high intensity finned radiator.

Above: Stand of Fahrzeugfabrik Eisenach with Dixi aircraft engines at ALA 1912 in Berlin. [J3, 1912]

This fan was located directly on the pump shaft and was driven by the pump. This combination of pump and fan had only been used by Fahrzeugfabrik Eisenach until then.

A starting device is provided at a right angle to the crankshaft with conical wheels, thus reducing the space requirement of the entire engine system to the smallest possible dimension. At the same time, all engine control elements are grouped within easy reach of the operator.

As is a matter of course with a powerful airship engine, which is subject to heavy inclinations, the lubrication was carried out in a very special way so that the engine receives full oil on all pistons etc.

even when it is standing at an angle of inclination of up to 30 degrees.

Lubrication of the airship engine was such that it can be considered a very simple combination of centralized and plunger lubrication; it unites the advantages of both types of lubrication in that the oil supply to the engine is constantly under control through a few sight glasses easily visible to the operator, while, unlike pure centralized lubrication, it allows the use of only a few oil points, which are therefore easy to overlook and operate. This has been achieved by the fact that the unique design of the crankshaft allows each crank chamber to be sealed off from the adjacent ones, so that there is mutual

Summary of Airship Engines Made by Fahrzeugfabrik Eisenach							
Power [hp]	Cyl.	Bore [mm]	Hub [mm]	RPM	Year	Weight per power [kg/hp]	Remarks
20	4	80	110	1500	1909	3,75	Magneto capacitor-discharge ignition
38	4	100	140	1400	1909	2,8	
64	4	120	170	1300	1910	2,58	Magneto capacitor-discharge and battery ignition
95	4	140	200	1200	1910	2,42	

This Goedecker Taube "Sturmvogel", equipped with a 100 hp Dixi engine, was part of the company capital of Fahrzeugfabrik Eisenach with 13,500 marks. [J3, 1912]

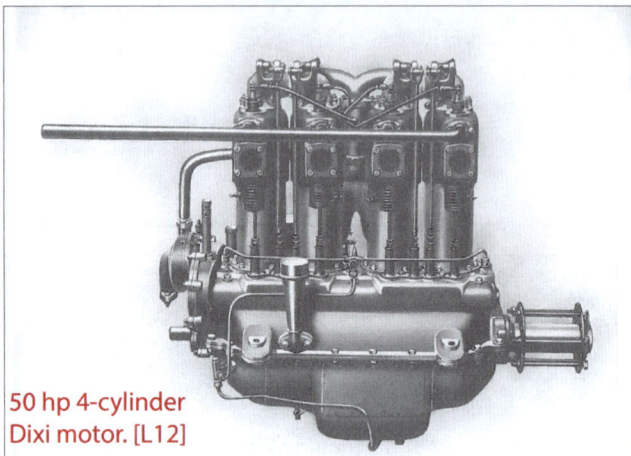

50 hp 4-cylinder Dixi motor. [L12]

Above: Advertisement for three different aero-engines built by Fahrzeugfabrik Eisenach. [J3, 1912]

communication only for the purpose of ventilation. The individual crank chambers were each constantly supplied with oil through a special oil line with a sight glass in the driver's cab, so that it was possible to maintain a constant quantity of oil in the crank chambers, in contrast to pure splash lubrication.

Through the dipping crank the necessary oil was now supplied to the cylinders, main bearings, piston pins and connecting rod bearings. By regulating the oil supply to the crank chambers, the machine operator is therefore able to influence the lubrication of the entire engine as required with certainty. The lubrication of the connecting rod bearings is further enhanced by the fact that the crank pins are pierced. The oil entering these holes is fed through radial lubrication holes to the sliding surface of the crank pins as a result of the effect of centrifugal force.

The individual crank chambers are separated from each other, which makes the lubrication so independent of the inclined position of the engine, which is common in motorboats and even more so in airships, that this type of lubrication could be

used without any problems in a recently built airship engine, whereby an inclination of the engine axis of up to 20 degrees from the horizontal was expected, an inclination which far exceeds that occurring in motorboat operation.

With the closure of the crank chambers, of course, there is also an oil-tight closure at both the front and especially at the flywheel bearing, so that the leakage of oil from this bearing, which occured in many engines, and the flinging of this oil around in the nacelle by the flywheel is completely avoided.

The lightest possible design of all parts has been considered for the present engine only in so far as the possible use of the same machine as a vehicle engine is permitted; this applies especially to the shape of the housing, which is of course modified appropriately for easy installation in airships.

75 hp Dixi motor, carburetor and exhaust side. [J3, 1912]

Aircraft Engines

The basic design and principles of operation of aircraft engines were similar to those of airship engines. There was no deviation from the basic principle of the 4-cylinder water-cooled 4-stroke engine.

In contrast to the airship engines, great importance was attached to optimizing the weight of the aircraft engines. Particularly noteworthy are the light pistons of the Dixi aircraft engines, which are made of a hard-aluminium alloy and are of extraordinary lightness, toughness and durability.

Goedecker-Taube and Dixi

In the early years, the several of Goedecker aircraft were delivered with Dixi aircraft engines. These engines were built as four-cylinder with adjacent single cylinders in the types of 50 hp, 75 hp and 100 hp.

The general agency of Goedecker Taubes for East Germany was in the hands of Dixi-Luftfahrt- und Bootsmotoren-Verkaufsgesellschaft m.b.H., Berlin, which was at the same time also the exclusive distributor of Dixi aircraft engines for the German Reich.

The technical details of the aircraft engines were similar to those of the airship engines described above. The valves were controlled by a common camshaft. The inlet valves were suspended in the cylinder heads and were operated by push rods and rocker arms, while the exhaust valves were controlled from below. Both valves are amply dimensioned. The valves as well as the carburetor are easily accessible due to the fresh and exhaust gas lines located on different sides of the engine.

The cylinders had copper water jackets and

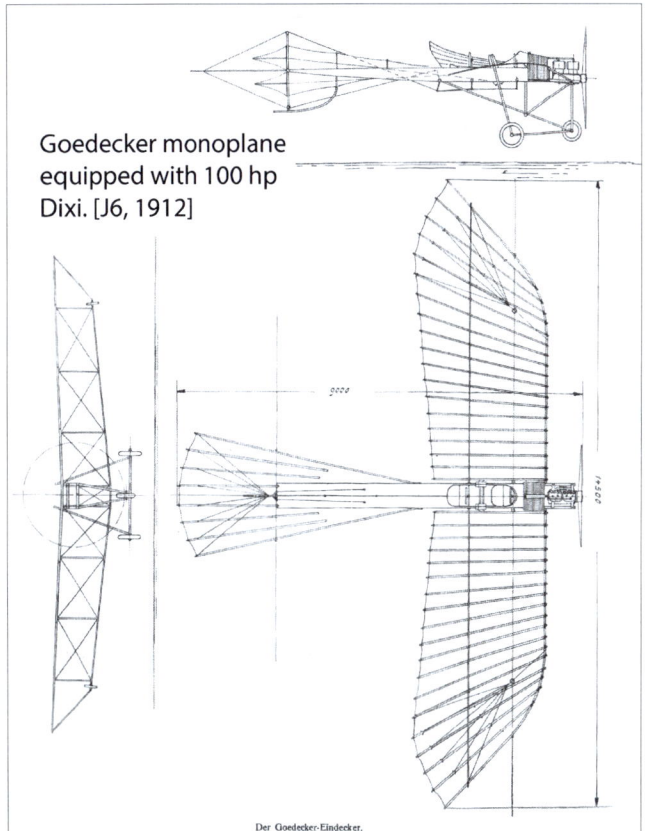

Goedecker monoplane equipped with 100 hp Dixi. [J6, 1912]

Der Goedecker-Eindecker.

received plenty of cooling from the cooling water delivered by a large centrifugal pump. The water pump itself was driven by gears.

Bosch arc ignition was used as ignition source for all three types. The two more powerful types also combine an accumulator ignition for easier starting of the engine. The magnet apparatus was driven by the same shaft that actuates the water pump.

The carburetor was a separate Dixi-piston carburetor. The carburetor was equipped with

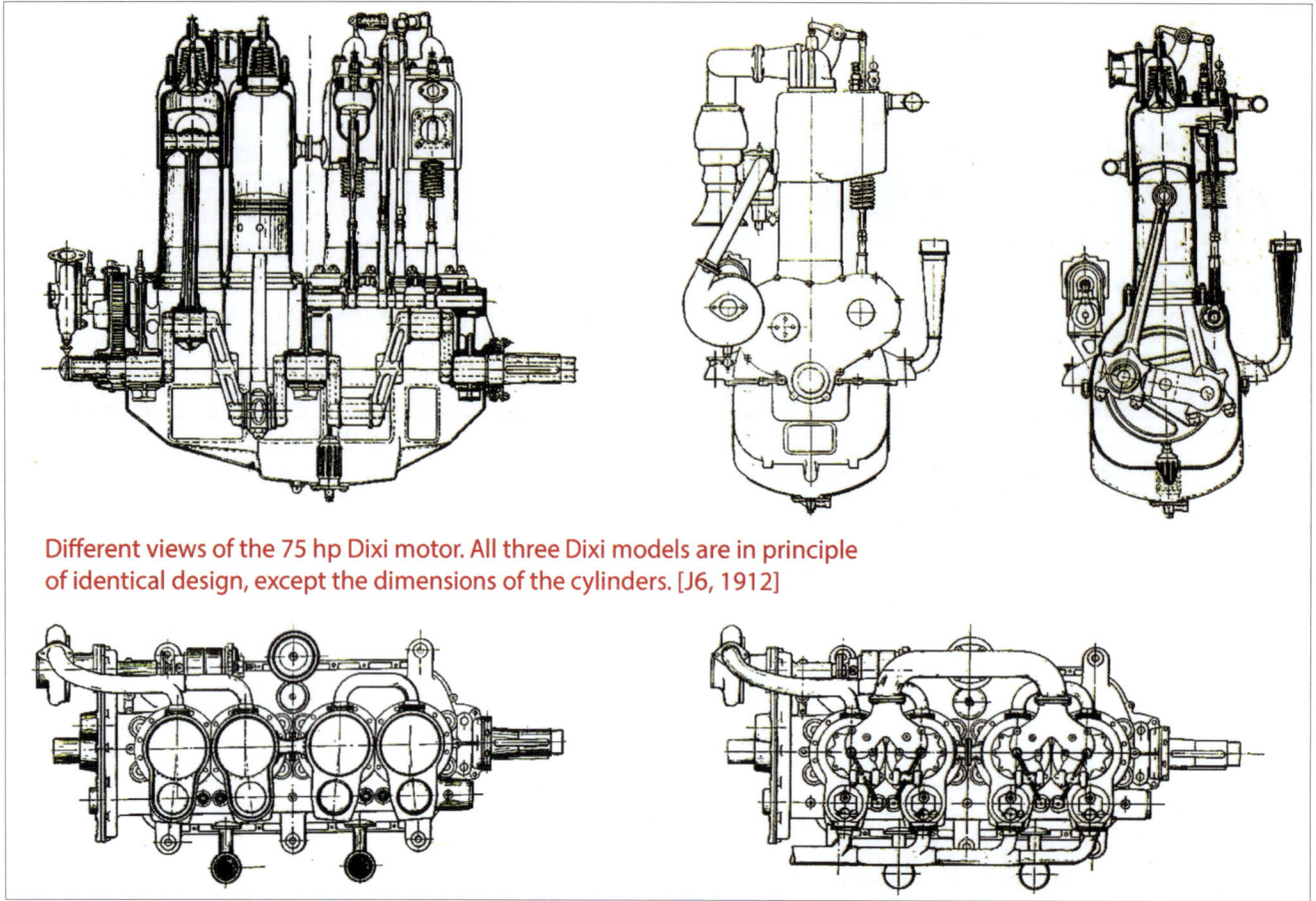

Different views of the 75 hp Dixi motor. All three Dixi models are in principle of identical design, except the dimensions of the cylinders. [J6, 1912]

On the right side is the common drive of the water pump and the magnet apparatus. [J6, 1912]

hot water preheating, which could be regulated accordingly, thus ensuring the entire function of the carburetor and significantly increasing the engine's

Above: Carburetor side of 100 hp Dixi watercooled aircraft engine. The pendulum (P) below the carburetor (float S) was originally used for regulation during steep ascents. However, flight testing showed that this component could be avoided. B - fuel supply fitting. [J3, 1912]

Summary of Dixi Aeroengines					
Power [hp]	Cyl.	Bore [mm]	Hub [mm]	RPM	Weight*[kg]
50	4	100	140	1400	ca. 90
75	4	120	170	1300	ca. 140
100	4	140	200	1200	ca. 205
* Cooler, cooling water, fuel, oil, fuel and oil tanks are excluded from the weight.					

performance according to the weather conditions.

Lubrication was carried out by a piston pump located in the middle of the lower part of the engine housing, which is set in rotation by an eccentric mounted on the crankshaft and thus always adapts itself to the speed of the engine with the oil supply. The oil that enters the pump is first fed by the pump into the crankshaft, which is pierced along its entire length for this purpose and allows the oil to enter the crankshaft through transverse holes in all crank and connecting rod bearings. From here, the oil rises in the connecting rods, which are also cannulated, lubricates the piston pins and passes through the bore in the latter to lubricate the pistons on the cylinder walls.

A reduction valve attached to the oil pump ensures that excess oil can return to the oil tank, thus preventing oiling or sooting. A single filling of the oil tank is sufficient for several hours for each type of engine, and the operator can check at any time whether the lubrication is working and whether the oil pump from the control unit is delivering enough oil to the various points by means of a pressure gauge located near the operator's seat.

As can be seen from the illustrations, all parts are mounted clearly and easily accessible and the greatest care has been taken to ensure that all parts are easy to handle.

Remarkable in the construction of the carburetor is the self adjustment of the float. The float could swing around an axis transverse to the longitudinal axis of the engine (flight direction). Due to the pendulum, the float should always be kept vertical. The designer overlooked the fact that a pendulum is not only subject to gravity but also to inertia. Therefore the pendulum would also swing out and thus the float would be displaced when the airplane changes its speed. This pendulum effect will be harmful to the float and thus to the carburetor if the airplane suddenly reduces its speed while climbing.

Therefore, the late 100 hp Dixi engines have returned to the fixed arrangement of the float.

One can only speculate why the Dixi-engines did not become established in aviation.

All 3 types of aircraft engines were entered for the Kaiser Prize 1912 for the best German aircraft engine but did not receive any recognition. It is possible that this failure contributed to the fact that the development of a more modern 6-cylinder engine was not started.

Right: Exhaust side of 100 hp Dixi motor. [B26]

3.22 Flugmaschine Rex GmbH, Köln

3.22.0 General

The company Flugmaschine Rex GmbH was founded in December 1914, i.e. after the beginning of the war. The aim of the company was the production of light monoplanes and biplanes, as well as the establishment of a flying school. The resulting aircraft did not meet the quality required for them to be recognized by the military administration as fit for war. Dr. Ing. Friedrich J. M. Hansen, first Technical Director and later also Managing Director developed aircraft and aircraft engines.

3.22.1 Swashplate Rotary Engine

Hansen went to England and studied the construction of rotary engines and developed the English Statax swashplate engine.. While working for the Rex flying machine, he built his own engine based on this principle. The engine itself was not convincing and thus got beyond the experimental stage.

3.22.2 Nine-Cylinder 130 hp Air-Cooled Rotary Engine (1917)

During the war, Rex GmbH Cologne, a flying machine company, brought out a new rotary engine which, with its design differing from the previous one in various respects, had shown quite excellent performance.

The engine did not have a piston valve, but only the single exhaust valve controlled by a cam. At the bottom dead center of the piston, air was sucked in through a vacuum previously created in the cylinder, and flooded gas through a specially separated opening in the cylinder, which was also controlled by the passing piston. It should be noted in particular that gas and air entered the cylinder completely separately and the crankcase of the engine did not contain any gasoline vapours or gas, so backfiring into the crankcase was not possible under any circumstances.

The engine had dual ignition by two independent magnetos and received its fuel through a pump, so did not have a carburetor. The power was specified as 130 hp. The engine was to be regulated so that its lowest number of revolutions was 90, while the highest was 1250 rpm.

Bore/stroke: 110/170 mm
Displacement: 14,5 l

A second rotary engine of the Rex flying machine appears in German literature: 7 cylinders and 100

Rex advertisment 1917. [A2]

REX
EINVENTIL-MOTOR
FLUGMASCHINE REX
KÖLN A/RH.
ANTWERPENERSTR. 18-22. FABR: OSSENDORF.
TELEFON A 7500   TELEFON A500

9-cylinder 130 hp rotary engine developed by Mr. Hansen, Flugmaschine Rex GmbH. [A2]

Above: 7-cylinder 100 hp Rex rotary engine. [A2]

Endnotes

1. A swashplate engine is a reciprocating piston engine that has a swashplate instead of the usual crankshaft. The conversion of the oscillating piston motion into a rotating motion, which can then be used for propulsion, is effected by the swashplate, which is mounted in a Z-shaped crankshaft. The first patent for a swashplate engine was granted to H.S. Smallbone as early as 1906. In 1913 Statax-Motor of Zurich, Switzerland introduced a swashplate engine design. Only a single prototype was produced, which is currently held in the Science Museum, London. In 1914 the company moved to London to become the Statax Engine Company and planned on introducing a series of rotary engines.

2. Rex D.17 – On this biplane, the lower small wings were adjustable in flight and served as air brakes during landing. The D 17 was influenced by the Nieuport fighter. It is said to have been built for Lt. Voss and was powered by a 100 hp Hansen engine.

hp. Such an engine was tested in 1917 in the Rex 7 (D.17) fighter single seater.

Neither type of rotary engine found widespread use.

Above & Above Right: Rex D.17, tested with Hansen 100 hp rotary engine. [J14, 1991]

3.23 Flugwerk Deutschland GmbH, Plant Munich-Milbertshofen

Flugwerk Deutschland GmbH was an aircraft and aircraft engine manufacturer whose headquarters were located in Brand near Aachen. The engine production line was founded in Schleissheimerstrasse 8 in Munich-Milbertshofen in 1912, where Karl Rapp[1] and Joseph Wirth developed its first aeroengines. This plant was created by taking over the Schneeweiß company, previously located in Chemnitz/Saxony (see there).

Besides aircraft engines, the Flugwerk Deutschland GmbH built and sold aircraft, machinery and equipment and operated airfields and aerodromes. Flugwerk Deutschland manufactured several biplanes and a monoplane, mostly the Taube.

The company took part in the competition for the best German aeroengine General 1912 (Kaiser-Prize) with their FD 1416 engine, designed by Karl Rapp.

The company was dissolved by a resolution of the shareholders on April 16, 1913, and Joseph Wirth was appointed as sole liquidator. After the liquidation process had been brought to an end, the company was wound up on August 8, 1916.

The 100 hp four-cylinder engine of Flugwerk Deutschland, GmbH, Munich, in contrast to the other engines, had intake and exhaust valves arranged in baskets and therefore easily removable. This advantage caused a considerable accumulation of components in the cylinder head, which made it difficult to cool the compression chamber. The cylinders have shafts made of steel and mounted cylinder heads and water jackets made of tempered cast iron. The inner joint of the water jacket is sealed by flanging. A vertical intermediate shaft drives the upper control shaft and two magnets located between the cylinder pairs from the center bearing. The water pump is coupled to the top of the rear end of the control shaft. The circulation lubrication is supplied by a small gear pump at the rear of the engine. An adjustable overflow regulates the oil pressure and the amount of oil supplied to the bearings.

Power: 90/70,4 hp at 1062 rpm
Bore: 140 mm
Stroke: 160 mm
Weight: 196,35 kg

Above Right: FD 1416, Flugwerk Deutschland 70,4 hp 4-cylinder inline engine, exhaust side. [A18]

Right: Advertisement [J3, 1913]

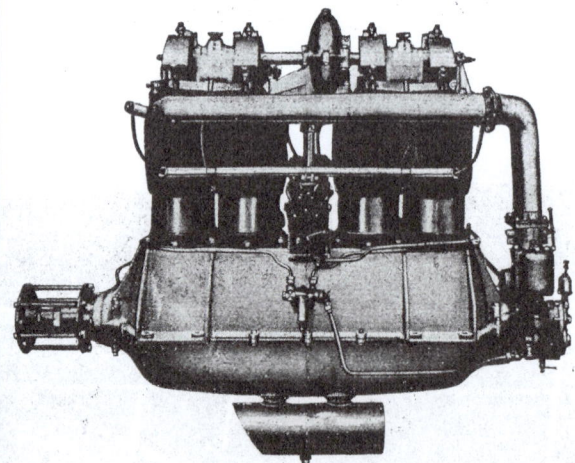

F.D. 100 PS Stahlzylinder Flugmotor

Benzinverbrauch 34,7 Liter
Oelverbrauch 1,5 Kilogramm } pro Stunde bei 1330 Touren
Gewicht 1,5 kg pro Pferdekraft mit 2 Magneten.

Im Flug erprobt.   □ □   Vibrationslos.
Demontable Ventile. Grösste Präzision.

Flugmotorenfabrik-Deutschland
G. m. b. H. :: MÜNCHEN.

Right: 70 hp FD engine as delivered to the Kaiser-Prize competition 1913. [B36, 1912–13]

Below Right: Carburettor side of Flugwerk Deutschland aeroengine. [B36, 1912–13]

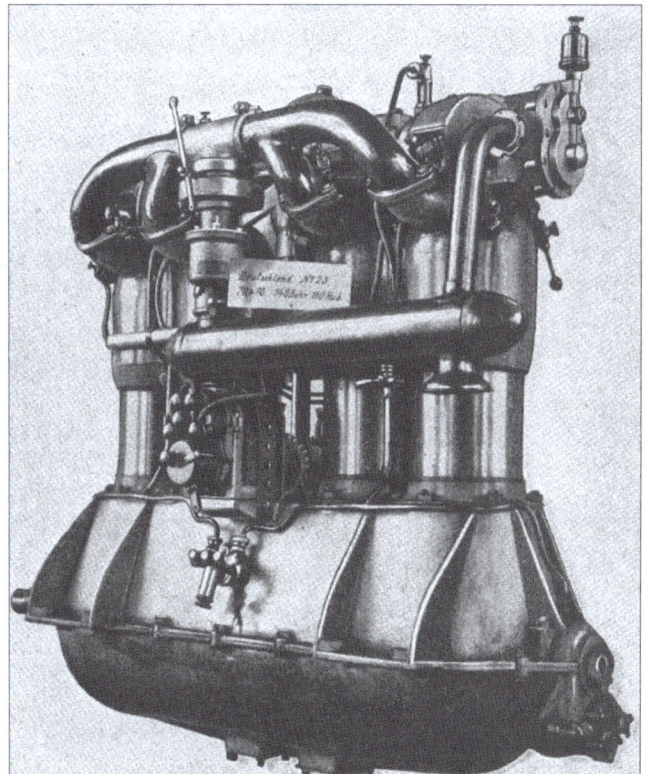

Endnote

1. Rapp later founded his own engine company and is also considered the founder of Bayerische Motoren-Werke (BMW).

3.24 Flugzeugbau Emil Freytag, Zwickau/Saxonia

3.24.0 General

Emil Freytag founded his aircraft manufacturing company in 1912 and moved into one of the aircraft hangars of the Württemberg Flying Club near the Cannstatter Wasen in Untertürkheim near Stuttgart. It is known that at least five "Baumann-Freytag" aircraft were built there, although they were not equipped with their own engines.

3.24.1 Ten-cylinder 50 hp aeroengine (1912)

On September 30, 1912, the engines admitted to the 1st Kaiser Prize for the best German aircraft engine were announced. The 24 companies included Emil Freytag, who was based in Zwickau/Saxony at the time of registration.

The only data available for this engine is that with which Emil Freytag entered the competition:

Operating mode:	two-stroke
Cooling:	air
Cylinders:	10 (fixed)
Power:	50 hp

No further information is available on the actual construction. It can only be assumed that it was a V-engine or a radial engine. Since this engine was not delivered in time for the competition, it must be assumed that this project was practically impossible to realize.

Above: Baumann-Freytag-Biplane (1912). [J4, 1913]

3.25 Gasmotoren-Fabrik Deutz (G.F.D.), Köln-Deutz

3.25.0 General

The oldest German factory for the production of internal combustion engines is located in Cologne, where Nicolaus August Otto[1], inspired by the French Lenoir engine, built his first atmospheric gas engine in 1863. This work took place in the workshops of M. J. Zons. Just one year later, N. A. Otto founded the company "N. A. Otto & Cie. KG" together with Eugen Langen, which was then transformed into the "Gasmotoren-Fabrik Deutz AG" from 1872. That same year, Gottlieb Daimler (1834-1900) and Wilhelm Maybach (1846-1929) joined the company as technical directors. Otto, meanwhile, took over the commercial management as director. In 1876, Otto presented the first four-stroke gas engine he had invented to the public.

In 1884, Otto developed the revolutionary magneto-electric low-voltage breakaway ignition system, which served as a model for Robert Bosch's high-voltage ignition system.

Between 1907 and 1912, Deutz also tried its hand at building automobiles, hiring another engineer with a big name in the industry: Ettore Bugatti. 1907 also saw the start of series production of diesel engines. In 1913, 3,400 workers and 700 salaried employees were working at the plant.

N. A. Otto's son Gustav, on the other hand, developed his own aircraft engines (see section 3.56).

3.25.1 Six-cylinder 180 hp Argus aeroengine As III Dz (1917)

In addition to the production of engines for land vehicles, Gasmotoren-Fabrik Deutz applied for the licensed production of aircraft engines. In 1917, the type examination for the Argus As III Dz license construction was passed and series production began (see section 3.4 for details).

The performance data was identical to that of the original. A further 252 engines[2] were delivered by the end of the war.

Endnotes

1. N. A. Otto, born June 10, 1832 in Holzhausen an der Haide in the Taunus; died January 26, 1891 in Cologne.
2. See Dan-San Abbott's German engine production list.

Above: The massive Lubeck-Travemünde F 2 used the obsolete but powerful Mercedes D IV straight-8 engine.

3.26 Gandenbergerische Maschinenfabrik Georg Goebel, Darmstadt

Above: Destruction of the production facility 1920.

3.26.0 General

The Darmstädter Maschinenfabrik Goebel AG was founded in 1851 by Peter Gandenberger. At that time, the production included scales, fire extinguishers and all kinds of other equipment, including lantern columns. In 1856 Georg Goebel joined the factory as co-owner. Under his leadership the production was changed over. Machines and equipment for the production and control of railroad tickets and ticket printing machines were newly added to the production range.

Between 1913 and 1918 four[1] rotary engine models were developed; the larger engine, known as Goe III, was used to a limited extent in active service before the signing of the Armistice.

The principal feature of the Goebel engines was the valve gearing. The exhaust valves were controlled from a single stationary cam; the tappet plungers, connected with the push rods and rocker levers, swung so that they passed the cam every other revolution.

Lubrication was of the pressure feed type. The inlet valves, situated in the tops of the pistons, were provided with counterweights. The pistons were built up in two sections, the lower section acting only as a guide.

The Gandenberger'sche Maschinenfabrik Georg Goebel was engaged since about 1913 in the construction of rotary engines designed by Georg Hoffmann[2]. The exact background of this product, which is not typical for the company, is not known. It can be assumed that the Goebel company had to contribute its direct share to the national defense and thus should become part of the armaments industry. At that time Motorenfabrik Oberursel created the UR III double radial engine, Siemens-

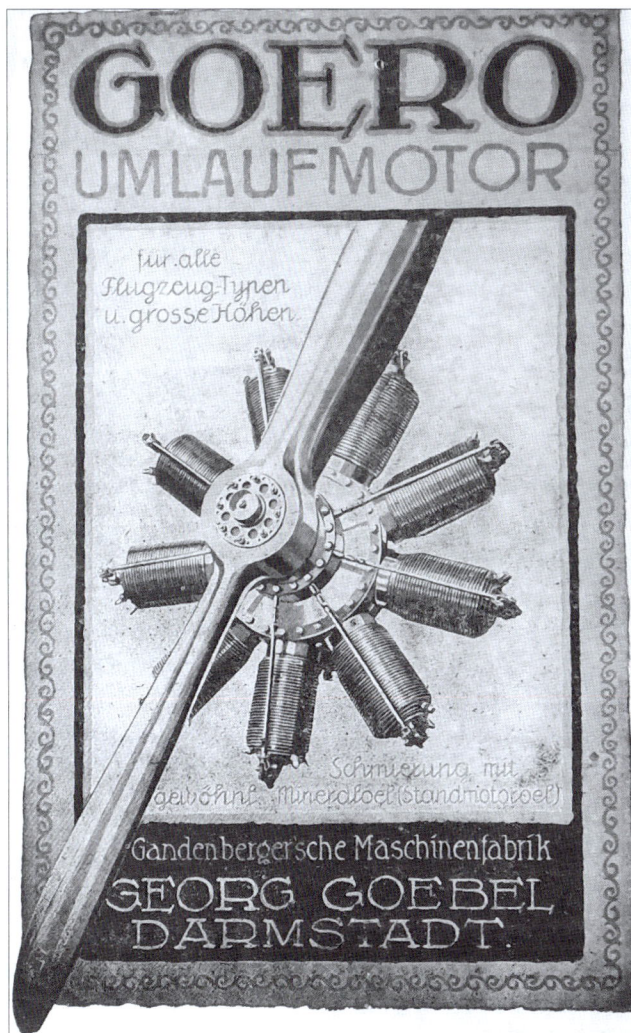

Above: Baumann-Freytag-Biplane (1912). [J4, 1913]

Halske the Sh III and Georg Goebel first designed the Goe II in 1913 and the Goe III in 1917. The latter engine model was designed for an output of around 180 hp.

Georg Hoffmann developed not only the Goe-motors, but in this context also the needle bearing, which was also widely used as a rolling bearing in engine construction.

3.26.1 Goebel Type VI

In Gilles' Engine Encyclopaedia the following information were given on the Type VI rotary engine: The 30/40-hp model had seven cylinders of 94 mm bore, 95 mm stroke, and a total displacement of 4,6 liter. The weight was said to be 55 kg. The engine operated from 1150 rpm minimum to 1200 rpm maximum, and consumed nearly·14,5 kg of fuel and 0,9 kg of oil per hr. The compression ratio was 4.6. Both inlet and exhaust valves were mechanically operated and had a clear diameter of 34 mm. The cylinders were provided with flanges for mounting. A Pallas carburetor supplied the mixture through induction pipes, and a Bosch magneto provided ignition. The overall dimensions were as follows: outside diameter 0,66 m, and length 0,9 m.

3.26.2 Goebel Type V

The Type V[3] was a larger seven-cylinder rotary engine, which operated at the same speeds, was rated at 50 to 65 hp. This engine had a 105 mm bore and stroke, and a total displacement of 6,4 litre. The weight was reported to be 75 kg, and the approximate fuel and oil consumption 21 and 4,5 kg/hr, respectively. The compression ratio was 5.2.

The cylinders were mounted by a threaded joint. Both valves are mechanically controlled, their diameter being 43 mm. The gas was fed through induction pipes from a carburetor, and a Bosch magneto supplied the ignition. The overall diameter was 0,70 m and the length approximately 0,96 m.

3.26.3 100 hp 7-cylinder rotary engine Goebel Goe II

In August 1915, Gandenberger'sche Maschinenfabrik Georg Goebel, Darmstadt, sent its rotary engine, which had originally been prepared for the second Kaiserpreis competition in 1913, to Adlershof to the testing institute and shipyard to obtain type approval. This certification test was mandatory for the engines to be used in German military aircraft.

In the design, the engineers around Georg Goebel had taken remarkable steps to avoid the

Above: Euler D.R.7 triplane fighter prototype fitted with a Goebel Goe II engine.

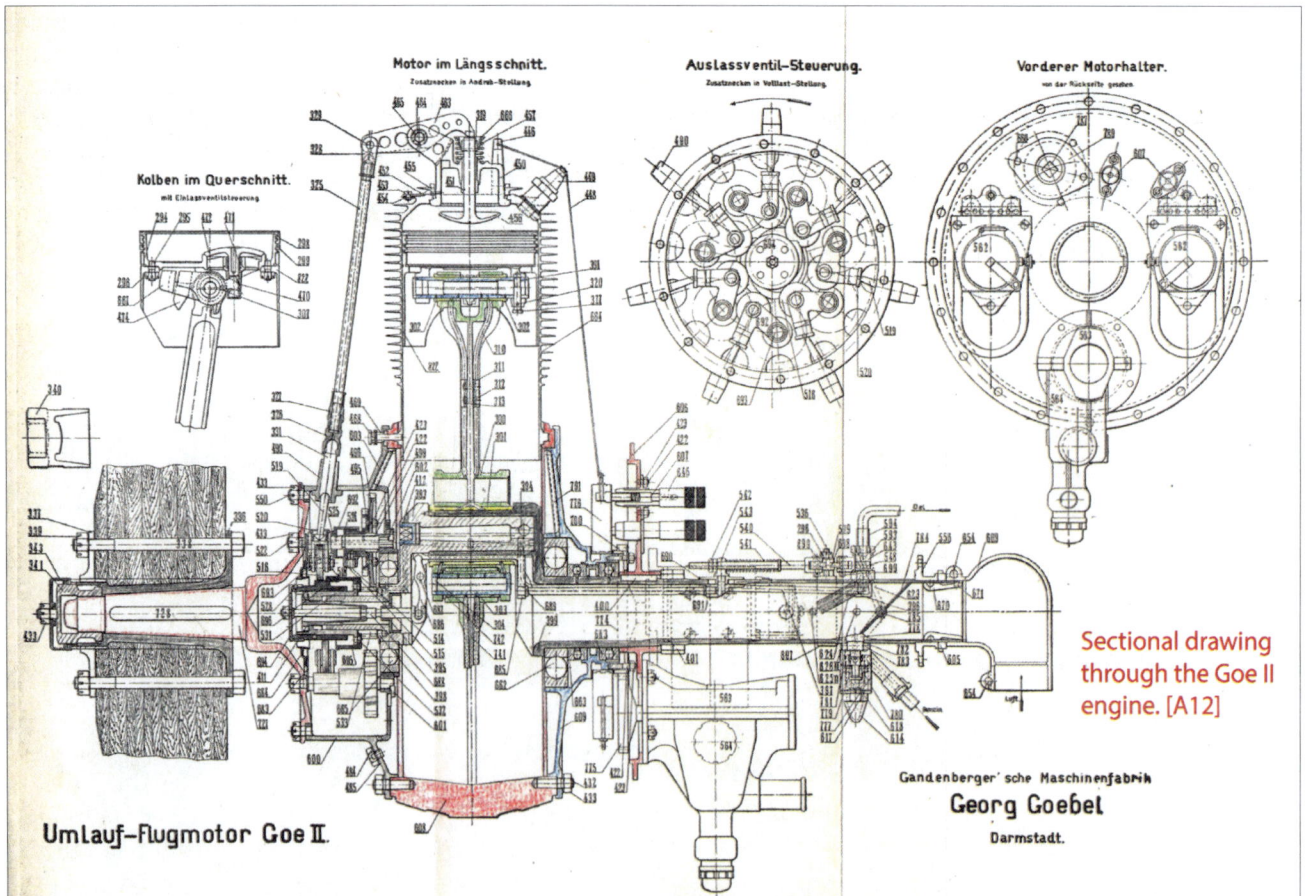

Sectional drawing through the Goe II engine. [A12]

weaknesses which were inherent in the Gnome engine: Although the intake valve was also located in the piston crown here, it was shifted from the center and controlled by a weight lever through the push rod in a semi-compulsory manner. The piston crown, which supported the pins, bearings and the

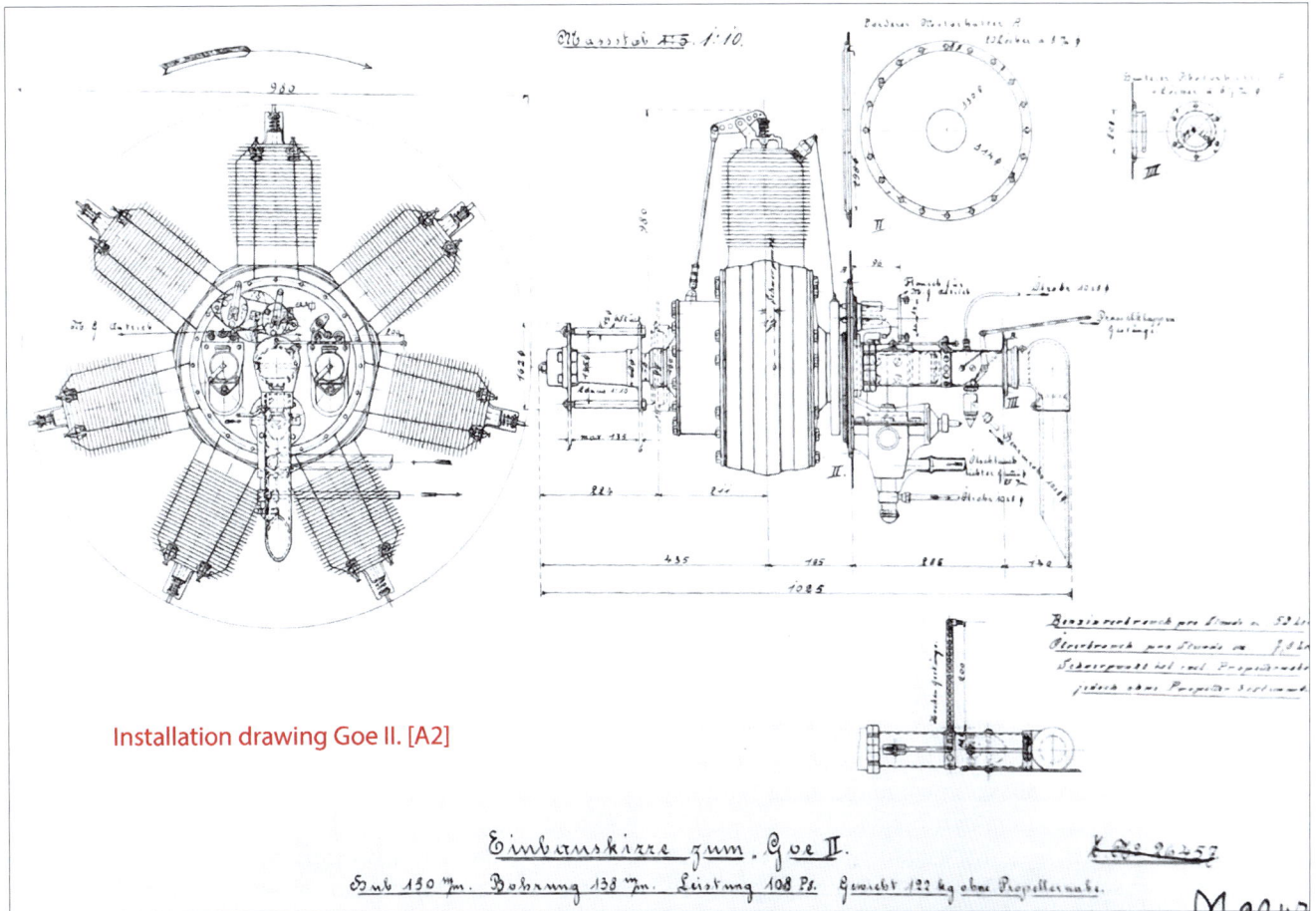

Installation drawing Goe II. [A2]

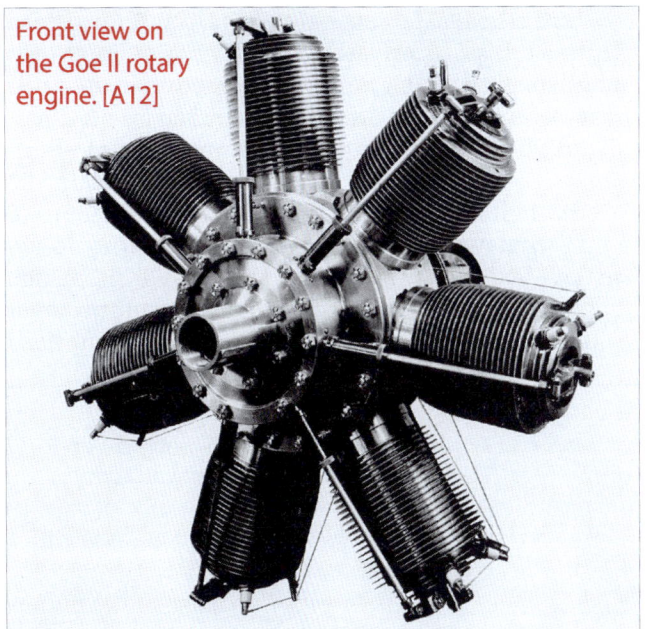

Front view on the Goe II rotary engine. [A12]

control elements of the intake valve, was made of steel; initially aluminum, later bronze, was used as the piston skirt material. In addition, the engine had a movable auxiliary cam in front of the main cam for easy starting and slow running. This cam could be actuated from the driver's seat via a linkage, and after switching on, the tappets opened the exhaust valves during the compression stroke. This device was valuable in terms of aeronautical engineering as it reduced the risk of the engine stopping.

However, the 7-cylinder engine, designed for an output of 100 hp, showed considerable weaknesses in the design of the exhaust valve cages and the rocker arm supports during the test runs at Adlershof in August 1915. Unfortunately, the company devoted its energies more to the design and testing of new designs of greater power output than to the flawless development of the 100 hp engine, so that the tests, which were repeated in the course of 1916, also had to be prematurely discontinued due to multiple fractures of the exhaust valve cages.

Only in the spring of 1917 (after about three years of development time) did this engine pass the type test without any complaints. It was registered under the designation Goe II with an acceptance test performance of 102 hp in May. However, the company's factory equipment was not sufficient for a significant production. This engine was built only in a small number of pieces, because the ldflieg rejected it as too weak. Nevertheless, the company worked

Above: Exhibit of a Goe III engine in the Deutsches Technikmuseum Berlin. [A8]

Detail view, spring loaded rocker arms of Goe III. [A8]

Above: Marking on the engine housing: EDUL - Entgegen Dem UhrzeigerLauf - Counterclockwise. [A12]

on a new, more powerful type, the later Goe III with 165 hp continuous power.

The cylinders were retained by a bayonet type joint. This model, as well as Goe III, employed automatically operated inlet valves. The inlet valves were 54 mm diameter and the exhaust valves 59 mm diameter in both models Goe II and Goe III engines. Further, the induction systems were alike; the gas being delivered to the cylinders through the crankshaft and case. The outside diameter of the Goe II design was 98 mm and the overall length approximately 101 mm.

3.26.4 170 hp 9-cylinder rotary engine Goebel Goe III

A 170 hp 9-cylinder engine in development since the autumn of 1916 could not be made available for type testing until December due to difficulties in the supply of stainless steel for engine parts, which had to be interrupted prematurely due to malfunctions in the cylinders and pistons.

This engine represented a more powerful version of the Goe II engine. It is remarkable that this oversized engine was the first German aircraft engine to have a power-to-weight ratio of less than 1 kg/hp. The Goebel Goe III was with 27 litres displacement also the largest German rotary engine in front line service. The final type approval was reached in May 1918. The test results were very promising: 160 hp continuous power at 1100 rpm, 200 hp 5-minute power at 1250 rpm and even 160 hp at 2100 m.

Each piston had a controlled intake valve in the piston base. The year of manufacture is 1917, but

it did not pass the type test until May 1918. The total number of engines built was only about 229 and they were used in several aircraft types, such as Fokker V.5 (prototype of Dr.I), Fokker D.VI, Fokker V.28 (prototype of D.VIII), Kondor E.III, LFG Roland D.XVI, Pfalz D.VI, Pfalz D.VII, Pfalz D.VIII. But also August Euler, based in Frankfurt a.M., used Goebel engines in three of his prototypes presented at the end of the war (Goe II: D.R. 7, Goe III: D.R. 6 & D 9).

A special advantage of the 200 hp Goero rotary engine, which was especially important for fighter pilots, was that it could be throttled down to 250 rpm. This was not possible with most other rotary engines.

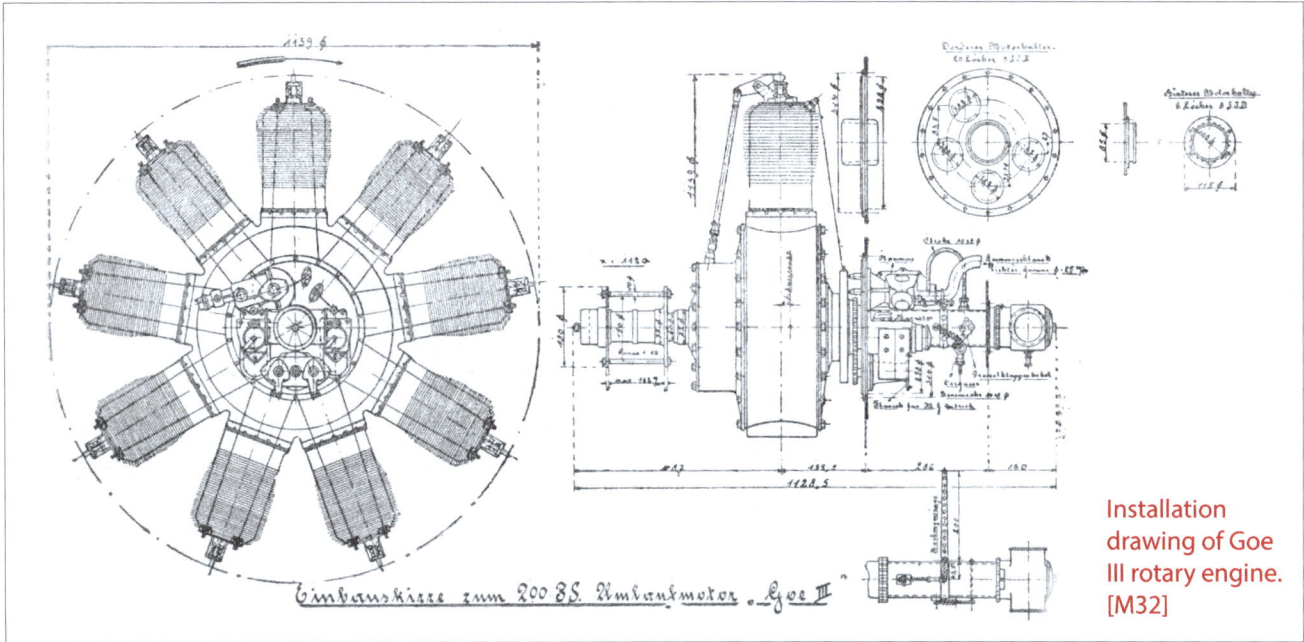

Installation drawing of Goe III rotary engine. [M32]

Construction of the Goe III engine (taken from the Technical Description of the "Goe" III rotary engine):

1. The exhaust valve is controlled by a common stationary cam. The plunger rollers, which actuate the exhaust valves in conjunction with the push rods and rocker arms, run according to the four-stroke cycle, one time over the cam and the other time past it. For easy starting and slow running of the engine, a movable additional cam is mounted in front of the main cam. When the engine is started, the tappet rollers pass over this short additional cam during the compression stroke, opening the exhaust valves for a moment. Part of the compressed gas escapes, so that the compression in the combustion chamber decreases. The additional cam is operated from the driver's seat.

2. the pistons are composed of two parts, the steel piston base and the piston guide. The piston base, which is hinged to the tie rod, absorbs the compressive and tensile forces. It carries the sealing rings without coming into contact with the cylinder itself. As its name suggests, the guide jacket serves firstly to guide the entire piston and secondly to distribute and dissipate the heat.

3. the inlet valve, which is located laterally in the piston crown, is balanced by a counterweight. The control is affected by means of an additional weight lever through the connecting rod. Both levers have their pivot point on the piston pin. To ensure that

Front view on the Goe III rotary engine. [A12]

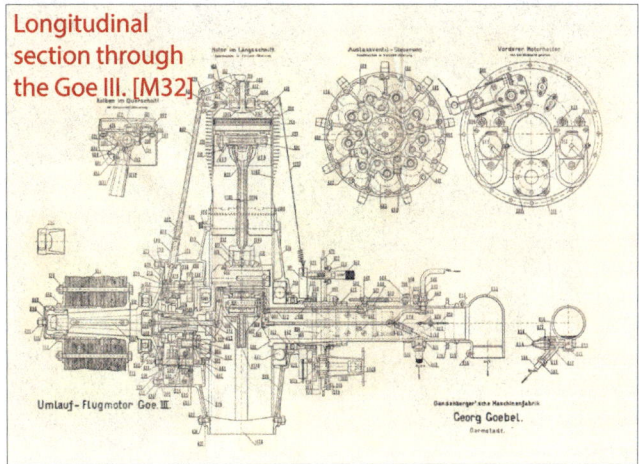

Longitudinal section through the Goe III. [M32]

Goebel Goe III installed on a test station.

the additional weight lever closes in all positions of the engine, a locking spring is fitted.

4. the cooling fins run thread-like around the cylinder barrel and continue over the sloped cylinder head. These winding cooling fins give the cylinder strength, elasticity and cooling capacity.

5. the cylinders are screwed into the crankcase and secured by a lock nut. Each cylinder can be screwed out of the crankcase individually after loosening the locknut and removing the exhaust valve lever with push rods.

6. each cylinder is equipped with two Bosch spark plugs with a ring electrode of 0.3 mm spacing. Two Bosch magnets, type "DAGn", are used to supply the spark plugs.

7. The motor is lubricated by an oil pressure pump with a ratio of 1 : 12.4. The plunger, designed as a slide, is moved by force. The output can be regulated by axial displacement of the cylinder jacket. The engine can run on castor oil as well as on castor oil substitute (mineral oil).

8. the carburetor consists of a replaceable petrol nozzle and a throttle valve in the hollow crankshaft. The throttle valve serves to limit the filling. Its actuating lever has a segment on which there is a red line, just like on the stop pin. If the red lines coincide, the position corresponds to an air pressure of about 760 mm. The approximate consumption of fuel and oil 35 kg/hr and 6,4 kg/hr, respectively.

3.26.5 230 hp 9-cylinder Goe IIIa (Goe IV)

At the end of the First World War, another 230/200 hp 9-cylinder rotary engine was under development. The performance of this engine was similar to that of the Goe III. Through technical improvements to the cylinders, a higher compression (over compressed, high altitude) was achieved, which resulted in an increase in power of about 20–30 hp. Therefore, an engine designation Goe IV (Performance class IV: 200–300 hp) would have been necessary. Practically however, in most cases it was described as Goe IIIa. This engine modification did not go into a wide serial production.

It is known that such an engine was again installed and tested by Euler-Flugzeugwerke in a D.9 biplane.

Franz Schneider, the successful chief designer of the Luft-Verkehrs-Gesellschaft A.G. and from 1918 owner of the Franz Schneider Flugmaschinenwerke mbH Seegefeld, reached a speed of 260 km/h with his last design at the end of the war, a single-seater fighter with a 220 hp Goebel engine.

Endnotes

1. Glenn D. Angle listed in his *Airplane Engine Encyclopedia* (1921) 4 different models. In the German literature no information was found so far about the 2 smaller engines (called as Typ VI and V)
2. Georg Hoffmann also developed his own "Rotor" rotary motors (see section Hoffmann 3.33).
3. Model designation Type VI and type V iaw. Gilles Encyclopedia

Above: Pfalz D.VIII fighter fitted with a Goebel Goe III high-altitude engine for evaluation; normal Pfalz D.VIII power was the Sh III.

Right: Advertisement for Pallas carburettor as used in Goe Type VI. [B13]

Cut through the Goe III oil pump. [M32]

Engine Datasheet	
Gandenberger'sche Maschinenfabrik Georg Goebel, Darmstadt	
Designation	**Goe II**
Year:	1916
Purpose:	Aircraft engine
Number of Cylinders:	7
Arrangement of Cylinders	Rotary piston engine
Bore [mm]:	138
Stroke [mm]:	150
Displacement [l]	15,71
Compression [Ratio]	4,5
Power [Hp]: norm./max.	100/110
RPM [min-1]: norm./max.	1150/1200
Power per Displacement [Hp/l]	6,4
Carburetor(s)	
No.:	1
Type:	Pallas SBL
Fuel consumption per hp per hour [g]:]:	350
Oil Pump	
No.:	1
Oil consumption per hp per hour [g/PS/h]:	80
Ignition No.:	2
Type:	Bosch "DAGn"
Firing order:	1 – 3 – 5 – 7 – 2 – 4 – 6
Weight of complete engine (dry) & ext. masses	
Total [kg]:	122
Weight per displacement [kg/l]:	7,8
Weight per hp [kg/hp]:	1,22

Remarks: Type certification in February 1917. 50 units were built.
Applications: Euler Triplane Dr.7.
* Listing has no claim to completeness!

Engine Datasheet	
Gandenberger'sche Maschinenfabrik Georg Goebel, Darmstadt	
Designation	**Goe III**
Year:	1917/18
Purpose:	Aircraft engine
Number of Cylinders:	9
Arrangement of Cylinders:	Rotary piston engine
Bore [mm]:	138
Stroke [mm]:	200
Displacement [l]:	26,92
Compression [Ratio]	6,0
Power [hp]: norm./max.	200/230
RPM [min-1]: norm./max.	1150/1200
Power per displacement [hp/l]	7,4
Carburetor(s)	
No.:	1
Type:	Pallas SBL 70/70
Fuel consumption per hp per hour [g]:]:	320
Oil Pump	
No.:	1(suction and pressure pump)
Oil consumption per hp per hour [g/PS/h]:	55
Ignition No.:	2
Type:	Bosch "DAGn"
Firing order:	1 – 3 – 5 – 7 – 9 – 2 – 4 – 6 – 8
Cooling	Air
Weight of complete engine (dry) & ext. masses	
Total [kg]:	183
Weight per displacement [kg/l]:	6,8
Weight per hp [kg/hp]:	0,91

Remarks: Type certification in April 1918. 229 engines were built.
Applications: Euler Dr. 6; Fokker V.26, Fokker V.28, Fokker V.31; Kondor E.IIIa; L.F.G. Roland D.XIV, Roland D.XVI; Schneider Fighter. * Listing has no claim to completeness!

Summary of Goebel Rotary Engines									
Model	Power [hp]	RPM	Cyl.	Bore [mm]	Hub [mm]	Disp. L.	Wt. [kg]	Comp	Year
Typ VI	40/30	1200/1150	7	94	95	4,61	55	4,6	
Typ V	65/50		7	105	105	6,4	75	5,2	
Goe II	100/110	1150/1200	7	138	150	15,71	123	4,5	End 1916
Goe III	200/230	1150/1200	9	138	200	26,92	183	6,0	1917/18
Goe IIIa (Goe IV)	220	1150	9	138	200	26,92			1918

Left: Kondor E.IIIa with Goebel Goe III high-altitude engine shown in postwar Swiss markings. The E.IIIa competed in the Third Fighter Competition.

Below: Schneider fighter prototype with Goebel Goe III high-altitude engine.

Right: Fokker Dr.I with Goebel Go.II engine installed; It is from Jastaschule I or II.

Left: Roland D.XIV prototype with Goebel Goe III high-altitude engine for evaluation.

Right: Roland D.XVI prototype with Goebel Goe III high-altitude engine. The D.XVI competed in the Third Fighter Competition.

3.27 Grade-Motoren-Werke GmbH, Magdeburg und Bork

3.27.0 General

Hans Grade[1] was born in Köslin on May 17, 1879. In 1903, Grade designed his first motorcycle. After completing his studies at the college in Berlin-Charlottenburg, Hans Grade founded a small engine factory in his father's town, which he later sold and moved to Magdeburg in 1904, where he opened a factory on a significantly larger scale, which has since supplied over 1000 units of the well-known Grade two-stroke engines. During his many years of experience in the engine business, Grade became convinced that the two-stroke engine, by virtue of its simplicity and lightness, but above all by virtue of its rational operation, was qualified to be used as an aircraft engine. At that time, Grade's two-stroke engines were initially used primarily in motorcycle and boat construction. In 1907, Hans Grade

withdrew from the management of his company and devoted himself to the construction of his first triplane aircraft, with which he made his first flight on the Cracauer Anger in Magdeburg on October 28, 1908. This triplane was equipped with its own six-cylinder two-stroke engine, which produced 36 hp. In 1910, with aviation gradually becoming established in Germany, Grade set up an aircraft factory in Bork near Berlin. There is much to suggest that the engine parts, such as pistons, crankshafts, casings, etc., were manufactured in Magdeburg - the assembly of the engines and the test runs took place in Bork near Berlin. The aircraft company, in which about 80 aircraft were built, existed until the beginning of World War I. Grade was one of the first successful German powered aviators. Grade was one of the first successful German powered aviators.

Summary of Grade Aero Engines 1908–1912						
Number	1	2	3	4	5	6
Year	1908	1908/09	1909/10	1909	1912	1912
No. of cylinders	4	2	4	6	4	4
Bore/Stroke [mm]	70/85	85/85	85/85	85/85	95/95	105/105
Displacement [L]	1,31	0,96	1,92	2,9	2,7	3,7
Max./norm. Power [hp]	20	12	24/16	36	36/24	45/40
at rpm	1700	1800	1700	1700	1800	1800
Mass	40		54			
Fuel consum. [g/hp/h]	500					
Grade-Type	Lanz-Prize		A, B	3D	B new	C
Taken from: *Typenhandbuch der deutschen Luftfahrttechnik*, Bruno Lange, Bernard & Graefe Verlag						

Summary of Grade Aero Engines 1912–1914						
Number	7	8	9	10	11	12
Year	1912	1912/13	1912/13	1912/13	1913	1913
No. of cylinders	4	2	4	8	4	4
Bore/Stroke [mm]	85/105	95/120	95/120	95/120	105/140	115/160
Displacement [L]	2,4	1,7	3,4	6,8	4,9	6,5
Max./norm. Power [hp]	30	24	45	90	70	100
at rpm	1700	1600	1600	1800	1500	1400
Mass			185			
Fuel consum. [g/hp/h]						35 liter/h
Grade-Type				Renn-ED, E (Milit)		

Above: Advertisement for the Grade 24 hp Type A engine [J4, 1911]

Above: Announcement for both aircraft and airship engines. Note: No Grade engine was ever used on airships. [J4, 1911]

His pilot's license dated February 1, 1910, issued by the Luftschiffer-Verband Berlin, bears the number 2, after August Euler, who was awarded the number 1.

Before the war, Grade Motoren-Werke produced only its own designs. The Grade engines were multi-cylinder air-cooled engines in which the cylinders were arranged in a 90° V-shape.

There was no significant series production. The Grade engines were used almost exclusively in his own flying machines. During the war, repair work was carried out on various types of aircraft engines at the Grade engine plant in Magdeburg.

3.27.1 Four-Cylinder 20/16 hp 2-stroke V-type Engine (1908)

The first grade monoplane, which was also used for the first dynamic takeoffs, was powered by a 20/16 hp aircraft engine of our own production. Like the majority of the engines to come, it was built in a V-shape. The basis of the Grade engines was a multi-fuel engine.[2]

The intake valves, which were located on the side of the cylinders, were designed as flutter valves. Fuel was fed to each cylinder individually via float chambers with distributor ring grooves downstream of the intake valves.

Subsequently, the 4-cylinder engines dominated, which are to some extent difficult to distinguish from each other. It seems certain that the spark plugs in the early engines were screwed into the cylinder cover at an angle. As can be seen from the above table, the cylinders were longer from 1912 than before, as Grade increased the stroke of the pistons by up to 50 mm.

3.27.2 Two-cylinder 2-stroke V-type Engines (1909/1912)

In the literature, several references can be found to two-cylinder aircraft engines with a low output of 12 or 24 hp.

Remarkable is a note from issue 9 of the magazine *"Flugsport"* of 1912, where it says:

Above: 16 hp Grade engine three-quarter view (Deutsches Museum Munich)

Above: Four-cylinder 16 hp V-type engine [Deutsches Museum Munich)

"For a particularly light flying machine, Grade has constructed a two-cylinder inline two-stroke engine, which results in an output of 16/24 hp and contributes considerably to operational safety by its simplicity and easy accessibility to the various individual parts."

In his book "*Motoren für Flugzeuge und Luftschiffe*" (Bibliothek für Luftschiffahrt und Flugtechnik, Vol. 14), Dr. Fritz Huth also describes another small two-cylinder 2-stroke engine with a bore of only 35 mm and a stroke of 120 mm. It seems extremely doubtful that this Grade engine, if it really existed with these dimensions, should develop a maximum power of 24 hp at 1600 rpm.

Illustrations of this engine are not known. Unfortunately, it cannot be clarified what exactly is meant by "standing" in the magazine "Flugsport". From the author's point of view, it would be very questionable to assume that Hans Grade developed a stationary engine consisting of 2 cylinders.

3.27.3 Four-cylinder 24/16 hp 2-stroke V-type engine (1909/10)

Increasing the bore to 85 mm while maintaining the stroke of 85 mm resulted in a 4 hp increase in power over the 1908 model.

Improvements were made to the cylinders, especially to improve its cooling.

3.27.4 Six-cylinder 36 hp 2-stroke V-type engine (1909)

It seems unusual that Grade used a 6-cylinder two-stroke engine for his triplane, i.e. the flying machine with which the first air jumps were achieved. This engine produced 36 hp at 1800 revolutions. The weight of the apparatus was almost 40 kg without gasoline and oil. No magneto ignition was used yet, so the engine had to be started by hand.

[J4, 1911]

Mit nur **16 PS** Touren-Maschinen

gelang es den

Grade-Fliegern

während der Sachsenwoche

erfolgreich gegen **70** u. **100 PS** Maschinen

32 Preise Im Gesamt-werte von **Mk. 20000** zu gewinnen

Chemnitz	Dresden	Leipzig

Mit nur 16 PS Motor erreichte Herr C. Schall nach eben bestandenem Piloten-Examen **in 23 Minuten**

2700 bis **2800 Metern**

Der Gradeflieger ist leicht und trotzdem stabil, auf demselben sind bis jetzt

ein Fünftel aller deutsch. Piloten ausgebildet

Er hält den **Rekord** der Betriebssicherheit und Gefahrlosigkeit, da bis jetzt noch **niemand mit ihm verunglückt ist**

Hans Grade Flieger-Werke Bork b. Berlin

Telephon Amt Brück i. d. Mark Nr. 13

Fliegerschule auf dem Flugfeld „Mars" Bork b. Berlin

Ausbildung für **Käufer** kostenlos
Für **Nichtkäufer** gegen Honorar Mark 1500 exkl. Bruchkosten

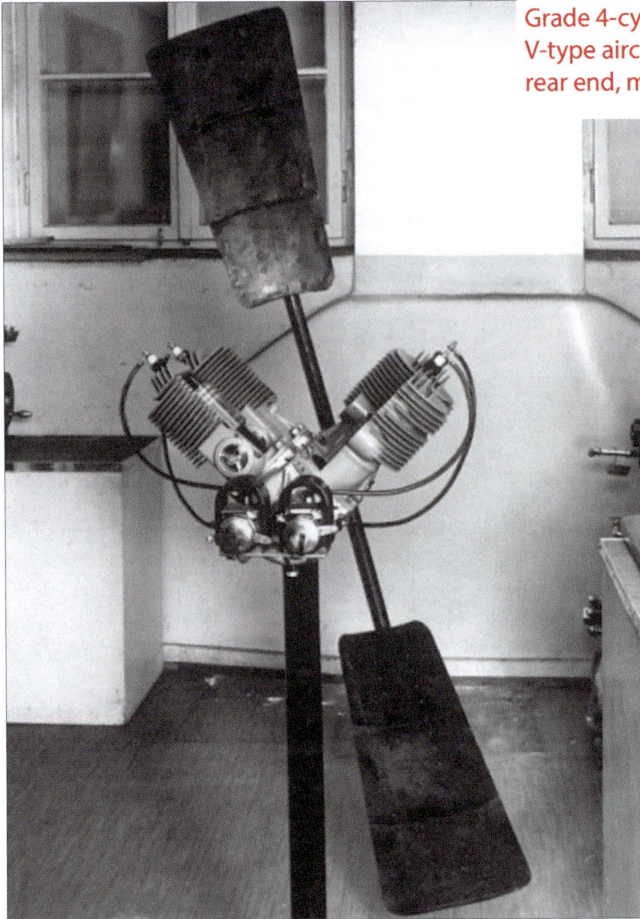

Grade 4-cylinder 24 hp V-type aircraft engine, rear end, magnetos. [A1]

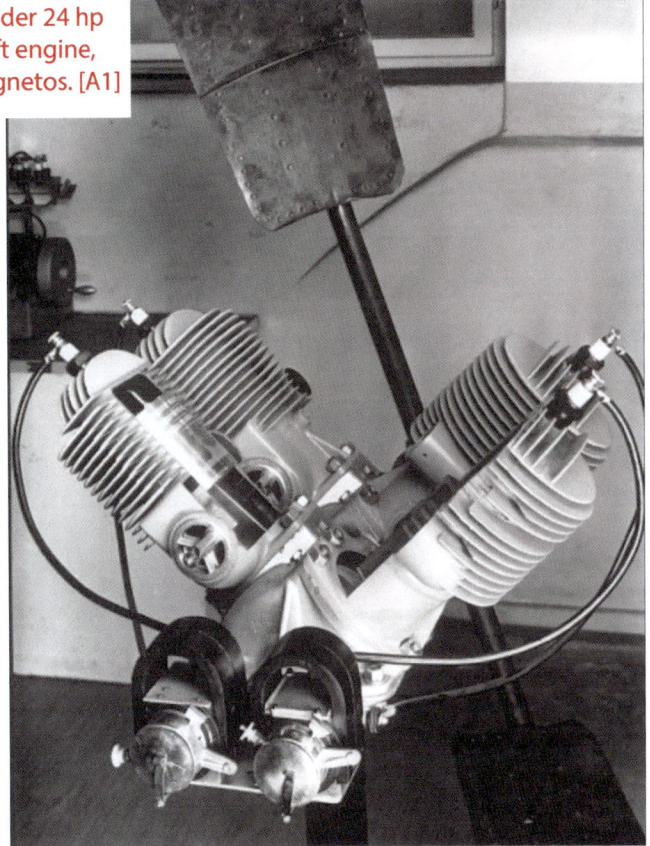

Grade 36 hp engine in his triplane.

3.27.5 Four-cylinder 36 hp 2-stroke V-type engine (1912)

 The Grade "military monoplane", with which Hans Grade took part in military exercises, partly out of competition, was already powered by a performance-enhanced 36 hp engine.

Starting in 1912, Grade experimented with different cylinder dimensions. This engine had a bore of 95 mm and a stroke also of 95 mm.

In the same year Grade brought out a next four-

Above: Hans Grade's triplane with which he achieved his first jumps in the air. [J3, 1909]

Above: Grade Monoplane with 36 hp Grade engine. The aircraft was used to carry privately airmail letters and cards. [B10]

Right: Early Grade monoplane with gondola in Berlin Aviation Museum (around 1940) 4 cylinders/24hp. [A1]

cylinder engine, which developed 45 hp, with a bore and stroke of 105 mm each.

3.27.6 Eight-cylinder 90 hp 2-stroke V-type engine (1912/13)

In 1912/13, Hans Grade developed a two-, four- and eight-cylinder engine based on the modular principle, using one type of cylinder with a piston diameter of 95 mm and a stroke of 120 mm. Each cylinder produced about 12 hp, making a total of 90 hp for the eight-cylinder engine. The number of cooling fins can serve as an external distinguishing feature. Instead of the usual 14, the new cylinders have 17 fins.

This engine with suspended cylinders was installed, among others, in a so-called "Military Type 1913". The cylinders were arranged in the usual V-shape, but in such a way that the cylinders arranged one behind the other were not at the top but at the bottom. This arrangement allowed a better shaping of the front part of the flying machine and did not obstruct the pilot's field of vision, as was the case with upward arranged cylinders. Due to the forced oiling of the cylinders and oil screen walls inside the housing, which is usual with Grade, the oiling of cylinders lying downward may have caused fewer difficulties in relation to others.

Above: Small deviation on this Grade monoplane: The exhaust pipes are directed outward. [J3, 1912]

3.27.7 Grade two-stroke V-type engine design

Hans Grade's vision was a light, uncomplicated flying machine, virtually an airplane for "everyone". However, this also required an equally uncomplicated and low-maintenance engine. These

Grade monoplane Type E with overhead seat and suspended eight-cylinder engine by Grade at the ALA 1912 in Berlin. [A1]

Above: Grade eight-cylinder 90 hp engine with inverse cylinders. [A1]

requirements were met by the air-cooled two-stroke engines, since components such as valves, control linkage, cooling water pump and piping were not necessary.

The vast majority of Grade engines had 4 cylinders, which ranged in power from 16 to up to 100 hp. To distinguish these engines is quite difficult.

As distinguishing features can be used:
A) Length of the cylinders: The engines from 1912 on have a longer stroke, therefore the cylinders are also slightly longer by 3 rips.
B) Position and installation position of the spark plug: either centered vertically or at an angle to the side.
C) Shape of cooling fins of the cylinder heads as shown on picture.

Except for the 6-cylinder engine, all subsequent engine types had a Bosch magneto ignition system consisting of 2 magnetos. Normally, only one spark plug was used per cylinder, and a second bore in the cylinder head was also used to accommodate a compression valve. With a normal 24 hp four-cylinder, the engine alone with piston, crank and crankcase weighed about 36 kg, the fittings, the oil and gasoline tanks and the piping about 10 kg. The magneto ignition brought an additional weight of 4.4 kg.

In all two-stroke engines, the four functions under consideration are: injection of fresh gas-air mixture into the cylinder, compression, ignition and expansion, and ejection of the burned gases, are

Left: Grade monoplane with 4-cylinder engine, exhibited in the Berlin Aviation Collection (about 1936). [A1]

Below: Cylinder head spark plug variants on Grade engines.

itself and in the case of the Grade engine was effected as follows (see also the diagrams).

The working process takes place on the upper side of the piston, while the mixture is formed on the lower side. For this purpose, the encapsulation of the crank gear is necessary, while in four-stroke engines the encapsulation is only done because of oiling and dirt.

When the piston K rises, a vacuum is created in

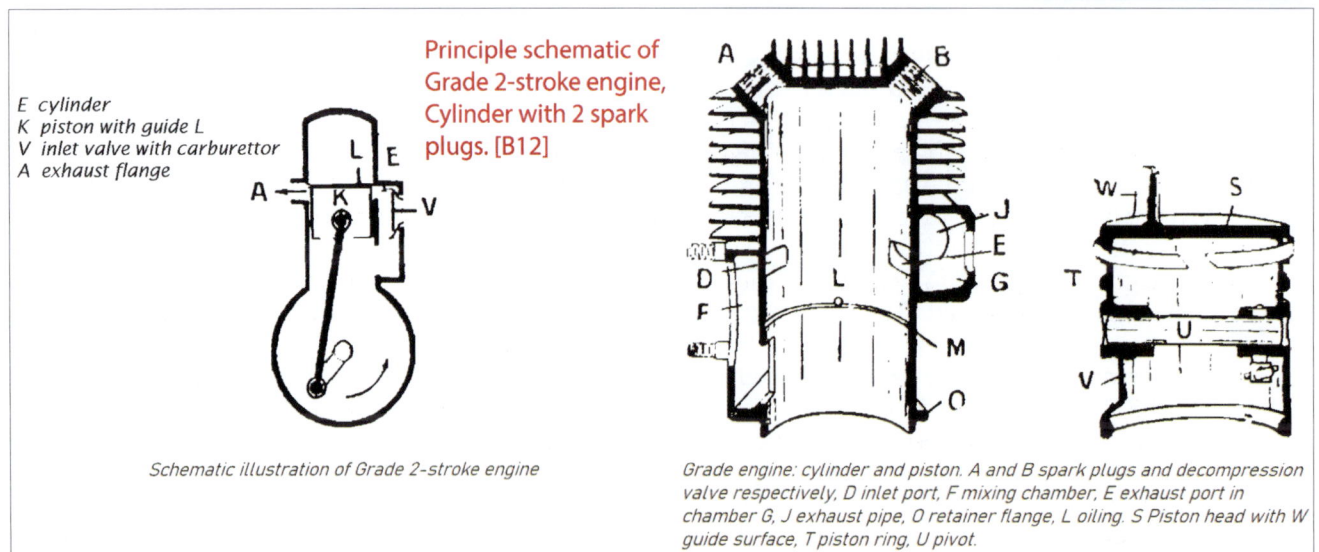

E cylinder
K piston with guide L
V inlet valve with carburettor
A exhaust flange

Principle schematic of Grade 2-stroke engine, Cylinder with 2 spark plugs. [B12]

Schematic illustration of Grade 2-stroke engine

Grade engine: cylinder and piston. A and B spark plugs and decompression valve respectively, D inlet port, F mixing chamber, E exhaust port in chamber G, J exhaust pipe, O retainer flange, L oiling. S Piston head with W guide surface, T piston ring, U pivot.

distributed over two piston strokes instead of four. Also worth mentioning for the valveless two-stroke engines is the absence of the control devices; the distribution of the operating processes to the two piston strokes is instead carried out by the piston

the crank chamber, or in the entire space under the piston, and this causes the opening of the suction valve V, through which fresh air with fuel enters. During the following descent of the piston, the sucked mixture is slightly compressed. During this

Side view and longitudinal section through a Grade two-stroke engine. [B28]

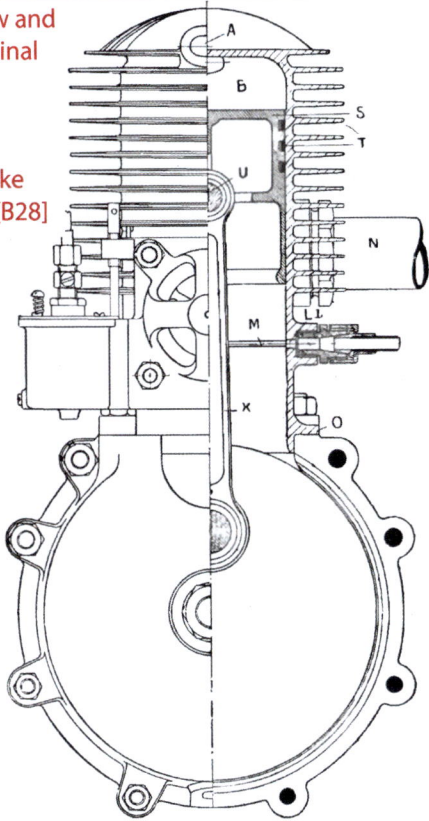

Cross view and section through a Grade two-stroke engine. [B28]

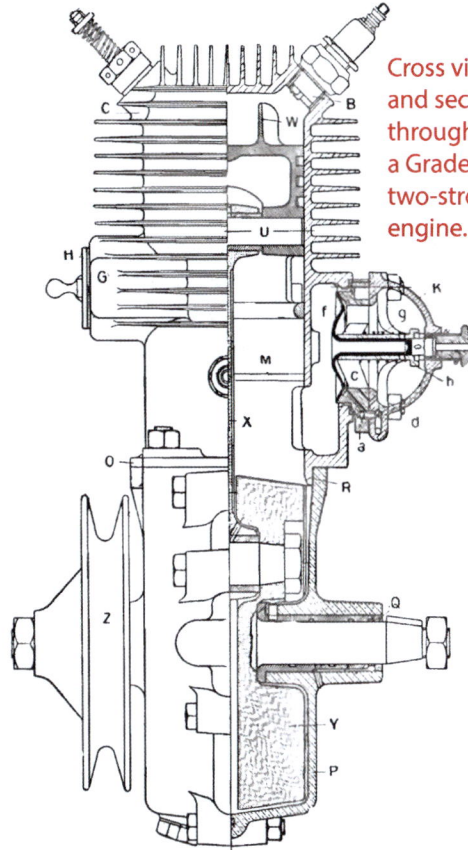

descent, a power stroke has been performed over the piston by the preceding charge as a result of explosion and expansion; the gases have expanded in the drawn piston position as far as seems expedient for their utilization. If the piston goes a little lower still, it opens the exhaust port A, and the pressurized gases puff out. This reduces their tension to near atmospheric and allows the new charge precompressed in the crankcase to enter the cylinder as soon as the piston clears the inlet port E on its further downward path. To prevent the new charge from shooting in at E and out again immediately at A, a guide vane L is attached to the piston, which forces the fresh charge to rise and, deflected by the cylinder floor, now fills the left-hand side space and, pushing the old, spent gases in front of it, fills the entire cylinder. -The process of exhaust and new charge thus takes place in the time during which the upper edge of the piston moves back and forth by the height of the exhaust port; thus a short piece is cut off from the expansion and compression stroke, which, together with the operations under the piston, replaces the first and fourth strokes of the four-stroke cycle.

When the exhaust port closes at the top of the piston, compression begins in the working cylinder, and ignition and explosion occur near top dead center, driving the piston down again.

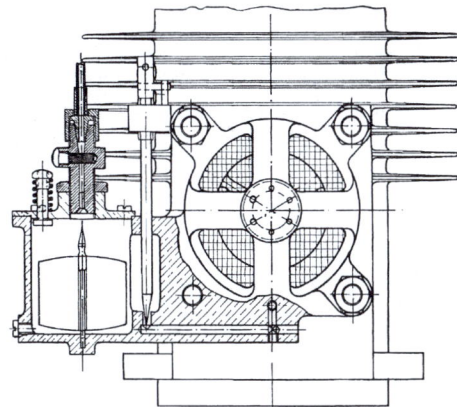

Grade carburettor, Cross section of float casing

Grade carburetor. [B11]

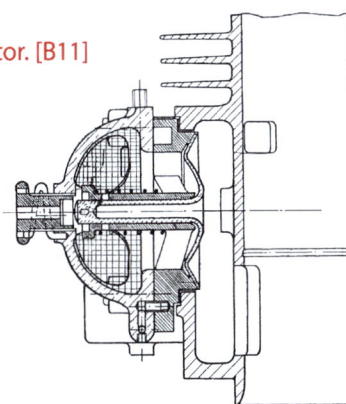

Above: Grade-Renneindecker. [J2, 1914]

Left: Grade 24 hp V-type engine. [A1]

Below: Four exhaust pipes visible on the Grade-Renneindecker [J2, 1914]

The illustrations opposite show the designs for engines with high numbers of revolutions. In the upper part, the cylinder had two openings A and B to accommodate the spark plugs and the compression valve. In the center were the control ports D for the intake of the fresh mixture and E for the exhaust of the exhaust gases, to which was connected the valve chamber F for the former and the exhaust chamber G for the latter. Attached to the exhaust chamber was a rotating disc H, the opening of which made it possible to turn off the muffler. In addition, there was an opening J on the side of the exhaust chamber, where the exhaust pipe N was connected by a union nut. An opening K led from the valve chamber at its lower end into the cylinder for the entry of the fresh mixture for precompression. The bore L served for oil supply, the groove M for distribution of the incoming oil over the entire cylinder periphery.

The cylinder was connected by flange O to the crankcase P, in the usual way by means of screws. The crankcase consisted of two identical sleeves made of aluminium. The piston S, made of a special alloy, was tightly sealed by three spring-loaded steel piston rings T and had the aforementioned guide vane W at the top. On the side facing the valve chamber, the I piston had a larger cut-out V, so that the connection between the valve chamber and the crankcase was maintained even in the lower piston position. The crankshaft was forged in one piece of steel with two flywheels Y and the crankpin. The two ends of the shaft were perfectly symmetrical, to have the possibility of taking the power on any or both sides. In the latter case, a special device is provided to drive the magnetic apparatus. An essential part of the engine is the carburetor valve in conjunction with the floating valve in front of it, which simultaneously causes the carburetion of the fuel, the intake of fresh mixture and the separating air stream, and regulated the flow of gasoline. The design of its carburetor is unique. In fact, the carburetor and intake valve are united. Instead of a nozzle, the Grade carburetor had two small holes

Above: 24 hp Grade engine, front view. [B39]

in the valve seat, which were exposed by lifting the self-acting valve during suction. The actual valve consisted of the valve seat a, the part of the seat surface c, the supply nozzles d for the fuel, valve f with coil spring g, counter plate h and pin i.

Above & Below: Experimental Grade aircraft, powered by a 4-cylinder engine. [J3, 1912]

Grade-Flieger

deutsche Konstruktion · deutsche Arbeit · deutsches Material

Ingenieur Hans Grade gewann den Lanzpreis der Lüfte in Höhe von

M. 40000.

Der Grade-Flugapparat ist der erste erfolgreichste deutsche Apparat einfach · leicht · schnell · stabil · elegant in Form und Bewegung

Ausbildung zum Piloten in der Fliegerschule auf dem Flugfeld „Mars" bis zur Erlangung des Fliegerdiploms

Bork, Post Brück i. d. Mark

Hans Grade
Flieger-Werke

Fernsprecher: Amt Brück Nr. 13

GRADE-
Aeroplan- und Luftschiff-
MOTOREN
bestbewährtes deutsches Erzeugnis
Grade-Motorwerke, Magdeburg

Left & Above: Advertisements 1911 [J4, 1911]

Above: The first German aeroplane, with Herr Grade starting the engine. [J7, 1909]

Above: Grade just before the start of the first stage Chemnitz-Dresden. [J6, 1911]

Left: Grade 4-cyl water monoplane; the engine was not powerful enough. [A1]

Above: Grade military monoplane.

Left: The Grade-Flugpostillon Pentz receives the first airmail from Bork to Brück on 18 February 1912. [L22]

Endnotes

1. Johannes Gustav Paul „Hans" Grade (* 17. May 1879 in Köslin, Pomeranian Province, Prussia, today Poland; † 22. October 1946 in Borkheide) was a German mechanical engineer, businessman and aviation pioneer.

2. As early as 1903, the German engineer Joseph Vollmer presented the first road train of NAG, the automotive division of AEG, which was powered by a multi-fuel engine. The gasoline engine with 50 hp worked with magneto ignition and a carburetor designed for both gasoline and spirit.

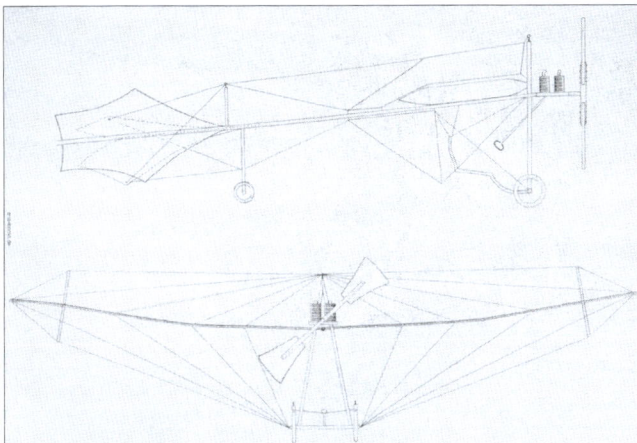

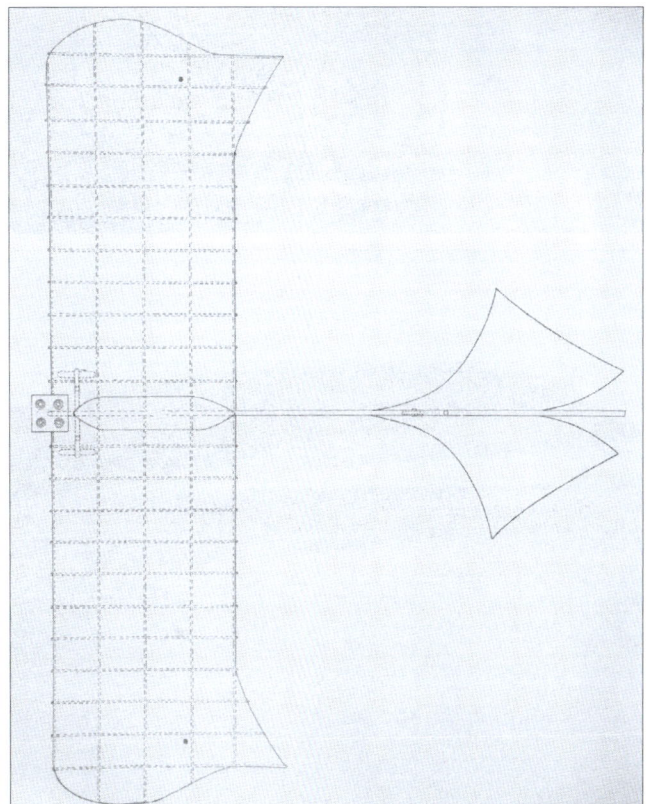

Left & Above: The Grade 1910 monoplane drawings. [J6, 1910]

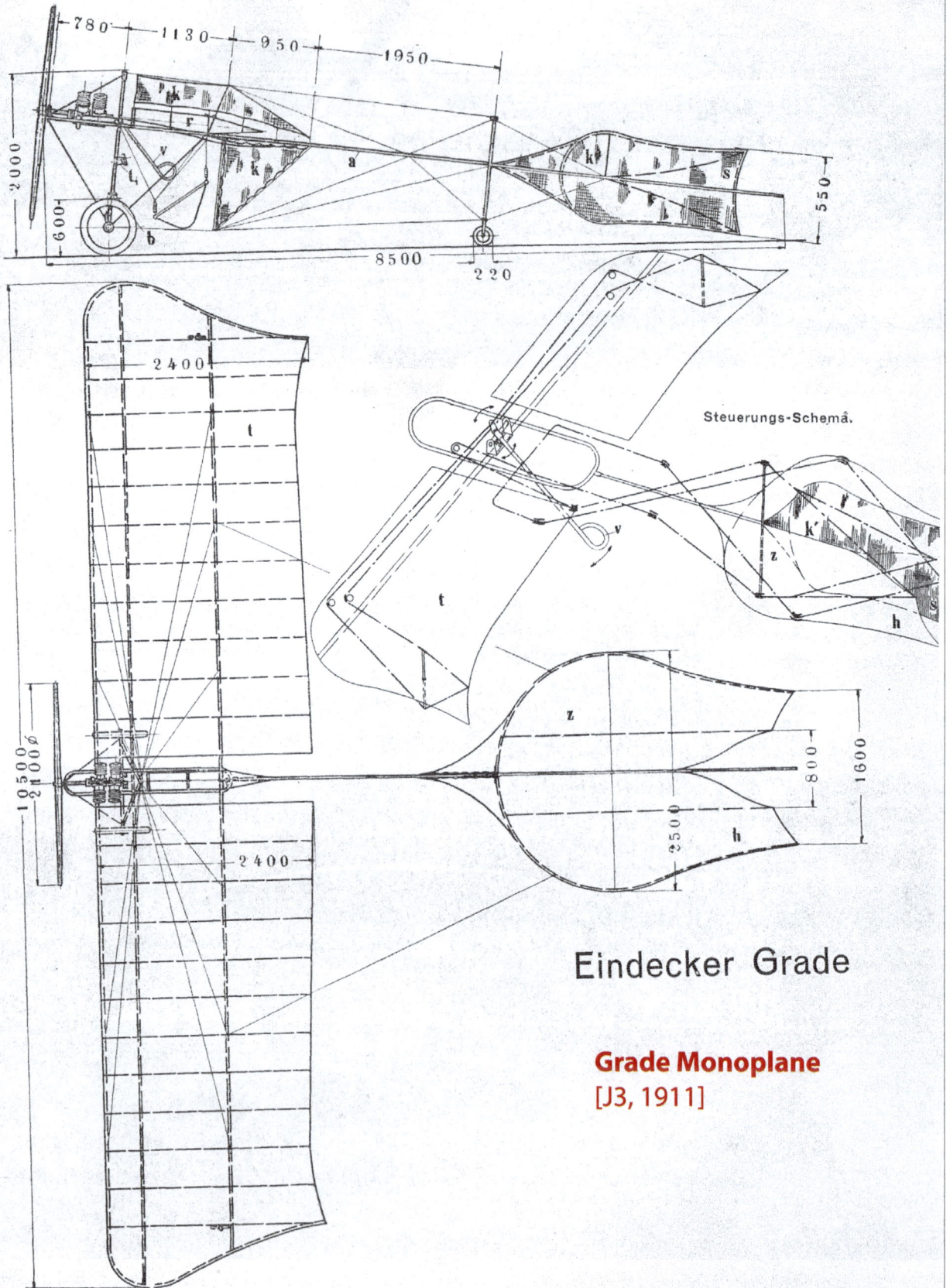

„Flugsport", Organ der deutschen Flugtechniker-Vereine 1911. Tafel XI

Steuerungs-Schema.

Eindecker Grade

Grade Monoplane
[J3, 1911]

Right: Grade 'hedgehog' of 1925.

Below & Bottom: Grade monoplane Type D with with overhead seat and suspended four-cylinder engine. [A1]

Above: Grade monoplane with nacelle fuselage and rotary engine. [A2]

Above: Grade fliers on the airfield Mars. From left to right: Miss Lager-Prague, Röpell, Bucher-Luzern, Lieutenant Hüttig, Lieutenant Böder, Pflug-Sidney. [J6, 1911]

Above: Early Grade monoplane No.6 during a flight competition. (B29]

Above: Engineer Grade in his airplane before starting the engine. [J3, 1909]

Above Right: German aviator Bozena Lagler with her Grade monoplane. [J3, 1909]

Above: Grade monoplane with boat and windscreen. [J3, 1912].

3.28 Güldner Motoren-Gesellschaft, Aschaffenburg

3.28.0 General

Güldner Motoren-Gesellschaft was a manufacturer of diesel engines and tractors. The company was founded in 1904 by Hugo Güldner, Carl von Linde, and Georg von Krauß in Munich and moved to Aschaffenburg in 1906.

3.28.1 Six-cylinder 180 hp Argus aeroengine As III Gü (1918)

From the beginning of 1918, the Argus As III was built under license as the As III Gü. A total of only 63 engines were produced by the end of the war. The performance data corresponded to the original (see also section 3.4).

Left & Below: The unusual Mercedes D IV straight-8 engine was quickly developed from the D III 6-cylinder as an interim measure pending availability of the D IVa 6-cylinder. The D IV was subject to failure in twin-engine bombers but was successful in the Albatros C.V (left) and LVG C.IV (below) reconnaissance aircraft, where its geared propeller gave it excellent efficiency and it could be fully cowled, reducing drag. These types were as fast as Allied fighters when they reached the front, allowing them to avoid interception.

3.29 Hermann Haacke Motoren-Fabrik, Berlin-Johannisthal

3.29.0 General

The H. Haacke Motoren-Fabrik was located in Berlin-Johannisthal and manufactured aircraft engines of various types from 20 to 60 hp since 1910. In 1917, the company was renamed "Hermann Haacke Motoren-Flugzeugteile-Fabrik." Haacke's factory in Berlin-Johannisthal was among those that successfully offered air-cooled engines in Germany in the manner of the Anzani engines. As with Anzani, the intake valves were uncontrolled. Lubrication was necessarily by a pump. The crankshaft of the engines ran in ball bearings.

3.29.1 Four-Cylinder 24/20 hp Haacke Engine HH 1

Air-cooled 4-cylinder V-shaped aircraft engine from 1911. The engine, equipped with a battery ignition, produced 24/20 hp at about 1200 rpm.

Bore/stroke: 95/110 mm.
Weight: 60 kg
Ignition: Battery

3.29.2 Four-Cylinder 35/30 hp Haacke Engine HH 1a

This air-cooled engine, also developed in 1911/12, was basically of the same design as the HH 1, but already produced 35/30 hp at 1400 rpm.

Bore/stroke: 105/120 mm.
Weight: 64 kg
Ignition: Battery

3.29.3 Four-Cylinder 35/30 hp Haacke Engine HH 1b

This V4 engine was the HH 1a, which was additionally supplied with a cooling fan. The power was also 35/30 hp at 1400 rpm.

Bore/stroke: 105/120 mm.
Weight: 65kg
Ignition: Battery

3.29.4 Three-Cylinder 40/35 hp Haacke Fan-shaped Engines HH 2 and Haacke HH 2a

This fan-shaped (72° offset) air-cooled 3-cylinder

Above: Haacke advertisement 1911. [J3, 1911]

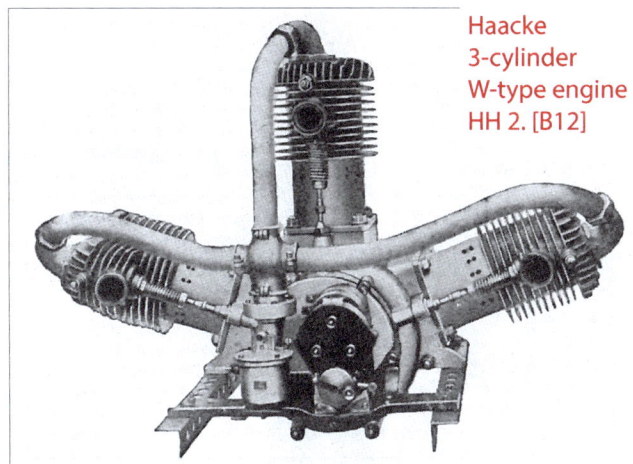

Haacke 3-cylinder W-type engine HH 2. [B12]

Haacke 40 hp HH 2a, Inlet valve controlled from above. [B12]

engine developed 40/35 hp at 1400 rpm.

HH 2a: Like its predecessors, the intake valve was controlled from above.

Bore/stroke: 120/130 mm
Weight: 75kg
Ignition: Magneto

3.29.5 Four-cylinder 50/40 hp Fan-shaped Engine Haake HH 3

In 1911, Deutsche Flugmaschinenbau GmbH (D.F.G.), Berlin-Rummelsburg, released a monoplane equipped with a 40 hp 4-cylinder air-cooled fan engine.

This 4-cylinder fan-type air-cooled engine, developing 50/40 hp at 1400 rpm, was constructively based on the type HH 1a.

Bore/stroke: 120/130 mm
Weight: 85 kg
Ignition: Battery

3.29.6 Five-Cylinder 60/55 hp Radial Engine Haacke HH 4

Air-cooled 5-cylinder radial engine (72° offset cylinders) of common design, 60/55 hp at 1400 rpm. This design was also built as a 10-cylinder twin-star engine on an experimental basis in 1913.

Bore/stroke: 120/130 mm
Weight: 100 kg
Ignition: Battery

3.29.7 Five-Cylinder 70/60 hp Haacke Radial Engine HH 4a

As HH 4, but with newly dimensioned cylinders:
Bore/stroke: 120/140 mm
Weight: 100 kg
Ignition: Battery

3.29.8 Six-Cylinder 60/55 hp Haacke Radial Engine HH 5

Four-stroke 6-cylinder radial engine (built 1913/14) with direct controlled intake and exhaust valves. In this type, the valves were suspended in the cylinder head.

Power: 60/55 hp at 1400 rpm
Bore/stroke: 105/130 mm
Weight: 85 kg
Ignition: Battery magneto ignition

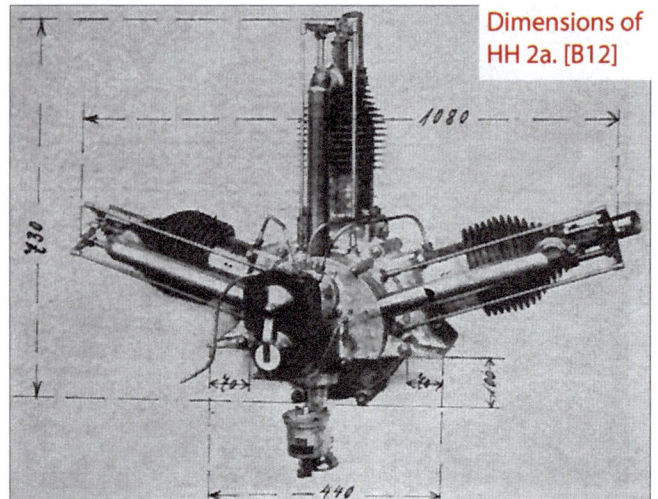

Dimensions of HH 2a. [B12]

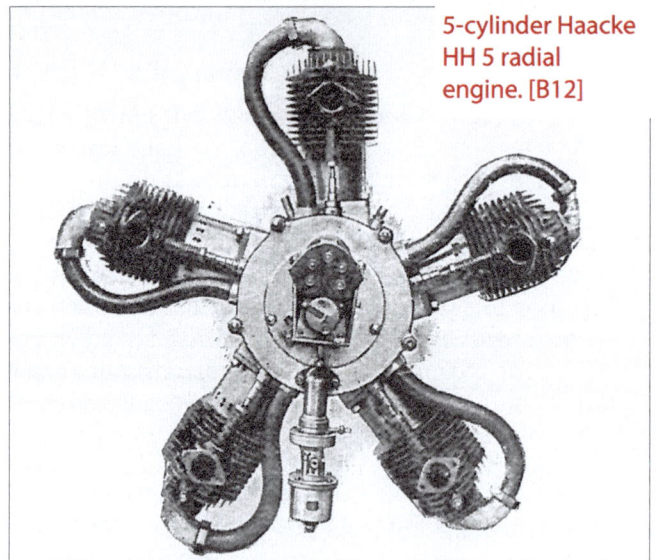

5-cylinder Haacke HH 5 radial engine. [B12]

Above: Monoplane of Deutsche Flugmaschinenbau-Gesellschaft equipped with 40 hp Haacke HH 3. [J3, 1910]

Facing Page, Bottom: Advertisement, showing front side of Haake HH 5 engine. [J3, 1910]

3X.14.9 Six-cylinder 90/80 hp Haake radial engine HH 5a

This 1913/14 engine was a more powerful version of the HH 5 with 120 mm bore.

Bore/stroke: 120/130 mm
Weight: 105 kg
Ignition: Battery magneto ignition

3.30 Deutsche Automobil-Industrie Hering und Richard, Ronneburg

3.30.0 General

The company was founded in 1902 under the name "Deutsche Automobil-Industrie Friedrich Hering" as a general partnership (oHG). Friedrich Hering had already operated a supplier company for bicycle and automobile parts as well as axles and chassis frames from 1888. Ball bearing axles were produced for Daimler-Motoren-Gesellschaft and Benz & Cie., and steel disc wheels with removable hard rubber rims for Michelin. In 1904, the industrialist Carl Richard, who owned a factory in Ronneburg, became a new shareholder; the company moved its headquarters there and now operated under the name "Deutsche Automobil-Industrie Hering & Richard".
In particular, the company was known for its light trucks under the brand "Rex-Simplex". These light commercial vehicles were one of the best-known trucks until the First World War.

The fact that the engine described here was not subsequently reported on suggests that the military administration was not interested, or that the engine did not pass type testing.

3.30.1 Six-Cylinder 100 hp Rex-Simplex Aeroengine

The six-cylinder "Rex-Simplex" aircraft engine, was developed in 1914/15 to participate in the German Army's armament program. The crankcase protruded a longer distance in front of the foremost cylinder, so that the propeller hub is at a greater distance from the cylinders. This design lengthens the overall length of the six-cylinder engine, but on the other hand makes it possible to fit a very low-drag engine cowling.

The six cylinders were cast together in pairs and placed so close together that the cooling water jackets of the individual castings butted against each other with their large openings. This meant that a narrow sealing ring could be used to connect the outer cooling jackets and the otherwise common pipe and hose connections could be avoided. The latter had the disadvantage that they always had to be sealed at two points and increased the resistance of the cooling water line not inconsiderably.

Similar to numerous Mercedes engines, the valves suspended at an angle in the cylinder head were controlled by a camshaft arranged above the cylinders in parallel with the crankshaft axis and interposed by short two-armed rocker arms. This design reduced the masses moved back and forth to actuate the valves by a considerable amount, since the long push rods otherwise still interposed were eliminated, and thus enabled a significant increase in the number of revolutions of the engine. Compared with this advantage, the disadvantages of the design are of little consequence. They consist mainly in the fact that the valves become less easily accessible and that a vertical shaft with two pairs of bevel gears had to be inserted between the camshaft and the engine shaft to drive it. The drive wheel for the two high-voltage solenoids placed transversely to it is also mounted on this vertical shaft located at the rear end of the engine.

In the downward extension of the vertical intermediate shaft located between the crankshaft and the camshaft, a second shaft was arranged which drove the water and oil pumps and was also driven by the bevel gear mounted on the end of the crankshaft. In this way, the Rex Simplex engine also succeeded in uniting the auxiliary units of the engine, namely the two solenoids and pumps, at the rear end of the engine, where they are clearly visible and accessible to the observer.

The gas mixture was fed to the six cylinders only through one Cudell carburetor. Since, as a result, the distances to be covered by the mixture to the individual cylinders are very different, an intermediate wall was fitted in the intake line to compensate for these differences. However, this partition increased the resistance in the suction line, which in its arrangement forces the mixture flow to change direction twice at right angles before entering the cylinders, not inconsiderably.

The Rex simplex engine had recirculating lubrication, dual ignition, and could be started by means of a starter. The engine produced about 100 hp at 1300 rpm. The cylinders had a bore of 120 mm and a stroke of 150 mm.

The ready-to-run engine weighed approx. 200 kg with all ancillary equipment.

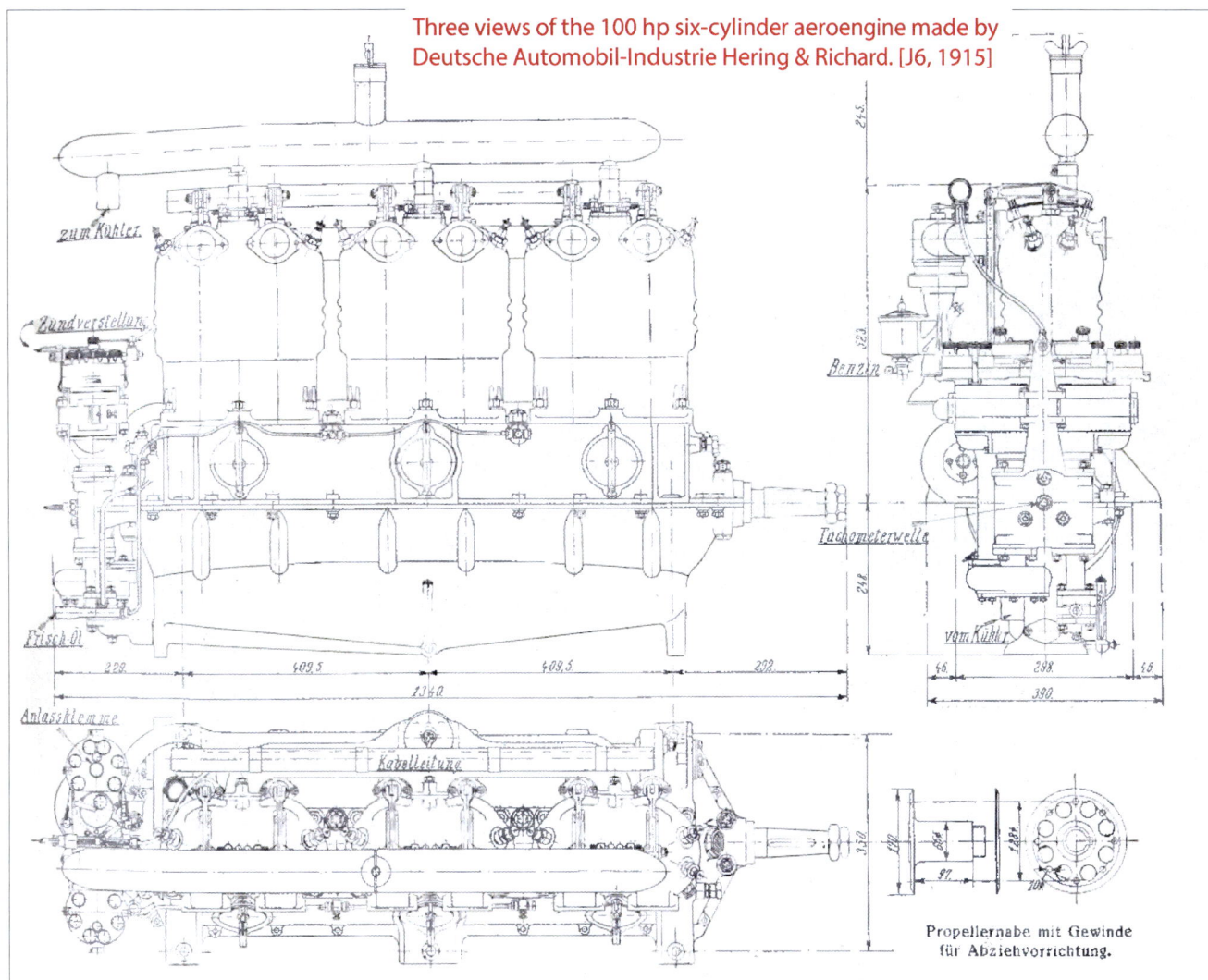

Three views of the 100 hp six-cylinder aeroengine made by Deutsche Automobil-Industrie Hering & Richard. [J6, 1915]

zum Kühler.
Zündverstellung.
Frisch Öl
Anlassklemme
Kabelleitung
Benzin
Tachometerwelle
vom Kühler

Propellernabe mit Gewinde
für Abziehvorrichtung.

Above: The revolutionary Roland C.II reached the front in March 1916. It was the first type to reach the front that was powered by the 160 hp Mercedes D III.

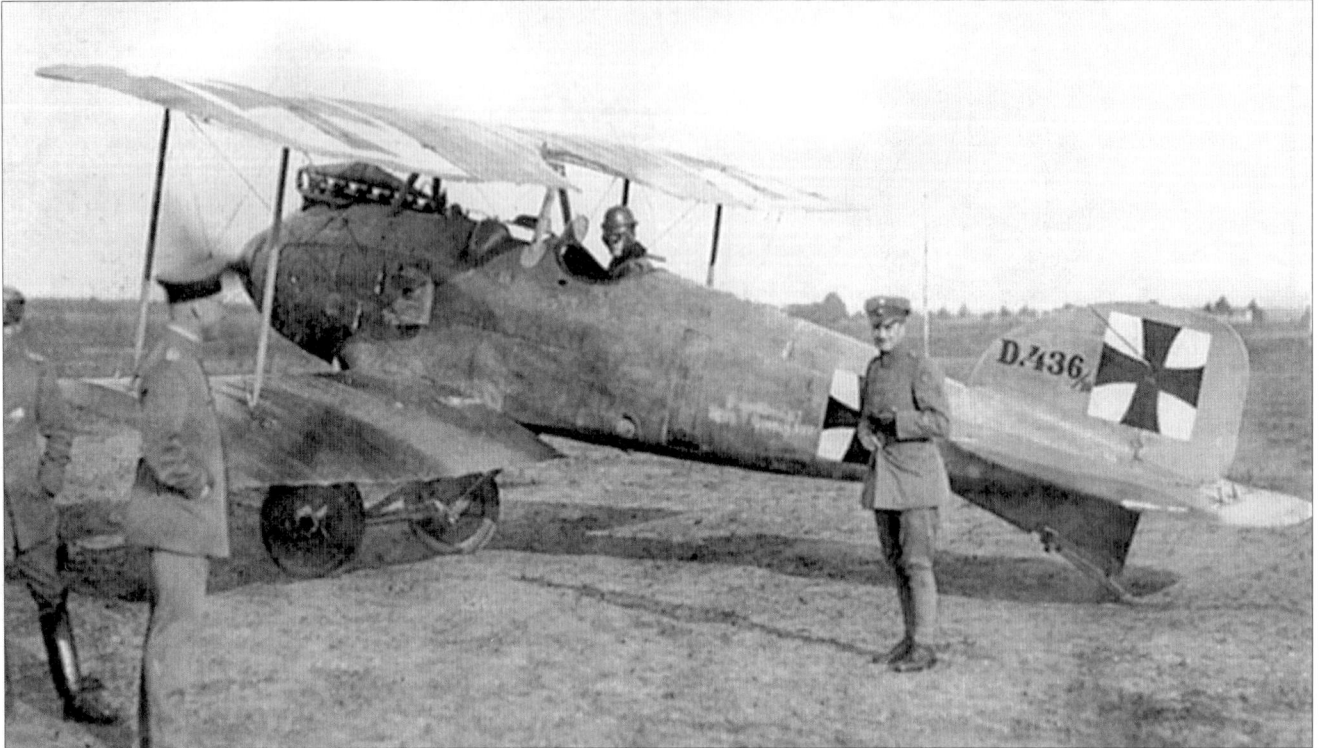

Above: The Albatros D.I reached the front in the late summer of 1916. It was the first of many fighter designs that were powered by the 160 hp Mercedes D III.

Right: The Roland D.I was also powered by the 160 hp Mercedes D III. It was built in small numbers; although fast it had poor handling qualities.

Left: The Pfalz D.III reached the front in the late summer of 1917. It was powered by the 160 hp Mercedes D III. Using the same engine, guns, and similar structural design, Its performance was similar to the Albatros D.I that appeared a year earlier.

3.31 Hilz-Motorenfabrik GmbH, Düsseldorf

3.31.0 General

The company "Hilz-Motorenfabrik, Gesellschaft mit beschränkter Haftung" was entered in the Düsseldorf Commercial Register in December 1910. It originated from the Düsseldorf company "L. Hilz", which was already involved in the construction of automotive spare parts and "Aeroplan engines" and whose partner was Max' Hilz's wife. Managing directors of the new company were the engineer Max Hilz and the businessman Theodor Sabatzky. Hilz-Motorenfabrik also concentrated on the production of automobile and aircraft engine parts.

The complete sale of the aircraft engines was transferred to the "Gesellschaft für Flugmaschinen-und Apparatebau mbH in Cologne, G.F.A. for short. The G.F.A. also manufactured complete aircraft of its own and other manufacturers' designs and was also involved in the supply of all accessories.

In the following years, Hilz-Motorenfabrik GmbH Düsseldorf was successful throughout Europe, especially with its light and reliable 3-cylinder fan-shaped aircraft engines[1], which were offered with air cooling, but also with water cooling on request. These engines were modeled after the well-known Anzani engines.

3.31.1 Hilz Type I – 25 hp Three-Cylinder Fan-Shaped Aeroengine (1910)

This engine was an air-cooled three-cylinder aircraft engine, which with its 25 hp was particularly suitable for smaller training machines, whereby it was mainly important that not too much speed was required of the flying machine.

The launch with this engine was extremely successful. By the end of 1910, over 100 engines had already been delivered, which in turn prompted the management to enlarge the production facilities and employ up to 100 people.

The air-cooled engine weighed 60 kg. The piston diameter was 105 mm, the stroke 130 mm. These cylinders were also used for the 6-cylinder radial engine. For more technical information on Hilz engines refer to the end of this chapter.

3.31.2 Hilz Type II – 30 hp Three-cylinder fan-shaped aeroengine (1910/1911)

Hilz responded to the increased customer requests and delivered the next, now 30 hp engine with either

Above: Advertising Hilz Aero engines and GEFA as General Supplier. [J4, 1911]

Below: Charlett monoplane with three-cylinder Hilz engine (1910). [A1]

25 hp three cylinder Hilz fan-shaped aircraft engine (1910). [A1]

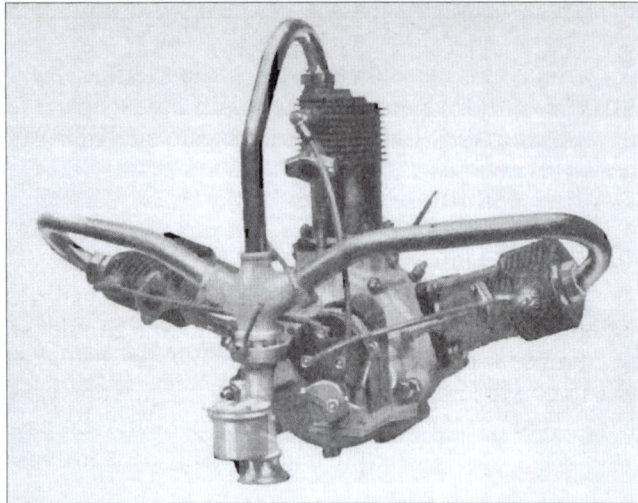

Above: General view of the 25 hp Hilz three cylinder aircraft engine, carburetor, spark plugs, ignition distributor, mixture distribution pipes. [B7]

GESELLSCHAFT FÜR FLUGMASCHINEN UND APPARATE BAU m.b.H.

CÖLN-OSSENDORF, Tel. Longerich 18. Telegr.: Flugtechnik Cöln.

VERKAUFSMONOPOL DER „HILZ" FLUGMOTORE.

BESTES DEUTSCHES FABRIKAT

NACHWEISBAR IN DEUTSCHLAND AM MEISTEN GEKAUFT.

VON JANUAR BIS DEZEMBER 102 GELIEFERT.

3 - 4 - 6 CYL. MOTORE VON 25—150 PS.

LUFT- u. WASSERGEKÜHLT.

TYPE No. I, 3 ZYL., 25 PS, LUFTGEKÜHLT.

Above: Advertisement Hilz 25 hp engine, more than 102 sold in 1910. [J3, 1910]

Above: Schulze monoplane powered by 25–30 hp Hilz three-cylinder engine (1911). [J3, 1912]

Hilz- Flugmotoren

3 Zylinder, Luftkühlung, Type 30 HP
4 „ Wasserkühlung, Type 50 HP

Ausprobiertes u. bestbewährtes deutsches Fabrikat. (Prima Referenzen.)

Nachweislich die meisten Flugmotoren in Deutschland geliefert. Vorzügl. Flugerfolge.

Hilz, Düsseldorf, Motorenfabrik.

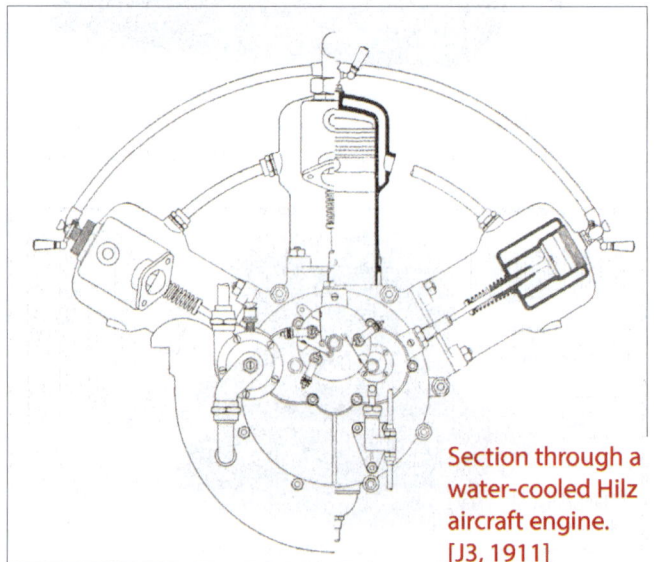

Section through a water-cooled Hilz aircraft engine. [J3, 1911]

Above: Advertisement for an air-cooled three-cylinder 30 hp Hilz engine. [J3, 1911]

Above Right: Advertisement for a water-cooled three-cylinder 30 hp Hilz engine. [J4, 1911]

Carburetor side of the 6-cylinder Hilz radial engine. [J3, 1912]

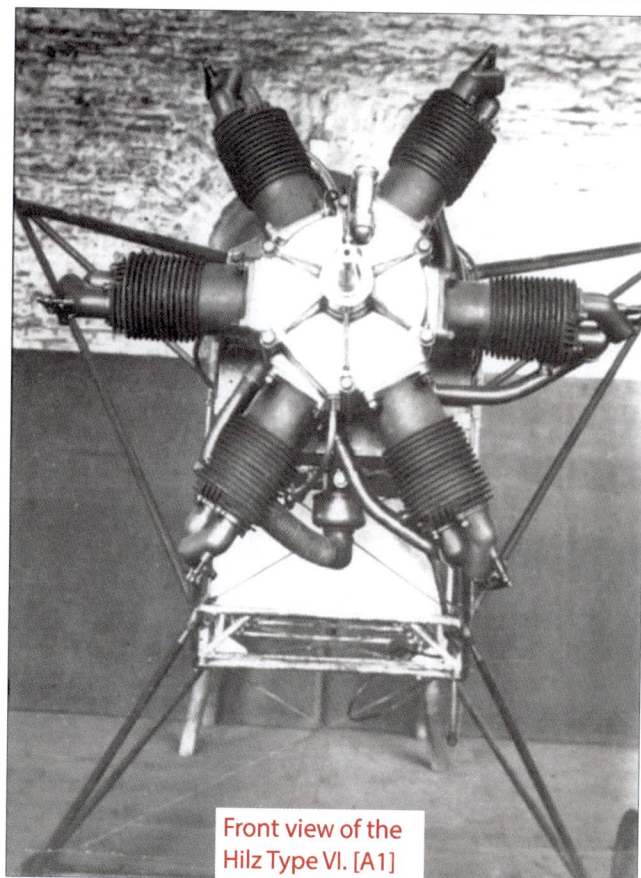

Hilz Type II engine installed on an monoplane made in Krefeld. [A1]

Front view of the Hilz Type VI. [A1]

Section through a 6-cylinder radial Hilz engine. [B26]

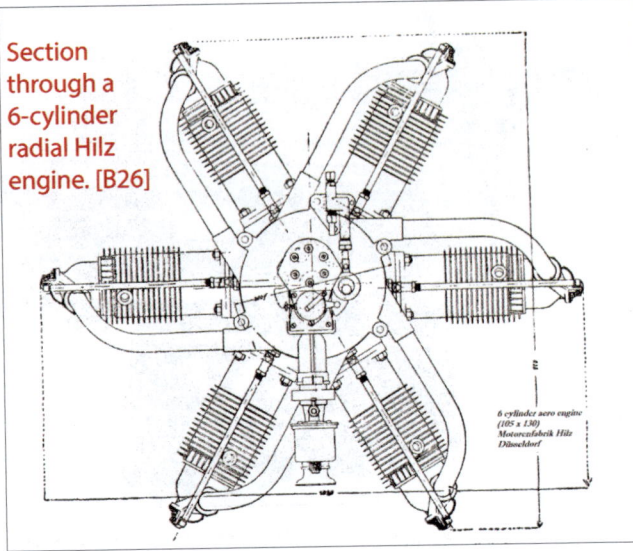

3.31.5 Hilz Type III – 50/45 PS Four-Cylinder In-line Aeroengine (1910)

The water-cooled 50/45 hp Hilz aircraft engine of 120 mm bore and 130 mm stroke was very similar to the usual automobile engine. Cylinder, pistons and piston rings are made of grey cast iron, the crankcase is made of nickel aluminum, the engine parts are made of high-quality steel. Intake and exhaust valves are positively controlled by a common camshaft. The engine had splash lubrication, a Hilz carburetor and a magneto high-voltage ignition.

This engine had a bore of 120 mm and a stroke of 120 mm and effectively produced a maximum power of 56 hp at a speed of 1200 revolutions per minute. The intake and exhaust valves were installed in the cylinder cover, so that the heat-damaging space or heat-absorbing surfaces, which are present e.g. in the valve chambers, could be avoided in the new arrangement, resulting in a far more favourable theoretical efficiency. The advantageous arrangement of the combustion chamber also resulted in a not insignificant weight saving, but this did not affect the solidity of the engine.

The control was very precise and simple, as only

water or air cooling. The basic design was retained, only the piston diameter was increased from 105 to 112 mm, the piston stroke was still 130 mm.

3.31.3 Hilz 50 hp Three-Cylinder Fan-shaped Aeroengine (1910/1911)

Similar to Types I and II, Hilz-Motorenfabrik developed a 50 hp air or water-cooled aircraft engine in fan shape. This type of engine did not become very widespread, probably because the Hilz company also offered an equally powerful water-cooled 4-cylinder in-line engine, which was more common.

3.31.4 Hilz Type VI – 50 hp Six-Cylinder Radial Aeroengine (1911/12)

In 1911/12, another Hilz engine was developed, which was a six-cylinder radial engine. This type was based on the good experience gained with Types I and II. The cylinders came from Type I, other elements, such as the valve actuation, from Type II. As can be seen in the picture, the cylinders received their gas-air mixture from a special ring chamber, to which the carburetor was connected by individual lines, in order to achieve a uniform filling.

A special lubrication system ensured that all cylinders and other rubbing parts were sufficiently lubricated.

The engine, weighing approx. 100 kg, had proven itself during continuous operation and had fulfilled the expectations placed on it in the best possible way. However, it is not known on which aircraft this type was used.

Right: Advertisement, placed in Deutsche Zeitschrift für Luftschiffahrt 1910. [J4, 1910]

Hilz-Morenfabrik, 50 hp four-cylinder in-line engine. [B7]

Above: Hilz-Morenfabrik, 50 hp four-cylinder in-line engine. [B7]

the exhaust valves were forced and the intake valves were controlled automatically.

The control shaft was located in the crankcase and was driven by built-in gears.

The carburetor with automatic air supply, always proportional to the speed, was a G. A. carburetor of the metal goods factory "Ideal", Opladen.

Ignition was by means of plugs, Mea or Bosch magnetic inductor. The weight of the ready-to-operate engine including all accessories was 120 kg.

3.31.6 Hilz Type IV – 55/50 hp Four-Cylinder In-line Aeroengine (1911)

In addition to the Type III, a 115 kg engine of 55/50 hp was built in the same dimensions, but with the valves suspended in the cylinder head, with only the exhaust valves controlled, while the intake valves operated automatically.

In a review by the renowned graduate engineer O. L. Skopik, head of the design office for aircraft construction and former lecturer for engine construction and aeronautical engineering, said:

The four-cylinder aircraft engine, factory no. 56, which I received from the factory, is of a normal design taken from motor vehicle construction. The cylinders, cast in pairs and made of special cast iron, have a bore of 120 mm; the intake valves are automatic, the exhaust valves are mechanically controlled. The dimensions of the valves and the

Hilz Type IV, 55 hp four-cylinder watercooled in-line aero-engine. [B7]

Above: Advertisement of Hilz Type IV, exhaust side, water pump , control rods. [J4, 1911]

intake pipe, as well as the opening times, are chosen in such a way that the speed of the intake gas complies with the proven standard of 55 m/sec.

The carburetor is from the G. A. Idealtype from Metallwarenfabrik Opladen.

The fuel consumption was determined by me on the basis of a test series of twelve tests, each lasting two hours, averaging 0.258 kg per hp/hour, that of the lubricating oil 0.75 liters per hour.

The weight of the ready-to-operate engine including all accessories was determined at 130 kg.

The aircraft engine in question showed the following performance:

Bore:	120 mm
Normal RPM :	1250 U/min
Stroke:	130 mm
Power (normal) in hp (N_n):	50
Power (maximal) in hp (N_m):	56,2
Fuel consumption:	0,258 kg
Weight per hp	2,6 kg

The tests, each lasting two hours, showed an effective output of 50 hp and a maximum output of 56.2 hp.

3.31.7 Hilz Type IVa – 65 hp Four-cylinder in-line aeroengine (1911)

The 65 hp type was designed in exactly the same basic construction as the types III and IV, only with the difference that it had a 124 mm bore and 140 mm stroke. This engine also had four cylinders and was water-cooled.

3.31.8 Hilz Type V – 115/100 hp Four-Cylinder in-line aeroengine (1913)

Hilz-Motorenwerke developed a 115 hp water-

Above: Hilz-Motorenfabrik Type IVa giving 65 hp (1911). [J3, 1912]

cooled aircraft engine after the conditions for the 1st Kaiserpreis for the best German aircraft engine became known. This engine was also duly entered for the competition, but was not delivered for unknown reasons.

3.31.9 Hilz 100 hp Eight-Cylinder V-type Aeroengine (1913/14)

Shortly before the closure of the company, tests were made with a 100 hp V8 engine. Results and illustrations are not known.

Above: Monoplane of GEFA (pilot Dr. Hoos) with 60 hp Hilz engine, here during a stop-over in Hannover, 1911. [A1]

Endnotes

1. Also known as GeFA, or GEFA.
2. At the 1911 fair in Düsseldorf a 2-cylinder air-cooled engine is said to have been exhibited, but no further information is available. See Ursinus, *Flugsport* 1911, issue 25.
3. See *Deutsche Zeitschrift für Luftschiffahrt* 1911, Heft 4.

Summary of Aero Engines Made by Hilz Motorenfabrik GmbH									
Type	Configuration	Cyl.	Power [hp]	RPM	Stroke [mm]	Hub [mm]	Disp. L.	Wt. [kg]	Weight [kg]
I	Fan type	3	30/25	1350	105	130	3,4	60	4,6
II	Fan type	3	40	1350	112	130	3,8	70	5,2
	Fan type	3	50		120	130	4,4		4,5
III	In-line	4	50	1350	120	120	5,4	120	6,0
IV	In-line	4	55	1350	120	130	5,9	115	
IVa	In-line	4	65	1350	124	140	6,8	120	
V	In-line	4	120/115	1200	150	205	14,5	120	
VI	Radial	6	50	1300	105	130	6,8	90	
	V-type	8	100		120	130	11,8		

3.32 Hellmuth Hirth Versuchsbau, Stuttgart

3.32.0 General

Hellmuth Hirth was born in Heilbronn on April 24, 1886. His father, the engineer and tool-maker Albert Hirth, sent him to the United States to train with the Edison General Electric Company as a mechanic. At this time, he developed an interest in aircraft, and on his return to Germany in 1909 Hellmuth Hirth became involved with the emerging industry. He built his own aircraft in 1910 and became a well-known and pilot (as well as his younger brother Wolf Hirth, a famous sailplane designer and manufacturer).

Since 1914 he was a Lieutenant of the Fliegertruppe, awarded with the Iron Cross II. Together with a small number of assistants he investigated in a test workshop (Versuchswerkstatt) several 2-stroke radial piston engines.

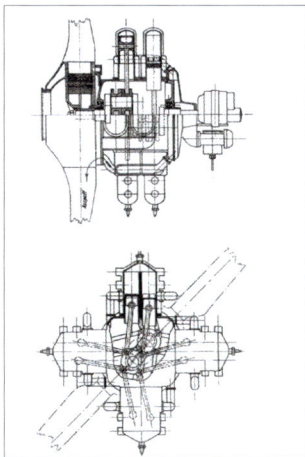

Above: Double-8-cylinder 300 hp twin star rotating engine, type Helmuth Hirth. [B4]

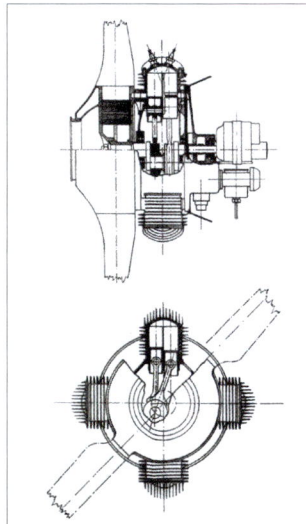

Above: 8 cylinder 40 hp rotating engine (principle H. Hirth). [B4]

Test rig for the 300 hp engine developed by H. Hirth. [B4]

3.32.1 Eight-Cylinder 350 hp Aeroengine (1917)

In 1917 Hirth got state financial resources within the framework of development order for a 12 litre aeroengine. This engine should develop 350 hp at 2400 rpm. A ZF gearbox reduced the speed to 1250 rpm.

The special feature of its design were two cylinders each joined to a "U" common combustion chamber. Two stars with four dual cylinders each formed the two-row engine. For the purpose of noise reduction, Hirth used his "exhaust propeller" in which the exhaust gases exited through the hollow blades at the blade tips. On the other hand, the exhaust energy should be exploited.

At the end of the war, work on this engine was stopped. The Benz company bought the engine and obtained the right to build, but did not proceed with the project.

Postwar development: 40 hp Hirth engine installed on a test car. [B4]

3.33 Georg Hoffmann, Frankfurt am Main

3.33.0 General

The great success of rotary engines in France prompted several designers to create an engine for Germany, although the story surrounding the Hoffmann engines was an unusual one, as the engineer Georg Hoffmann only owned a design office in Frankfurt. His engines were manufactured by Kieling & Pulver, also based in Frankfurt, and the distribution of the engines was transferred to Deutsche Fluggesellschaft. Nearby, at August-Euler in Frankfurt-Niederrad, G. Hoffmann found an old Euler biplane, which had been converted from pressurized to traction propeller drive for flight test purposes.

After Hoffmann's efforts to have his engines manufactured in Oberursel failed (they had acquired the Gnôme license themselves in the meantime), his own engine development was terminated in 1913. Hoffmann moved to Goebel, where he successfully worked on the development of Goebel engines.

3.33.1 Four-Cylinder 45/40 hp Hoffmann In-line Engine GHF

The first aircraft engine developed by G. Hoffmann in 1909/10 was based, as was usually the case, on a automobil engine. This was adapted to the requirements for installation in a flying machine. Such an engine was used, among other aircraft, in the "Poelke" airplane. The engine was water-cooled. Its 4 cylinders developed between 40 and 45 hp.

The 4 cylinders were cast into a block with the water jacket. In addition, the channel for the suction line for good preheating of the gas by the cooling water was also cast into the cylinder block.

The operating mechanism for the oil pump consists of a hardened eccentric, on which a hardened ball also runs, which actuates the pump plunger. The camshaft was driven by means of a chain. Each cam actuated two valves, so that only 4 cams were required for 8 valves. The valves were arranged horizontally in the cylinder head.

Above: Advertisement of Georg Hoffmann with the product range from 1910. [J3, 1910]

Above: Poelke aeroplane with water-cooled 4-cylinder 45 hp in-line GHF engine. [J4, 1911]

The arrangement allowed the largest possible dimensioning of the valves, intensive cooling of the exhaust valve, easiest accessibility and replacement of the same, as well as a good formation of the compression chamber.

The stroke movement was transmitted from the cams to the valves by means of balancing levers, which were identical and interchangeable. These were exposed.

Bore/stroke: 122/105 mm

3.33.2 Three-Cylinder 45/40 hp Hoffmann Rotary Engine "Rotor"

Not much is known about this 35/30 hp engine. It is questionable whether such an engine was ever sold.

The adjacent advertisement from the magazine *"Flugsport"* from 1910 shows engines which were also very probably never realized, e.g. a 10- and a 14-cylinder aircraft engine.

3.33.3 Five-Cylinder 55/50 hp Hoffmann Rotary Engine "Rotor"

Also among the less fashionable engines was the five-cylinder rotary engine. This engine from 1910 was of the usual design, i.e. with a carburetor of its own construction and magneto ignition, but still had uncontrolled intake valves.

As the illustration opposite shows, the crankcase rotated around the stationary crankshaft. The latter was hollow and served to supply the gas mixture. The piston crowns contained the suction valves, which are relieved. To reduce exhaust noise, an

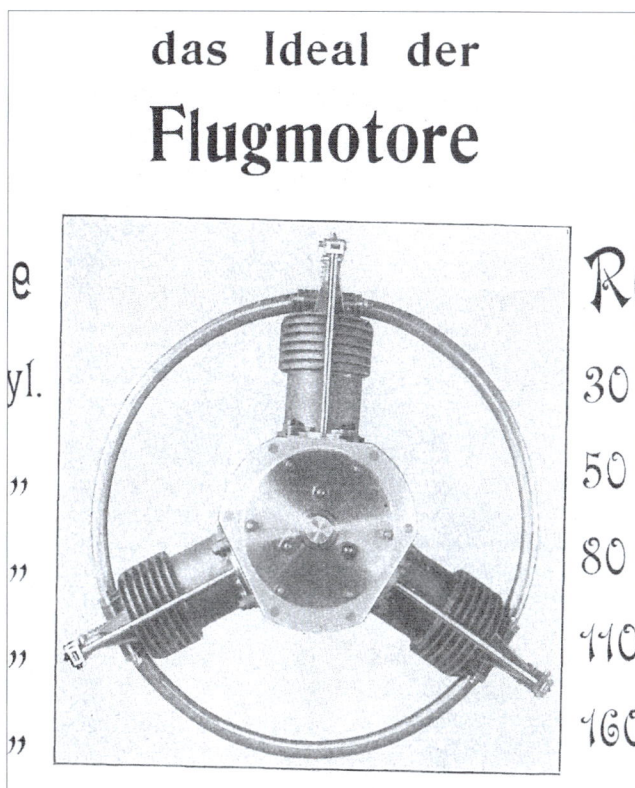

exhaust pipe, which also served to stiffen the cylinders, was arranged in a circle. The weight of this new engine was 1.3 kg per hp.

The propeller could be either flange-mounted directly or driven by chain transmission in the familiar manner. Particular importance was attached to the lubrication of the cylinders. Suitable design and arrangement of the pistons prevented the oil

G.H.F. Motore
Type „Rotor"
≡ D. R. P. angemeldet ≡

— 3, 5, 7, 10 und 14 Cyl. —
Das Ideal des Flugmotors

Georg Hoffmann
Frankfurt a. M.
— Schillerstrasse 30. —
Telegr.-Adr. „Rotor". Teleph. Amt I, 3475.

Above: Designer Ing. Georg Hoffmann demonstrating the rotary principle of his engine. [J3, 1910]

Left: Advertisement showing the 5-cylinder Hoffmann rotary engine. [J4, 1910]

from being thrown out of the cylinders in excess as a result of centrifugal action.

3.33.4 Seven-Cylinder 70 hp Hoffmann Rotary Engine "Rotor"

One of the most successful Hoffmann rotary engines was the 7-cylinder 70 hp engine (at approx. 1100 rpm).

In 1910, Gebr. Sommer of Frankfurt a. M. brought out a biplane with a front-mounted propeller that was powered by a 70/60 hp Hoffmann rotary engine.
Bore/stroke: 110/150 mm
Displacement: 9.97 liters
Weight: approx. 90 kg

3.33.5 Nine-Cylinder 90 hp Hoffmann Rotary Engine "Rotor"

Georg Hoffmann exhibited the trademarked 9-cylinder rotary engine for the first time at the ALA 1912. Lubrication of the "9-cylinder Rotor" was completely automatic by means of an oil pump. The type protected connecting rods transmitted the piston pressures centrally to the crankpins, thus avoiding uneven running of the cylinders. The intake valves were located in the piston and operated automatically, the exhaust valves were located in the cylinder head and were controlled by a cam wheel.

This engine, which had already been manufactured by the Goebel company (see above), also took part in the competition for the best German aircraft engine (1st Kaiser Prize 1913) and won 8th prize. The 9-cylinder was tested on a Fokker monoplane. Nevertheless, this engine did not achieve widespread use.
Bore/stroke: 110/150 mm
Displacement: 12,82 liters
Power: 90 hp at 1100 rpm
Weight: approx. 110 kg

Only ball bearings were provided as bearings. In the case of the "Rotor", it was possible to avoid the alternately accelerated masses; in addition, the very significant centrifugal forces of pistons, piston pins, connecting rods, etc. counteracted the piston pressure, so that the specific bearing pressures are extremely low. In addition, this also reduced the stress on the crankshaft and connecting rods to a minimum.

The gas mixture was formed by a regular

Hoffmann 7-cylinder rotary engine on a test bench at Goebel-Werke (1911/12). [A1]

Above: The ring between the cylinders was used as a collector for the exhaust gases and at the same time served to increase the stability of the cylinders. [J3, 1912]

Right: 7-cylinder 70 hp Hoffmann rotary engine powering an aircraft designed by the Sommer brothers. [J3, 1911]

carburetor of our own design and fed to the cylinders through the hollow-bored crankshaft and the inside of the housing. By using this regular carburetor, the number of revolutions was highly variable and adjustable.

The mounting in the aircraft allowed two possibilities: 1. mounting to the crankpin without support, and 2. to the crankpin with support, which would have been necessary only for the 14 and 18 cylinder "rotor", or if indirect drive of the propeller was provided.

Above: Last Hoffmann developement: 9-cylinder 90 hp rotary engine. [J3, 1912]

Above: Given the great demand for the Mercedes D III to power fighters, it is surprising that it was used in the NFW B.I trainer. NFW built a small number of NFW B.I trainers to supply the NFW flight school at Johannisthal.

Right & Below: The Mercedes D IIIa was the most popular fighter engine and was used in the bizarre Naglo D.I, a quadraplane inspired by the Albatros fighters.

3.34 A. Horch & Co., Motorwagenwerke, Aktiengesellschaft, Zwickau

3.34.0 General

The great success of rotary engines in France prompted several designers to create an engine for Germany, although the story surrounding the Hoffmann engines was an unusual one, as the engineer Georg Hoffmann only owned a design office in Frankfurt. His engines were manufactured by Kieling & Pulver, also based in Frankfurt, and the distribution of the engines was transferred to Deutsche Fluggesellschaft. Nearby, at August-Euler in Frankfurt-Niederrad, G. Hoffmann found an old Euler biplane, which had been converted from pressurized to traction propeller drive for flight test purposes.

After Hoffmann's efforts to have his engines manufactured in Oberursel failed (they had acquired the Gnôme license themselves in the meantime), his own engine development was terminated in 1913. Hoffmann moved to Goebel, where he successfully worked on the development of Goebel engines.

6-cylinder 70 hp Horch rotary engine (1912). [B36, 1912–13]

Horch engine with propeller. [B7]

3.34.1 Four-cylinder 45/40 hp Hoffmann in-line engine GHF

The first aircraft engine developed by G. Hoffmann in 1909/10 was based, as was usually the case, on a automobil engine. This was adapted to the requirements for installation in a flying machine. Such an engine was used, among other aircraft, in the "Poelke" airplane. The engine was water-cooled. Its 4 cylinders developed between 40 and 45 hp.

The 4 cylinders were cast into a block with the water jacket. In addition, the channel for the suction line for good preheating of the gas by the cooling water was also cast into the cylinder block.

The operating mechanism for the oil pump consists of a hardened eccentric, on which a hardened ball also runs, which actuates the pump plunger. The camshaft was driven by means of a chain. Each cam actuated two valves, so that only 4 cams were required for 8 valves. The valves were arranged horizontally in the cylinder head. The arrangement allowed the largest possible dimensioning of the valves, intensive cooling of the

Above: Advertisement 1912, showing the carburettor side of Horch 6-cylinder rotary engine. [J3, 1912]

Above: Front view with removed cover. [B7]

exhaust valve, easiest accessibility and replacement of the same, as well as a good formation of the compression chamber.

The stroke movement was transmitted from the cams to the valves by means of balancing levers, which were identical and interchangeable. These were exposed.

Bore/stroke: 122/105 mm

3.34.2 Three-Cylinder 45/40 hp Hoffmann Rotary Engine "Rotor"

Not much is known about this 35/30 hp engine. It is questionable whether such an engine was ever sold.

The adjacent advertisement from the magazine "Flugsport" from 1910 shows engines which were also very probably never realized, e.g. a 10- and a 14-cylinder aircraft engine.

3.34.3 Five-Cylinder 55/50 hp Hoffmann Rotary Engine "Rotor"

Also among the less fashionable engines was the five-cylinder rotary engine. This engine from 1910 was of the usual design, i.e. with a carburetor of its own construction and magneto ignition, but still had uncontrolled intake valves.

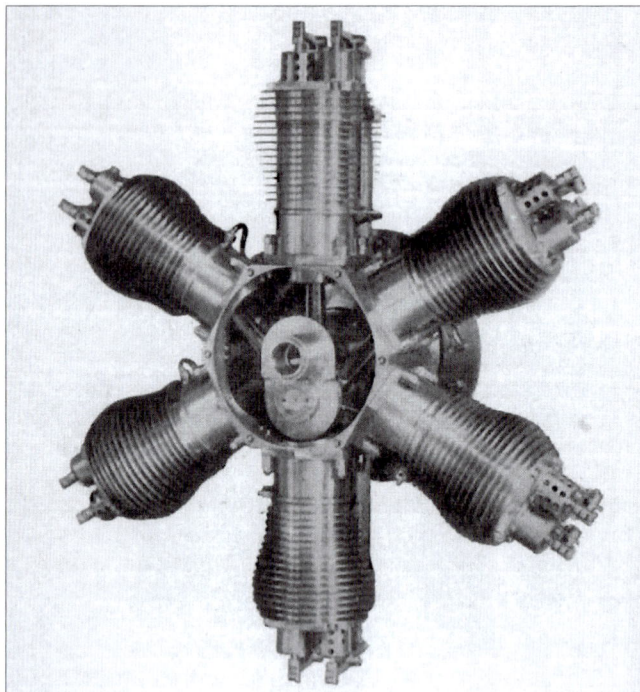

As the illustration opposite shows, the crankcase rotated around the stationary crankshaft. The latter was hollow and served to supply the gas mixture. The piston crowns contained the suction valves, which are relieved. To reduce exhaust noise, an exhaust pipe, which also served to stiffen the cylinders, was arranged in a circle. The weight of this new engine was 1.3 kg per hp.

The propeller could be either flange-mounted directly or driven by chain transmission in the familiar manner. Particular importance was attached to the lubrication of the cylinders. Suitable design and arrangement of the pistons prevented the oil from being thrown out of the cylinders in excess as a result of centrifugal action.

3.34.4 Seven-Cylinder 70 hp Hoffmann Rotary Engine "Rotor"

One of the most successful Hoffmann rotary engines was the 7-cylinder 70 hp engine (at approx. 1100 rpm).

In 1910, Gebr. Sommer of Frankfurt a. M. brought out a biplane with a front-mounted propeller that was powered by a 70/60 hp Hoffmann rotary engine.

Bore/stroke: 110/150 mm
Displacement: 9.97 liters
Weight: approx. 90 kg

3.34.5 Nine-Cylinder 90 hp Hoffmann Rotary Engine "Rotor"

Georg Hoffmann exhibited the trademarked 9-cylinder rotary engine for the first time at the ALA 1912. Lubrication of the "9-cylinder Rotor" was completely automatic by means of an oil pump. The type protected connecting rods transmitted the piston pressures centrally to the crankpins, thus avoiding uneven running of the cylinders. The intake valves were located in the piston and operated automatically, the exhaust valves were located in the cylinder head and were controlled by a cam wheel.

This engine, which had already been manufactured by the Goebel company (see above), also took part in the competition for the best German aircraft engine (1st Kaiser Prize 1913) and won 8th prize. The 9-cylinder was tested on a Fokker monoplane. Nevertheless, this engine did not achieve widespread use.

Bore/stroke: 110/150 mm
Displacement: 12,82 liters
Power: 90 hp at 1100 rpm
Weight: approx. 110 kg

Only ball bearings were provided as bearings. In the case of the "Rotor", it was possible to avoid the alternately accelerated masses; in addition, the very significant centrifugal forces of pistons, piston pins, connecting rods, etc. counteracted the piston pressure, so that the specific bearing pressures are extremely low. In addition, this also reduced the stress on the crankshaft and connecting rods to a minimum.

The gas mixture was formed by a regular carburetor of our own design and fed to the cylinders through the hollow-bored crankshaft and the inside of the housing. By using this regular carburetor, the number of revolutions was highly variable and adjustable.

The mounting in the aircraft allowed two possibilities: 1. mounting to the crankpin without support, and 2. to the crankpin with support, which would have been necessary only for the 14 and 18 cylinder "rotor", or if indirect drive of the propeller was provided.

Above & Right: The Mercedes D III and D IIIa engines were mostly used in fighters. One of the most unusual types to use the D IIIa was the Gotha WD27, a prototype long-range maritime reconnaissance floatplane. It appears to have been developed to the same requirement as the unusual Friedrichshafen FF60. Was the D IIIa chosen for its reliability given the WD27's design role?

3.35 Dr. Fritz Huth, Berlin

3.35.0 General

Dr. Fritz Huth[1], born on February 23, 1872, was a selfless German inventor, a creator, not a merchant. He was a senior teacher and at the same time the owner of a technical office for aircraft and engine construction. Dr. Huth founded the Association of German Aeronautical Engineers. Since 1909 he published various scientific articles for the technical press, but above all he became known for publishing several technical books on the construction of aircraft and aircraft engines. Various of his publications were also used in this book (see bibliography).

Dr. Huth also developed and built aircraft, which were used, among other things, to test his aircraft engine.[2]

3.35.1 Six-cylinder 50 hp double row fan-shaped engine

The double-row fan-shaped aircraft engine developed by Dr. Huth was based on the Esnault-Pelterie type. It had six cylinders and differed from the French original by a new type of cylinder arrangement and specially designed valves.

Compared to the Esnault-Pelterie fan engine, which has an odd number of cylinders, five or seven, Dr. Huth's engine has only six cylinders. Therefore, it was not possible to achieve an equal spacing of the ignitions. Three cylinders each operate on one crankpin, and the distance between the two crankpins was 180°.

The cylinders had a bore of 110 mm and 110 mm stroke. At 1200 rpm, the engine produced 50 hp. The weight of the engine including carburetor and ignition apparatus was 90 kg, i.e. less than 2 kg per hp.

The cylinders were cast in one piece with the valve chamber, but without water jackets. The water jackets were separately fitted from corrugated brass tubing. The control for inlet and outlet of the gases was similar to that of the Esnault-Pelterie engine by means of a combined valve, or a valve with a circular slide valve, but the trouble was avoided that both channels are open at the transition from the exhaust to the suction position. Instead, the suction channel is opened only after the exhaust channel is closed. Just before the valve closed, the exhaust channel was reopened for a moment, but this was of little significance, since the gases escaped directly into the free air, as is usual with aircraft engines.

Three cylinders each had a common carburetor.

Above: Huth 50 hp 6-cylinder radial engine. [B25]

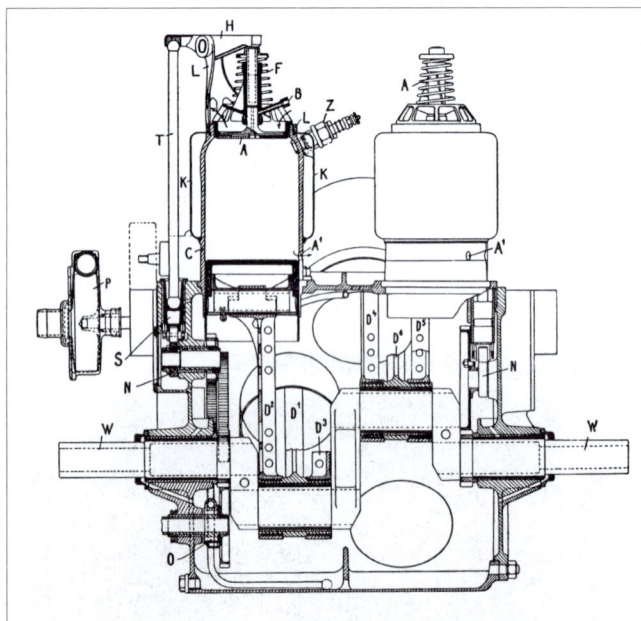

Above: Longitudinal section through the Huth motor. A - valve, B - fuel inlet, C - valve spring, L - bearing block for lever, H - rocker arm, T - valve actuation, C - cylinder, K - cooling jacket, exhaust, D1-D6 - connecting rods, N - control shaft, W - crankshaft, oil pump, P - water pump. [B25]

As already mentioned, the ignition distance could not be uniform, and the same was once 90° and once 150°; consequently, it was possible to get along with a magneto if the same made correspondingly high number of revolutions. Three pistons each (1, 4, 5

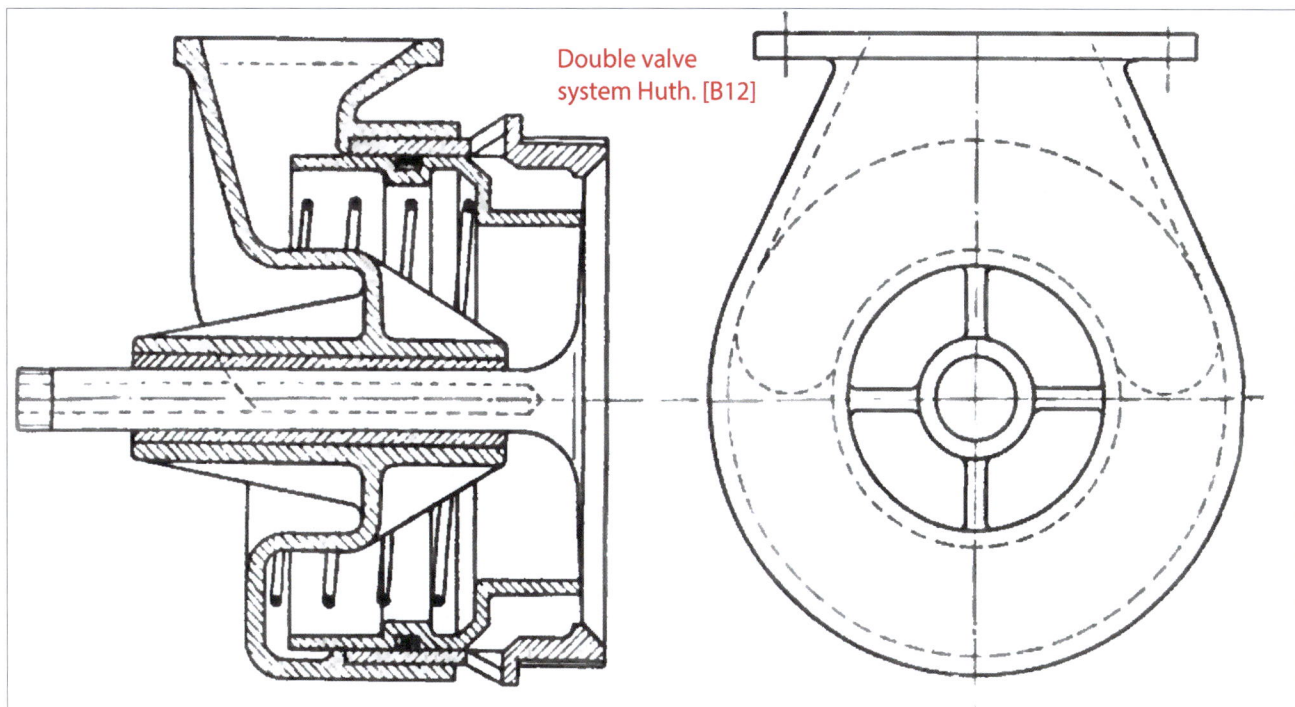

Double valve
system Huth. [B12]

and 2, 3, 6) work on a crankshaft in such a way that
the middle connecting rod completely surrounds the
crank, and the other two grip around the sleeve of
this middle one.

For technical reasons, not all induction positions
of the plunger could be utilized. The magneto was
mounted on the crankcase between the cylinders
and was driven by a chain. The firing sequence of
the cylinders was as follows: First firing cylinder 1,
then cylinder 4, cylinder 3, 6, 5 and 2, after which
cylinder 1 fired again after two revolutions.

The double valve used is shown in the adjacent
figure. A slider rested on the valve disc and was
pressed down by a spring. When the valve lowered,
the exhaust was released. When the valve continued

to move downward, the slider touched down
and closed the exhaust port. The valve disk now
continued downward on its own and opened the
inlet.

Endnotes

1. Dr. Fritz Huth obtained his airplane pilot
   certificate 615 on a monoplane (Rumpler-Taube)
   on December 3, 1913.
2. The company "Flugmaschinen- und Motoren-
   Gesellschaft m. b. H.", founded in 1910, intended
   to exploit the flying aircraft designs and engines
   developed by Dr. Huth, as well as the patents
   granted on them.

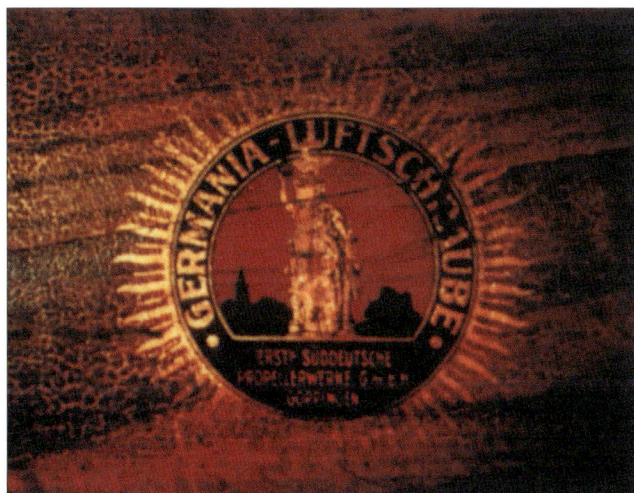

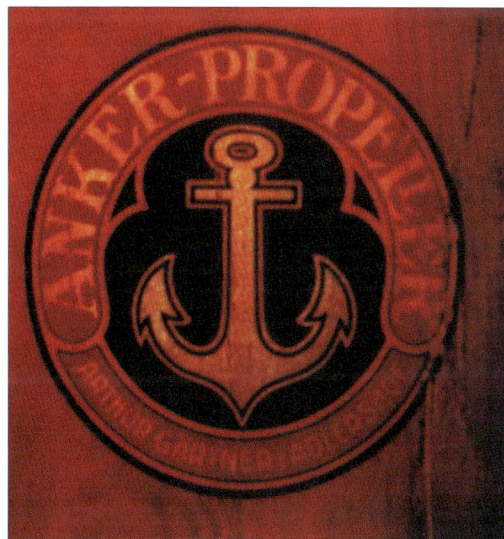

3.36 Stahl-Motoren-Gesellschaft Ernst Jaenisch & Co., Berlin

3.36.0 General

In 1912, Stahl-Motoren-Gesellschaft Ernst Jaenisch & Co. entered a 4-cylinder 60 hp (1350 rpm) water-cooled inline four-stroke engine for the 1st Kaiser Prize for the best German aircraft engine.

Probably only one engine was built, but it was not delivered.

The Stahl Motoren Gesellschaft have offered to build four-cylinder vertical water-cooled engines in 50, 75, and 100-hp sizes. The cylinders were constructed in pairs from steel with a common welded-on water jacket.

56/60 hp Stahl engine (1912). [B1]

Above & Left: The Mercedes D III and D IIIa engines were widely used in fighters. One of the most unusual types to use the D IIIa was the Friedrichshafen FF60, a prototype long-range maritime reconnaissance floatplane. It appears to have been developed to the same requirement as the Gotha WD27. The FF60 was completed just as the war ended and was test flown in November 1918. The D IIIa may have been chosen for its reliability given the FF60's design role.

3.37 Hamburger Motoren-Fabrik GmbH, Carl Jastram

3.37.0 General

Carl Jastram founded a locksmith's workshop in Hamburg-Bergedorf in 1873, which he expanded into a small factory in 1887. Jastram's engines, in particular a petroleum engine of 2 hp power, were quite successful. This engine, which reached a speed of 260 rpm, won an award at the Hamburg Industrial Exhibition in 1889, which in turn led to the founding of the "Hamburger Motoren-Fabrik Carl Jastram".

Due to its location, the main focus of this company was naturally on boat engines. Nevertheless, in 1909, Carl Jastram, inspired by the flights of the Wright brothers in Europe and also in Germany, began to design an aircraft engine.

Monoplane designed 1912 by Thele, but it failed to fly. It could only make some jumps of 20–30 meters. [L18]

3.37.1 Sechs-Zylinder Reihenmotor

"Jastram" built a six-cylinder engine with suspended cylinders, a design that was still relatively uncommon in Germany at the time. The determining factor in the choice of this cylinder arrangement was that it prevented the accumulation of lubricating oil in the crankcase. This, in turn, prevented the lower heads of the connecting rods from flinging the oil around in the crankcase and avoided excessive lubrication of the pistons and the associated oiling of the spark plugs. The engine, after passing test runs well, was installed in an airplane designed by a constructor named Thele, but it failed to fly. It could only make sets of 20-30 meters, but could not stay aloft for any length of time. This led Carl Jastram not to continue building aircraft engines. Instead, he continued to build marine engines.

Above: Six-cylinder aeroengine developed by Jastram with inverted cylinders. The engine can now be seen in the Schleswig-Holstein Engine Museum in Lütjensee. [Source: Christian Schupp, www.motorenbau.eu]

3.38 Junkers & Co., Dessau

3.38.0 General

Junkers Motorenbau-Gesellschaft mit beschränkter Haftung" was entered in the Magdeburg Commercial Register on June 24, 1913. As far as is known, no aircraft engine production was carried out at this location. However, this company was already closed in 1915.

The first designs for lighter, high-speed engines had already been started at Professor Junkers' research institute in Aachen as early as 1913. They were intended for later use of the Junkers engine as a drive for tractors and aircraft..[1] Zu einem Serienbau von Junkers-Motoren vor Kriegsende kam es nicht. Bei allen hier vorgestellten Motoren handelt es sich um Versuchsmotore.

3.38.1 Four-Cylinder 400 hp Junkers Experimental Engine M 0 3

The first experimental type, the M 0 3 (also known as the M 0.3), already appeared as a horizontal twin-shaft engine with four cylinders, each with a bore of 80 mm and 2 x 120 mm stroke. The engine operated on the two-stroke principle and was a diesel engine running on kerosene with airless injection. Scavenging was performed by a piston pump driven by the face crank of one of the two outer shafts.

3.38.2 Junkers Experimental Engine M 0 8 (1915)

The difficulties encountered with regard to perfect combustion of the fuel and with the control system due to leaking valves, as well as shaft breaks in the bevel gearbox mounted separately in front of the engine, led to the design of the M 0 8 (also M 0.8) experimental engine.

The first tests with this six-cylinder explosion engine with mixture scavenging according to Oechelhaeuser (bore and stroke of M 0 3 (M 0,3)) took place in November 1915 in Dessau.

The faults that occurred: Precipitation of the gasoline used as fuel on the cylinder walls, scavenging explosions and fires led to the transition to direct injection of the fuel into the dead space. The injected gasoline was detonated by spark plugs.

This injection process required the development of a reliable high-pressure fuel pump (Pat. No. 312 878), which was tested using split nozzles in subsequent intermediate trials and various designs.

Purging by a piston pump was initially retained,

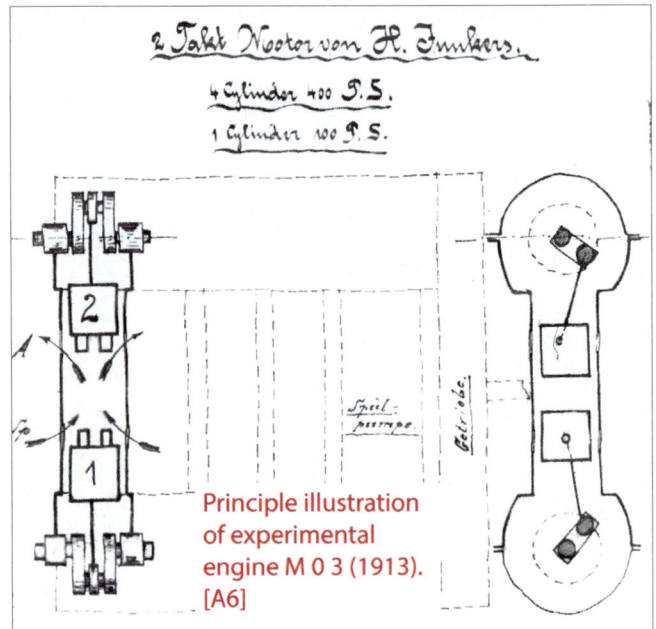

Principle illustration of experimental engine M 0 3 (1913). [A6]

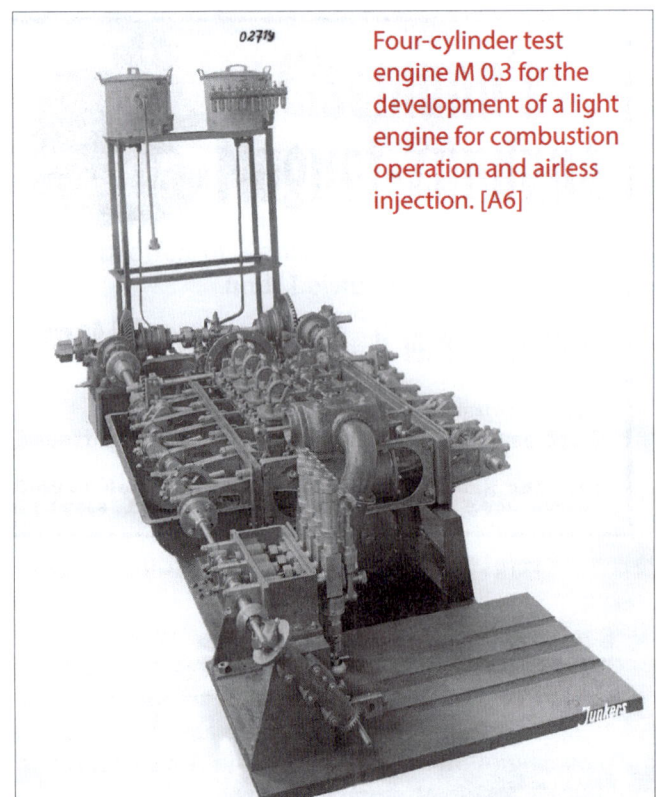

Four-cylinder test engine M 0.3 for the development of a light engine for combustion operation and airless injection. [A6]

but later extended by a rotary piston auxiliary blower (Pat. No. 328 332).

Parallel tests were carried out on the single-cylinder M I (M 1) engine from March 1916 to July 1916, continuing the work interrupted on the M 0 8 (M 0.8) engine and serving to design a 400

Dessau test stand: engine and test stand (March 1916). [A6]

hp aircraft engine and to study the influence of thermal expansion on the overall structure of such engines. The guiding idea was to use the crankcase simultaneously as a beam and the cylinders as tie rods.

The results of the tests, which were available by the outbreak of the war, encouraged the company to enter into negotiations with the army administration on the design and construction of light high-speed engines.

3.38.3 Six-Cylinder 500 hp 2-Stroke Double Piston Experimental Aeroengine Fo.2 (1916)

The design was relatively closed in aluminium. The two crankshafts were coupled by gears to a common propeller shaft mounted for power transmission.

The scavenging pump was mounted as a rotary piston pump. The gasoline used as fuel was injected as a spray by the above-mentioned high-pressure pump and ignited by spark plugs.

Bore/stroke: 110/2 x 150 mm, Displacement: 17.1 l, Weight: 1200 kg.

Fo.2 test engine during assembly. [A6]

Fo.2 test engine after completion. [A6]

Test engine Fo.2: Assemblies of the "scavenging air pump" before assembly. [A6]

Test engine Fo.2: Scavenging air pump after assembly. [A6]

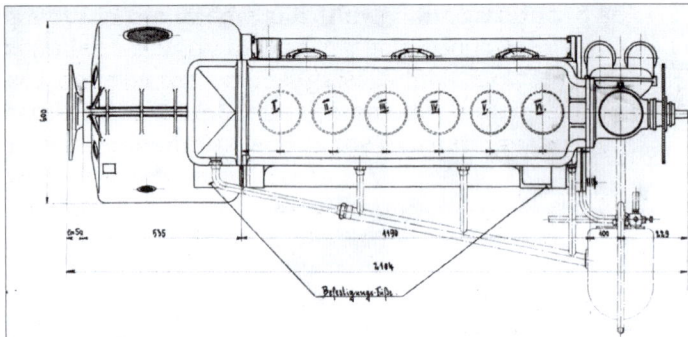

Design drawing of the 500 hp E.Fo.2 aircraft engine. [A6]

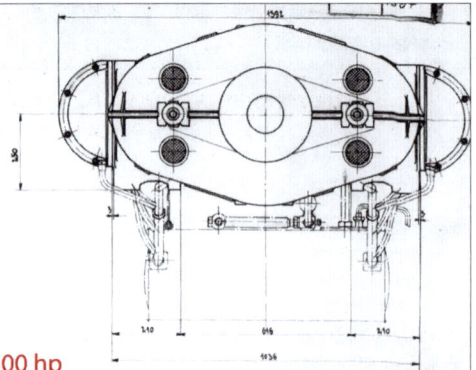

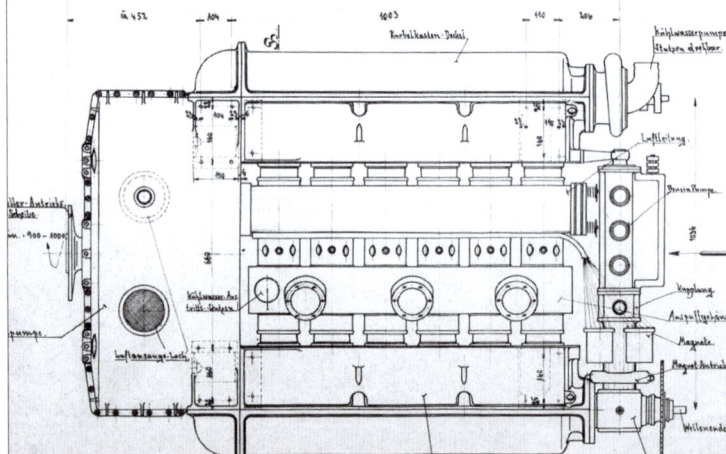

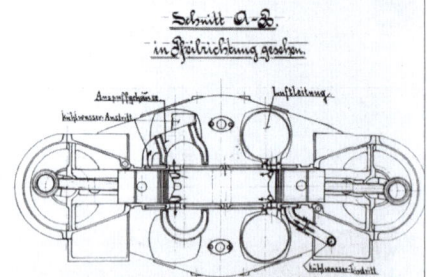

3.38.4 Six-Cylinder 2-Stroke 500 hp Double Piston Experimental Engine E.Fo.2 (1916)

The first engine built by Linke-Hoffmann (for Junkers) arrived at Dessau in October 1916 on the test stand for complete finishing and testing. This type E F O 2 (or E.Fo.2) corresponded in its structural arrangement to its predecessors M O 3 (M 0.3), M O 8 (M 0.8) and F O 2 (Fo.2).

The end of the war put a temporary end to work on this type of engine. The six E F O 2-[E.

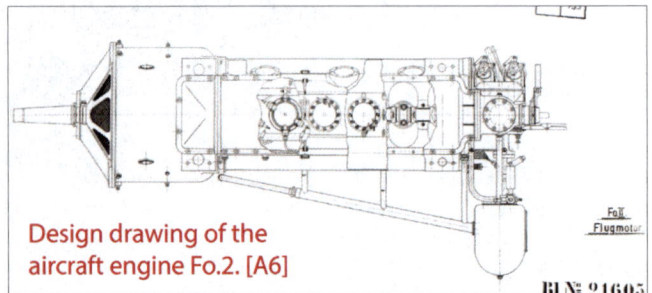

Design drawing of the aircraft engine Fo.2. [A6]

Fo.2] engines built for wartime purposes had to be smashed. A casing of this engine type is on display in the Junkers Works Museum in Dessau.

3.38.5 Six-Cylinder 1000 hp 2-Stroke Double Piston Aeroengine (1917/18)

The 1000 hp 6-cylinder two-stroke Junkers aircraft engine is also a opposed piston arrangement of 6 parallel side-by-side cylinders. Designed in 1917, the engine had 2 crankshafts (one on each side of the cylinder) connected underneath by gears. Power was taken from the center gear. The engine had no valves, but had intake and exhaust ports controlled by the piston.

A novel feature of this engine was piston cooling, which was achieved by partially filling the tightly bolted cavity of the piston with a liquid that was shaken violently back and forth during operation. The hot piston crown heated the liquid, which transferred its heat to the cooled cylinder jacket. The tests showed that this piston cooling system worked perfectly even at high speeds of 2000 rpm. The piston crown heated up to only 250° C in this case.

Compared to other two-stroke engines, the Junkers engine offered the advantage that high power could be achieved at medium pressures. This engine was still in the experimental stage at the end of the war.

But development on these twin-cylinder engines continued throughout the 1920s. In 1928, an aircraft installation of an F 0 3 engine was shown at the ILA in Berlin (developed in 1926).

Endnotes

1 The information in this section is taken with the kind permission of Bernd Junkers from "Dokumente zur Firmengeschichte der Junkerswerke, Geschichte des Junkers-Motorenbaus Teil V", edited and published by the Bernd Junkers archive.

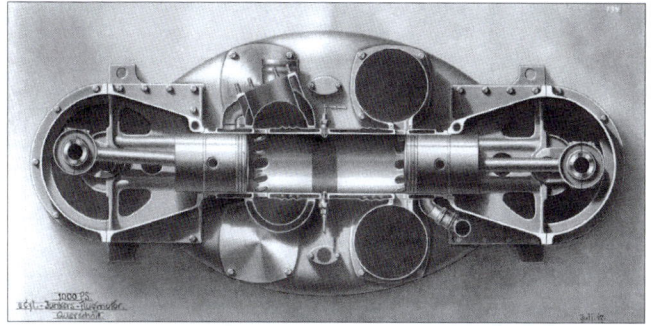

Above: First draft drawing for a 1000 hp Junkers light engine (July 1917). [A6]

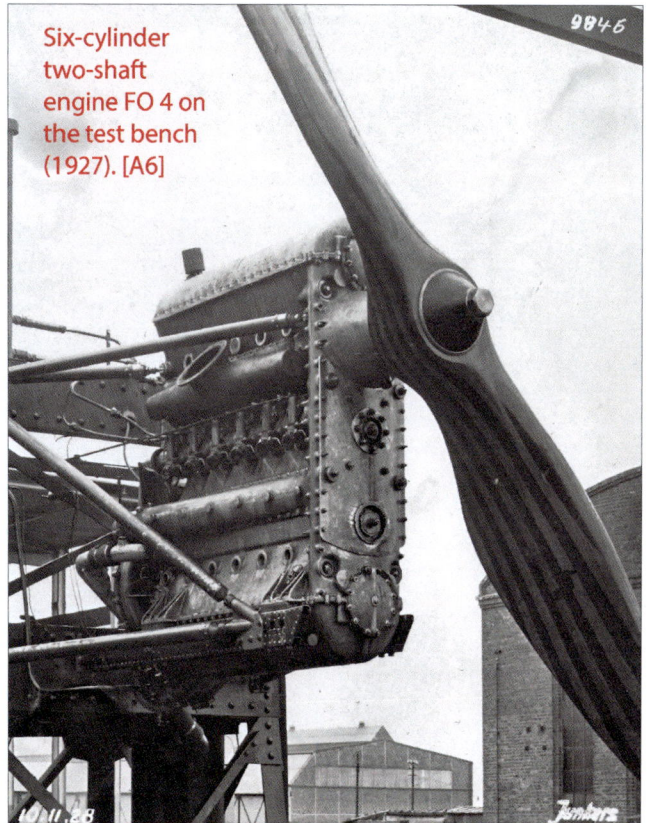

Above: First draft drawing for a 1000 hp Junkers light engine (July 1917). [A6]

Six-cylinder two-shaft engine FO 4 on the test bench (1927). [A6]

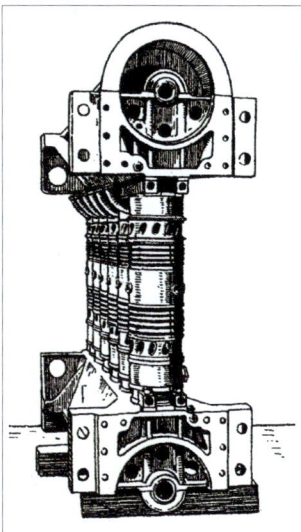

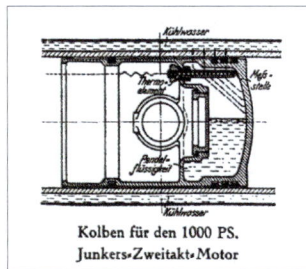

Above: Cut through a piston of the Junkers 1000 hp engine. [B4]

Left: Arrangement of pistons in the 1000 hp Junkers engine project. [B4]

3.39 Oscar Kersten, Berlin

The Kersten aircraft engine consisted of two opposing water-cooled cylinders located exactly on one axis. The water jacket made of sheet brass was pressed together by a ring, which had a groove, by means of a sealing ring and screwed together. The valves were located in the cylinder head and were extremely easy to access. The carburetor was located in the exact center of the crankcase so that the engine could be started from the rear. The float chamber of the carburetor was located exactly below the carburetor chamber, which kept the center of gravity in the middle and allowed the gasoline to be supplied regularly in case of fluctuations. Heating was done by the exhaust gases, which enclosed the carburetion chamber in a completely sealed cavity. The water pump as well as the magnetic apparatus were driven by gears.

Bore/stroke: 125/120 mm
Power: approx. 25 hp at 1600 to 1700 rpm
Weight: approx. 45 kg

According to the German press, this engine was also produced as a four- and six-cylinder version, but it is not known whether any engine ever powered a flying aircraft. From 1912 onwards, no more reports of Kersten engines appear in the technical magazines.

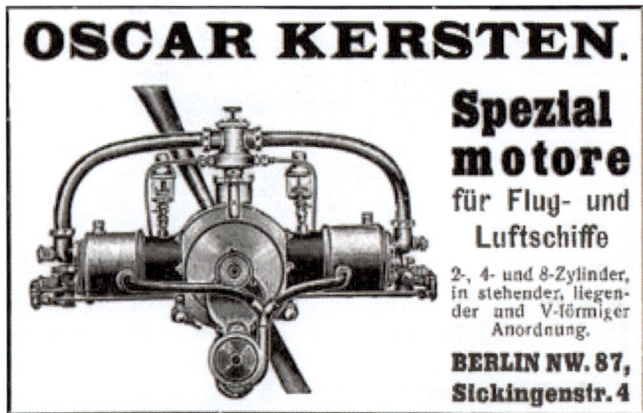

Above: Advertising of Oscar Kersten showing the 2 cylinder boxer engine. [J4, 1910]

Below: Two-thirds of production Fokker D.VII fighters were powered by the Mercedes D IIIa and one third by the over-compressed BMW IIIa. Here is a lineup of D.VII fighters at Jasta 72 with the Staffelführer's aircraft at left. Carl Menckhoff, the Staffelführer, achieved 39 victories and won the Pour le Mérite.

3.40 Kieling & Pulver Maschinenbauanstalt GmbH, Frankfurt a.M.

3.40.0 General

The company Kieling & Pulver in Frankfurt am Main, founded in 1909, initially manufactured the circulating engines of the Hoffmann company (see also Section 3.33). However, after Georg Hoffmann stopped developing his own engines, Wilhelm Kieling, as managing director, made his own attempts to develop aircraft engines. But this failed in all areas, because not even one product led to success, let alone series production.

3.40.1 Four-Cylinder 60 hp In-line Engine

Unsuccessful water-cooled four-stroke engine from 1912.

14-cylinder rotating aero-engine developed by Kieling & Partner. [J3, 1910]

Advertising of Kieling & Pulver GmbH, 4-cylinder in-line and 7-cylinder ratating engines. [J3, 1910]

3.40.2 Four-Cylinder 100 hp In-line Engine

Unsuccessful water-cooled four-stroke engine from 1912.

3.40.3 Seven-Cylinder 50 hp Rotary Engine

In 1912, the German Emperor Wilhelm II called for a competition for the best German aircraft engine. Kieling & Pulver registered their 7-cylinder, air-cooled, four-stroke rotary engine for this competition, but it was not delivered.
Bore/Stroke: 110/120 mm

Power: 50 hp at 1250 rpm
Weight: 76 kg

3.40.4 Fourteen-Cylinder 100 hp Rotary Engine

The adjacent advertisement from the magazine "*Flugsport*" (1910) shows the 14-cylinder, approximately 100 hp four-stroke rotary engine. Nothing is known about its practical use.
Weight: approx. 115 kg

3.40.5 Seven-Cylinder 80 hp Rotary Engine

With this engine, the Kieling & Pulver company intended to be able to participate in the armament program of the German Reich in 1916. In order to achieve this goal, it was necessary to pass the required type test in Berlin-Adlershof. But already in the first run, the complete test engine failed due to defects in the pistons, valves and control organs. In addition, the exhaust valves arranged laterally in the cylinder head failed several times as a result of the higher slideway pressures on the valve stems caused by the centrifugal forces.

Although the 7-cylinder 80 hp engine had a favourable power-to-weight ratio of 1.5 kg/hp, no further work was done to eliminate the defects.

Weight: approx. 100 kg

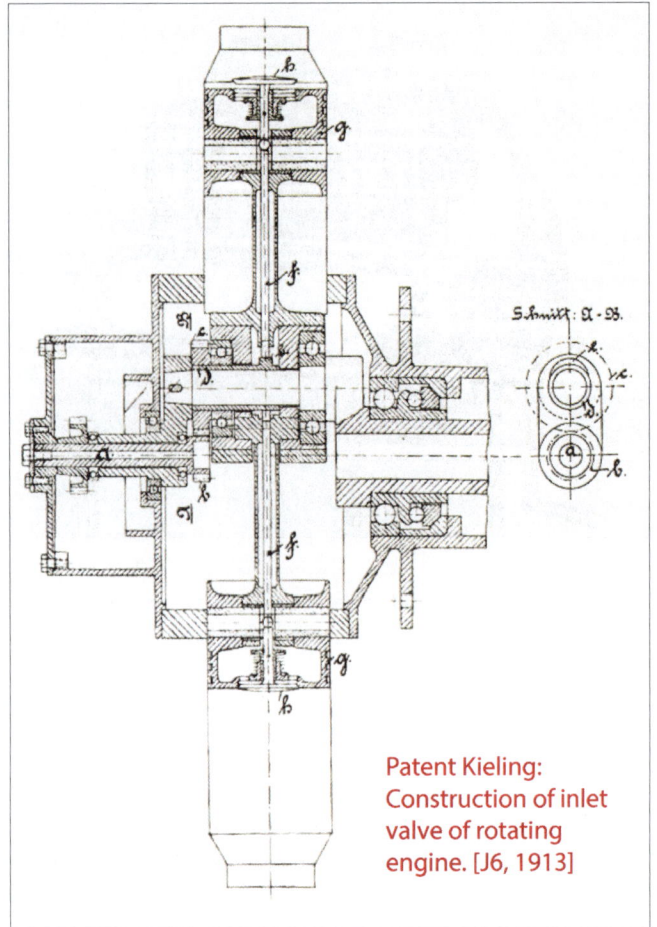

Patent Kieling: Construction of inlet valve of rotating engine. [J6, 1913]

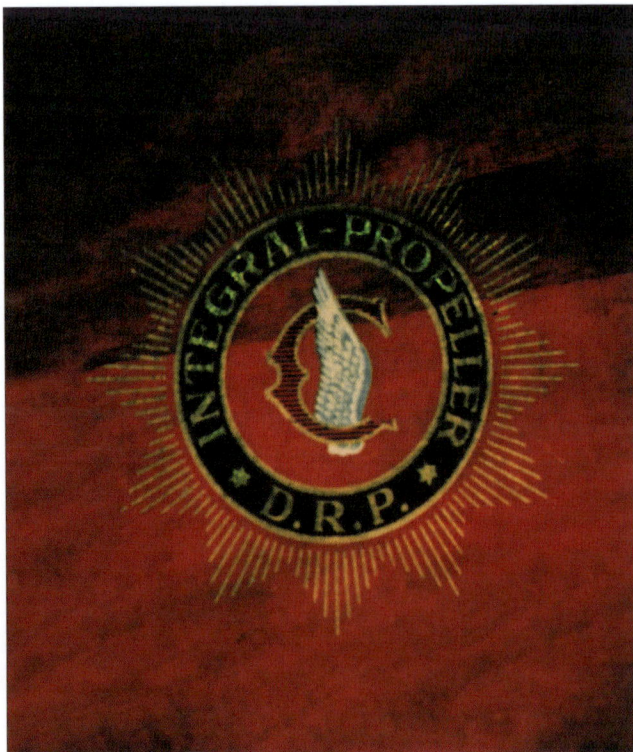

One obvious means of reducing fuel consumption seemed to be to control the fuel inlet valve.

Control of the valve located in the piston in the usual way presents very great difficulties in terms of design. An attempt to solve this problem was shown by the patent of Kieling (see illustration). In this, the suction valve is pushed open by a rod *f* guided along the inside of the connecting rod. This rod is actuated by a cam disk *e* rotating on the crank pin.

The latter is driven by gears *b* and *c*. The shaft of *b* passes through the hollow crankshaft and is driven from outside in the prescribed gear ratio. The assembly of the individual parts is, as can be seen from the illustration, rather complicated, and it is questionable whether all parts can be made to work properly. Unfortunately, nothing more is known about the success of this design.

3.41 Gebrüder Körting AG, Körtingsdorf near Hannover

3.41.0 General

The company Körting goes back to the brothers Ernst and Berthold Körting. In 1871 they built a small factory in Hannover for process engineering equipment like injectors, exhausters, water jet condensers, etc. From 1884 on, finned tubes for vapour and hot water heating systems were produced. Soon Körting was the largest manufacturer of heating pipes in Germany.

In 1904, Körting AG started to supply two-stroke petroleum engines for submarines. These engines with 6 or 8 cylinders were delivered to the Imperial Navy until about 1912. Two such 6-cylinder engines were also installed in the first German submarine "SM U1".

However, as early as 1904, the Körting brothers offered Count Zeppelin two 80 hp 2-stroke engines as a gift for the LZ-2 airship under construction at the time as part of the collection of donations for German Zeppelin airship construction program. The reasons why Graf Zeppelin finally chose Daimler instead of Körting are not known.[1]

The Körting brothers were among the first German companies to build airship and aircraft engines. The first practical engines built by the Körting brothers were used by aviation pioneers and aircraft construction companies such as Wright, Oertz, Dorner and others. The engines initially had a power of 30 to 40 hp, in 1906 already an engine for the Parseval airship of the Royal Airship Battalion in Berlin-Tegel with already 80 hp. Remarkable is the V-engine, which was not widely used in aircraft construction at that time.

In the following years further airship engines were developed, for example a 6-cylinder in-line engine with a power of 200 hp! Several such engines were used in military airships of the Gross-Basenach type, but also in the airships of Parseval.

A proof of the quality of the Körting engines, which were offered from 1906 with an output between 25 and 200 hp, was the fact that the German, Austrian, Russian and Japanese army administration ordered these Körting airship engines.

The Gebrüder Körting AG had also founded a company in Austria, in which, among other things, an airship was built. So, it is not surprising that they used engines from their own production (see also further information about 8SL 116).

The Prussian military administration's lack of

Above: Advertisment (*Flugsport* 1911), stating the deliveries to the goverments of Germany, Austria, Russia, and Japan. [J3, 1911]

interest in the development of aviation led to the fact that the further development of pure aircraft engines by Körting AG was initially postponed. Only when the necessity of a German military aviation system was recognized did Gebr. Körting AG resume the construction of aircraft engines based on the experience of earlier years. Powerful 8- and 12-cylinder V-engines were developed, whereby in particular the larger engine (military designation Kg IV) was used in the German Air Force, albeit in small numbers.

Exhaust side of Körting 4SL 101 (24 hp). [B25]

Carburettor side 4SL 101. [B10]

3.41.1 30/24 hp 4-Cylinder Airship and Aircraft Engine, 4SL 101

Not much is known about the origin of this engine. It was probably created as early as 1903/04, and nothing is known about its actual use.[2]

Using the same cylinder dimensions, an 8-cylinder V-engine with the designation 8SL 101 was developed in parallel (see below).

Bore/stroke: 101/100 mm, Total mass: 86 kg.

3.41.2 40 hp 4-Cylinder Airship Engine 4SL 111

The first Körting engine designed exclusively as an airship engine was a water-cooled 4-cylinder in-line engine from 1906, which developed about 45/40

Delivered Körting Airship Engines (Source: *Moedebecks Taschenbuch für Flugtechniker*, 3rd edition 1911)					
Expl.	Type	HP	Airship	Recipient	Year
1	4SL 111	30/40	Experimental airship,	Royal Airshipman Battalion, Berlin-Tegel	1906
2	8SL 116	à 75	Military airship M I	Prussian Army Administration	1907
6	8SL 116	à 75	Military airship M II and M III	Prussian Army Administration	1909
2	8SL 116	à 75	replacement	Prussian Army Administration	1909
3	6SL 185	à 200	2 x for M IV (before conversion to Daimler)	Prussian Army Administration	1913
1	4L 111	36	Military airship	Russian Airshipman Battalion, St. Petersburg	
2	4L 111	à 36	Military airship "Yamada I"	Japanese Governement	1910
2	4L 111	à 36	Airship "Boemches II"	Austrian Maschinenbau AG Körting, Wien	1912
2	8SL 116	à 36	Military airship M.III	Austrian Maschinenbau AG Körting, Wien	1910
2	6SL 185	à 180	Parseval PL 11 (P.III)	Motorluftschiff-Studiengesellschaft Berlin	1911
1	8SL 116	75	Airship "Golub"	Ischora-Works, Kolpino near St. Petersburg	1910
2	8SL 116	à 75	Airship "Albatros"	Ischora-Works, Kolpino near St. Petersburg	1914

hp at 1300/1200 rpm. The engine had oppositely controlled valves (outlet from below, inlet from above). This engine was delivered to the Royal Airship Battalion in Berlin-Tegel in 1906 to be installed in the experimental airship M.V. Bore/stroke: 116/126 mm

3.41.3 36 hp 4-Cylinder Airship and Aircraft Engine 4L 111

After the positive tests with the 4SL 111 airship engine, Körting AG made efforts to gain a foothold in the aircraft market. With a slightly smaller piston diameter (111 mm instead of 116 mm) than before, a new engine was offered, which should meet the requirements of the airship and aircraft manufacturers.

Initially it was the German aviation pioneers, such as Jatho, Oertz, Werntge and others, who were inspired by this engine. In 1907/08 Karl Jatho ordered such an engine for his biplane Jatho IV and in 1910 for the monoplane Jatho V, but also the famous Hamburg boat builder Max Oertz and

Above: Carburettor side 4SL 101. [B10]

the Flugmaschine Wright GmbH used this 36 hp 4-cylinder engine in their flying machines.

The water-cooled 4-cylinder in-line engine 4L 111 already developed 42/38 hp at 1300/1200 rpm on the test bench.
Bohrung/Hub 116/126 mm, 3,0 kg/PS.

Right & Below: Side, aft, and top views of 4L 111 engine. [J4, 1909]

Below Right: Dorner aircraft owned by Werntgen with 36 hp Körting engine 4L 111. [B42]

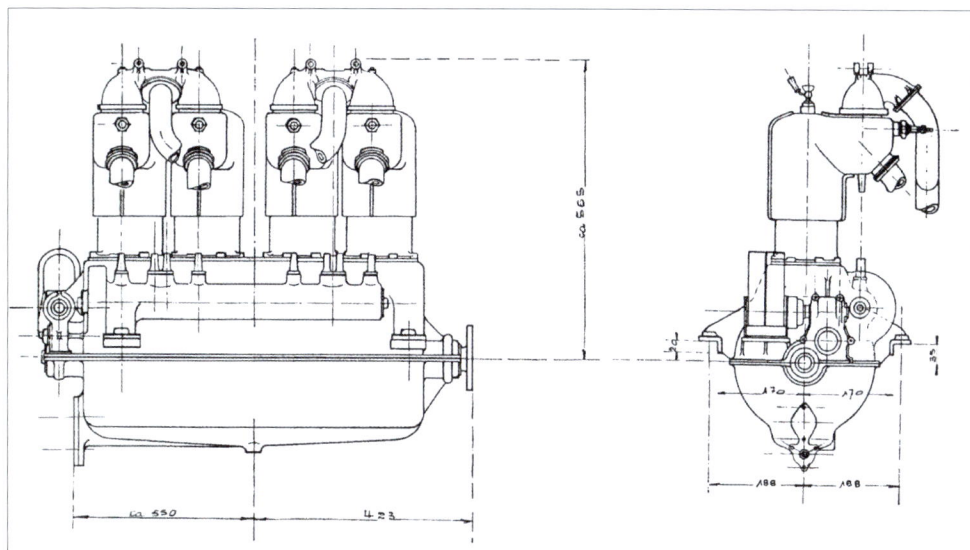

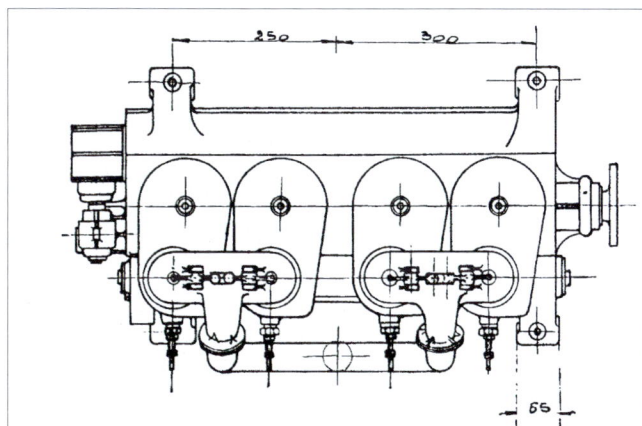

3.41.4 42/38 hp 4-cylinder aircraft engine 4L 111b

After the successful launch of the 4L 111 engine, which was used intensively by the first aviation enthusiasts, the Körting brothers introduced an improved engine especially for airplanes by increasing the stroke to 136 mm. With this increase in displacement it was possible to increase the power output to 45/40 hp.

Similar to the engine described above, the basic construction is comparable to the 36 hp airship engine. The engine had four vertical cylinders. The weight of the flywheel, if one became necessary, was 20 kg.

Die Ignition and lubrication of the engine was the same as for the large 8-cylinder engine described later, and the construction of the cylinders is also basically the same.

The fuel consumption of both engines was about 260 g, the lubricant consumption about 18 g per hp and hour.

Above Right: Körting 40 hp aircraft engine 4L 111b, exhaust side. [B14, 1914]

Below, Bottom, & Right: Körting 4L 111b, different views. [B25]

Körting 40 PS.

Bohrung: 116 mm.   Umdrehungen: 1250
Hub: 136 mm.   Gewicht: 116 kg.

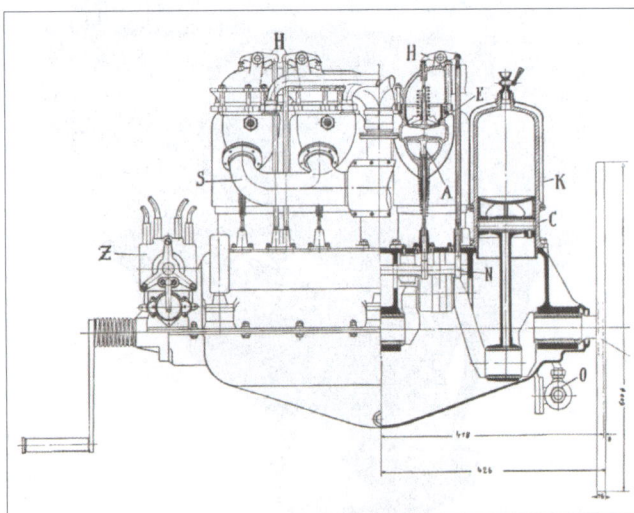

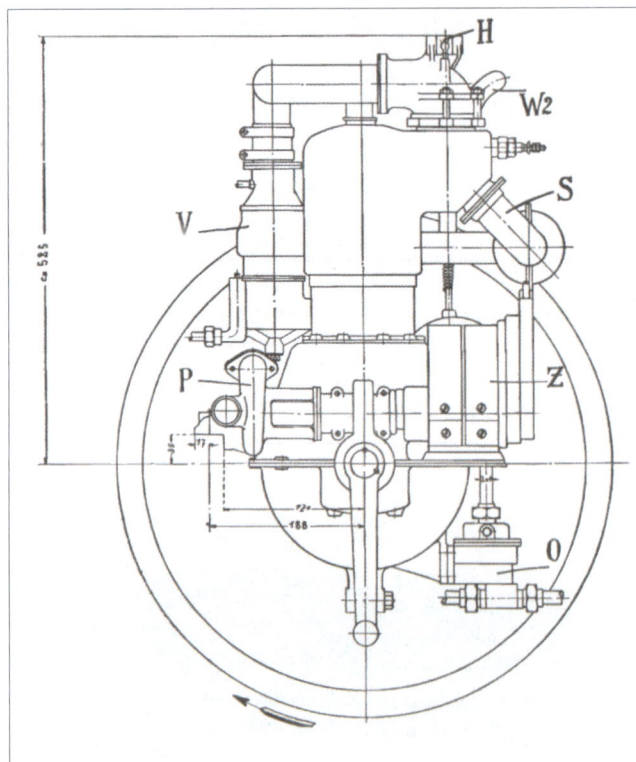

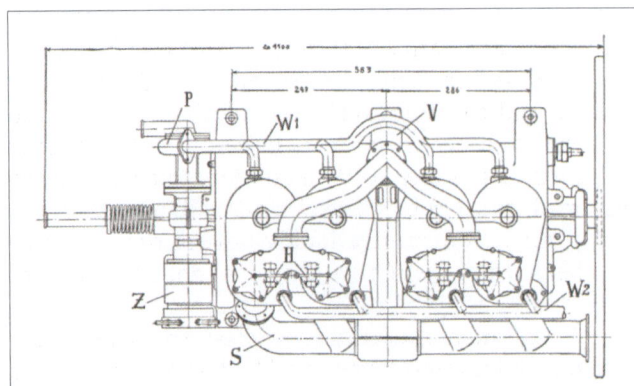

3.41.5 200/180 hp 6-cylinder airship engine 6SL 185

In 1909 the engineers of Gebr. Körting AG developed a 200 hp water-cooled in-line engine with the designation 6SL 185 (bore/stroke 185/180 mm, total weight 600 kg).

The first application of this engine was in the airship M IV, completed in 1911, in which two examples of this engine were initially installed in two nacelles. With a total power of 400 hp this airship exceeded all previously built airships.

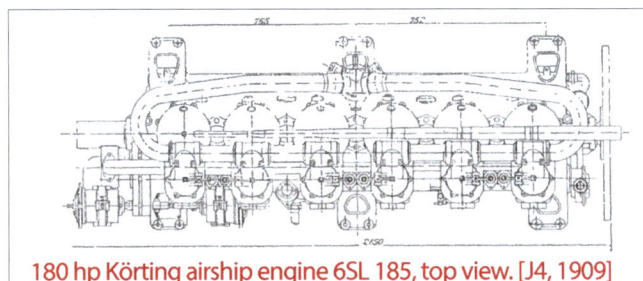

180 hp Körting airship engine 6SL 185, top view. [J4, 1909]

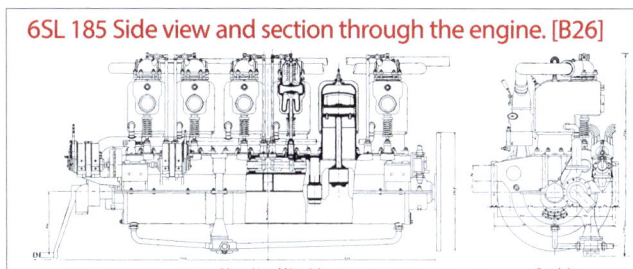

6SL 185 Side view and section through the engine. [B26]

Körting 6SL 185 Exhaust and Carburettor sides. [B10]

Parseval also used two of these powerful 6-cylinder in-line engines in the airship PL 11 (1911). The PL 11 was acquired by the military administration as a "fast ship", it had two 200/180 hp Körting six-cylinder engines and two chain-driven propellers, counter-rotatable for reverse travel. The engines could be switched to either of the two propellers.

3.41.6 50 hp 8-cylinder airship engine 8SL 101

The design and weight ratios of the 4SL 101 and 8SL 101 engines are a compromise between balloon and flying machine engines, so that these engines, especially the four-cylinder engine, could be used with advantage for flying machines. The 8SL 101, especially designed as an airship engine, is a quasi-doubling of the Körting engine 4SL 101, whereby the cylinder rows were arranged at 90° to each other.

In the 8-cylinder engine, the rows of cylinders were at a 90° angle to each other, just like the other

V-engines from Körting AG (with the exception of the Kg IV). In this design, a doubling of the power was achieved (55/48 hp at 1500/1300 rpm), but as an aircraft engine it was too heavy at 125 kg. The specific power-to-weight ratio was 3.5.

In 1910/11 the Flugmaschine Wright-Gesellschaft mbH, Berlin-Reinickendorf and Johannisthal presented its new "Record" racing biplane, which could be delivered either with a 50 hp Argus or 55 hp NAG or with a 50 hp Körting 8-cylinder engine. The flying machine reached a speed of 95 km/h after all.

Bore/stroke: 101/100 mm

3.41.7 75 hp 8-cylinder airship engine 8SL 116

One of the better known early water-cooled airship engines of Körting AG was the V8 engine with rows of cylinders offset by 90°. Initially, in 1907, two of the engines developing about 75 hp each at 1400 rpm were installed in the German military airship M I.

On September 12, 1908, the airship M l completed the longest flight of 13 hours ever made until then, covering a distance of over 400 km in this time. The 8SL 116 engines of the military airship M II were subjected to an even greater endurance test during the flight of 16½ hours carried out on August 4, 1909. Ship and both engines passed this trial without any problems.

Left: Flugmaschine Wright-Gesellschaft mbH, Berlin-Reinickendorf, presenting the Wrigh "Record" racing biplane equipped with 50 hp Körting 8-cylinder engine.

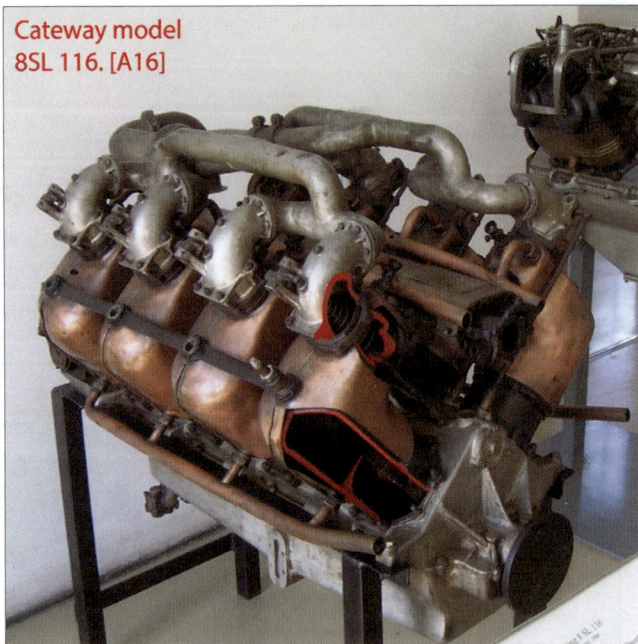

Luftschiffmotor von Körting ältere Ausführung.
A Auspuffventil, E Einlaßventil, N Steuerwelle, V Vergaser.

separately for each row of cylinders and are provided with ribs for better cooling

Initially, an electrical system with battery ignition was tested for the engines. However, after a short

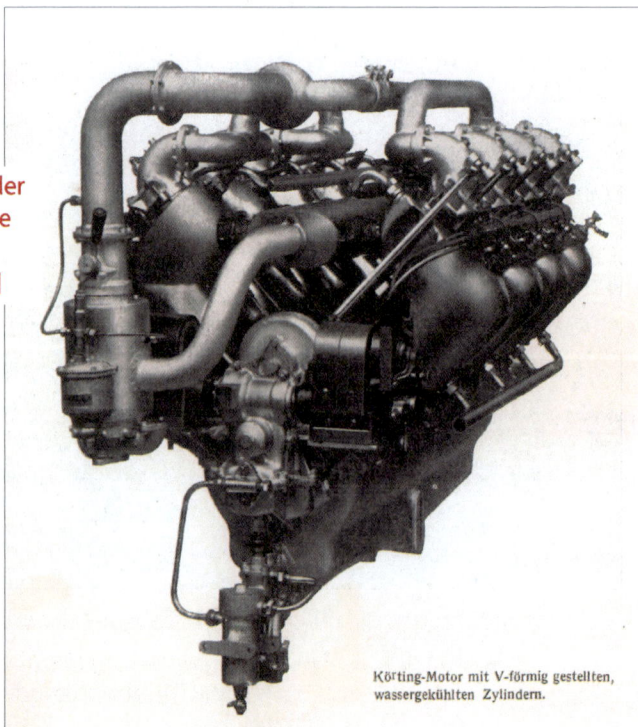

75 hp 8-cylinder Körting engine 8SL 116 (later version). [B10]

The adjacent figure shows the first version of the V8 airship engine. In this older version, only one intake manifold extends from the carburetor, through which the fuel-air mixture is fed to the cylinders via branch lines. With this arrangement, the distances that the mixture had to travel from the carburetor to the individual cylinders were unequal in length, which is why this problem was solved in the newer arrangement by forking the intake manifold at the carburetor into two main lines for four cylinders each. The exhaust pipes are arranged

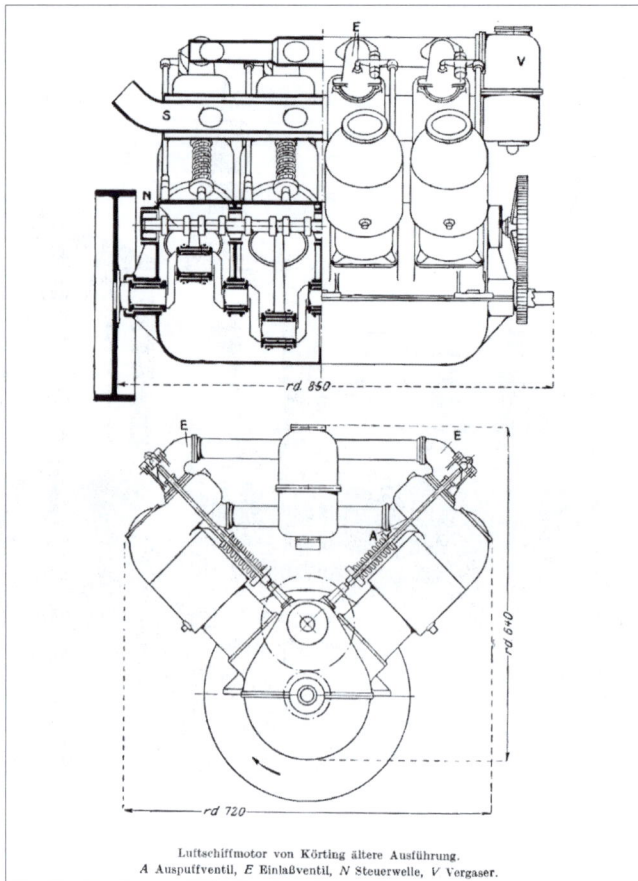

Körting-Motor mit V-förmig gestellten, wassergekühlten Zylindern.

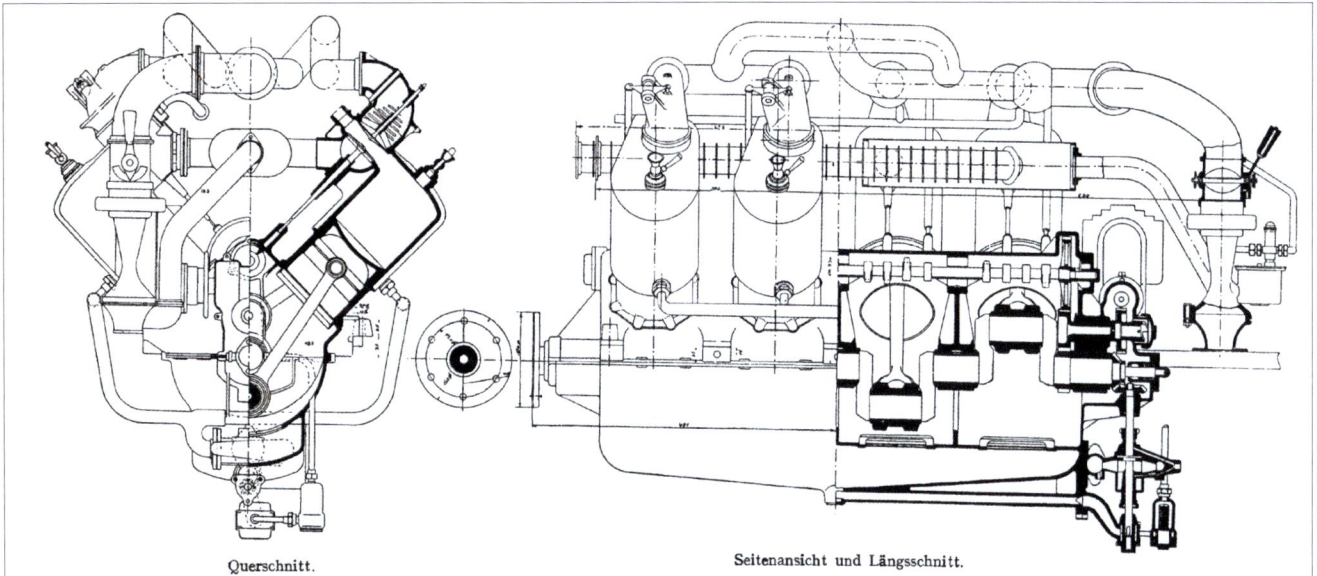

Querschnitt.

Seitenansicht und Längsschnitt.

Above: Cylinder as for stationary engine. Water pump with standing shaft driven by conical gears, solenoid by screw gears. For 8 cylinders only 1 carburetor. [B26]

time, technical shortcomings led to the engines being fitted with two magnets each.

At the end of 1909, the third ship, M III, was completed. Instead of the two Körting engines used so far, 4 of these 8SL 116 engines, each with 75 hp, were installed in the nacelle. The airship M III was the fastest of all balloons ever built.

Even though this engine was originally built for airship purposes, it has been installed in several aircraft of that time.

Although the design of the engine in a V-shape had already been successfully tested in the

automotive sector for some time, it represented a novelty in German aircraft construction. To the chagrin of the aircraft industry, this design was not intensively pursued. It even came to the point that until the first years of the war, such engines were deliberately excluded from production by the

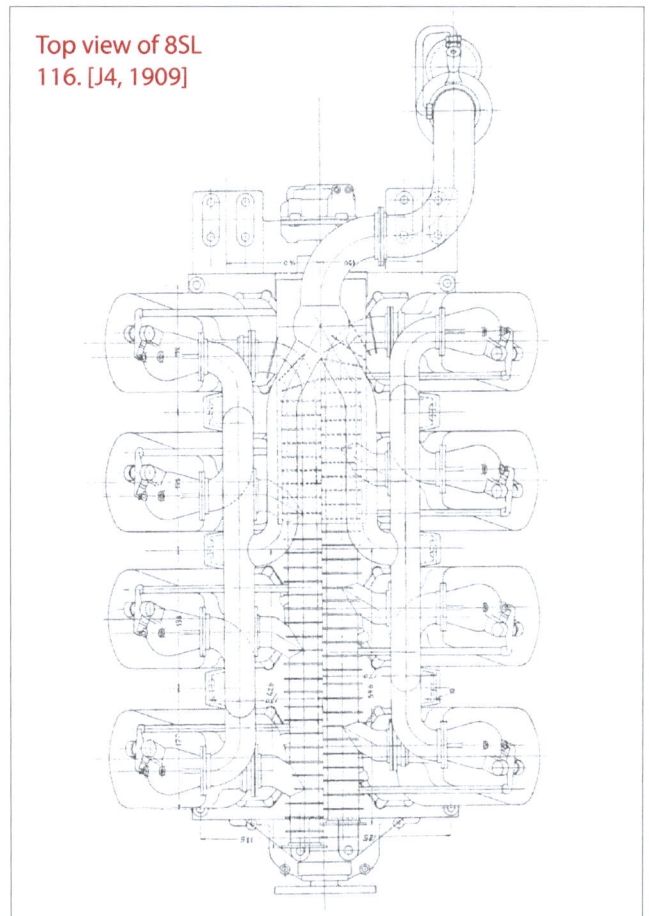

Top view of 8SL 116. [J4, 1909]

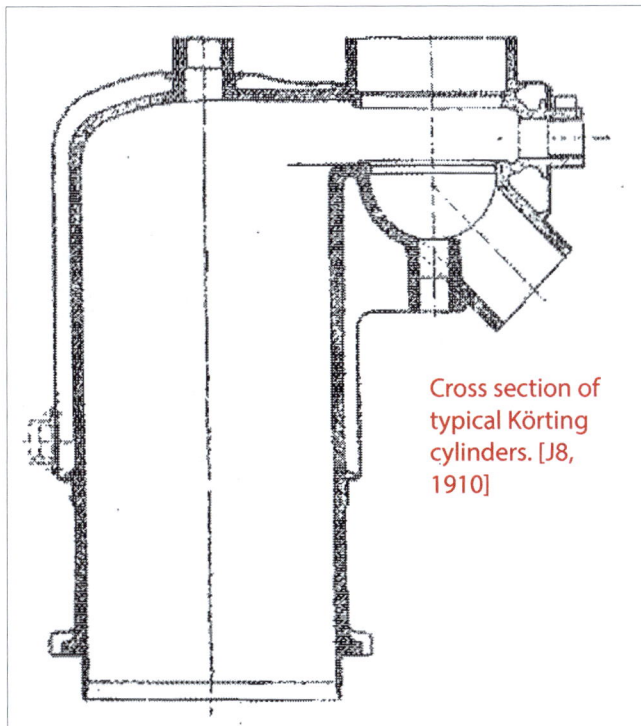

Cross section of typical Körting cylinders. [J8, 1910]

Left: Gondola of military airship M III with engine installation. [B10]

Below: First AEG airplane with 75 hp Körting, built in 1910. [A1]

Right: Propulsion of Austrian military airship M III with two 75 hp Körting engines. [B10]

Below: Advertisement 1910. [J4, 1910]

MOTOREN
für
Luftschiffe und Flugmaschinen
von 24—200 PS

geliefert an die deutsche, russische und japanische Regierung.

Gebr. Körting, Aktiengesellschaft
Körtingsdorf b. Hannover.

Below: Advertisement 1910. [J4, 1910]

Gebr. Körting Aktiengesellschaft
Körtingsdorf bei Hannover
liefert:

Luftschiffmotoren

Elegante leichte Ausführung, dabei grösste Betriebssicherheit. Gleichmässig ruhiger Gang. Sparsamster Benzinverbrauch.

Mit Körtings-Motoren ausgerüstet, konnte das lenkbare Militärluftschiff eine 13stündige Dauerfahrt vollenden, ohne dass sich der geringste Motordefekt zeigte.

military authorities.

The drawings shown here illustrate the design of the 8SL 116 engine, which effectively produces 75 hp at its normal speed of 1250 rpm. The maximum output of the machine is approx. 85 hp at 1300 rpm.

This engine had 8 pairs of V-shaped cylinders of 116 mm bore and 126 mm stroke, facing each other at 90°. The water jacket, in which the water used to cool the cylinder and the valve chambers circulates, is made of copper and is not, as in many other constructions, cast iron cast together with the cylinder to save weight on the one hand, but also to prevent any tension in the material that could easily arise as a result.

Cast together with the cylinders are the valve housings, which are arranged at the upper end of the cylinders in such a way that the intake valves are directly opposite the exhaust valves. This arrangement made it possible to control all the valves from a single common camshaft: the exhaust valves were controlled directly from below by means of pushrods, while the intake valves were controlled from above by means of rocker arms.

The pistons were made of cast iron, as this had proved to be the most suitable quality and had been machined for the purpose. The forged iron connecting rods of two opposing cylinders, each transmitting the piston pressure to the crankshaft, worked on one and the same crankshaft journal and the head of one rod was split so that that of the other rod was engaged in between. This peculiar design reduced the specific surface pressure on the crankshaft journal to a minimum, thus avoiding rapid wear and easy warm-up of these points. Like all bearings on the engine, these had bronze bearings, which were filled with white metal. Pistons and piston rods were precisely balanced to avoid vibration as much as possible.

The shaft, made of finest nickel chrome steel, with all cranks in one plane, was, as can be seen in the adjacent drawing, drilled out to reduce weight and mounted in 5 plain bearings. At one end of the crankshaft there was a pair of bevel gears, which transmitted the rotation to a vertical shaft leading downwards. On this shaft there was a very large cooling water pump and a small oil pump.

The lower part of the crankcase, which was made of aluminium and divided in the plane of the crankshaft, was designed as an oil sump and had a bag-shaped bulge at its deepest point. This design ensured that the crankcase was always kept free of oil and that the oil pump always found sufficient oil even when the engine was tilted. The lubrication was actuated by two oil pumps, one of which pumped the lubricant from the inside of the engine into the collecting tank, from which it could flow under static pressure to the actual lubrication press pump. All bearings of the machine were thus lubricated under pressure. Three strainers, which were arranged at different places, ensured that the oil was kept clean.

At the end of the engine, the carburetor is common to all cylinders and is equipped with a regulating throttle valve to regulate the speed of the engine.

The exhaust pipes were arranged separately for each cylinder bank and provided with ribs, i.e. lamellas, for better cooling.

An intermediate gear was driven by the crankshaft, which operated the camshaft (valve control) on one side and a worm gear on the opposite side of the casing.

A transverse shaft, which was driven by the worm gear, had a claw clutch, according to whose respective position one of the Bosch magneto ignition devices arranged on both sides was activated. In normal operation, only one of these devices worked; the other one served as an auxiliary and could be put into operation immediately in case of a possible malfunction by engaging the clutch. These double ignition devices had proved themselves very well in operation of the military airship.

A flywheel of 20 kg weight was sufficient for the engine, which, if such a flywheel was required at all, had to be adapted to the respective drive conditions. In such cases, where the engine was directly connected to the propellers without any wheel, belt or cable transmission, a special flywheel was not necessary.

The engine was started up by hand using a crank handle, which was specially adapted to the local conditions and transmitted the rotation to the crankshaft by means of a link chain.

The weight of the complete operable engine including all piping within the engine's boundary line, the two oil pumps, the carburetor, the two magnetos, etc. was only 200 kg, despite its robust construction, but without fuel and without water filling in the cylinder cooling chambers.

Bore/stroke: 116/126 mm, fuel consumption 240 gr/hp/h.

3.41.8 195/180 PS 8-Zylinder V-Motor Kg III(a) (1916)

In the early years of World War I, the Körting factories were more involved in the production of submarine and ship engines than in the development of aircraft engines. Nevertheless, from 1916 onwards, work was carried out on a water-cooled 8-cylinder engine in a 90° V-shape, which generated 195/180 hp at 2150/2000 rpm on the brake stands. This

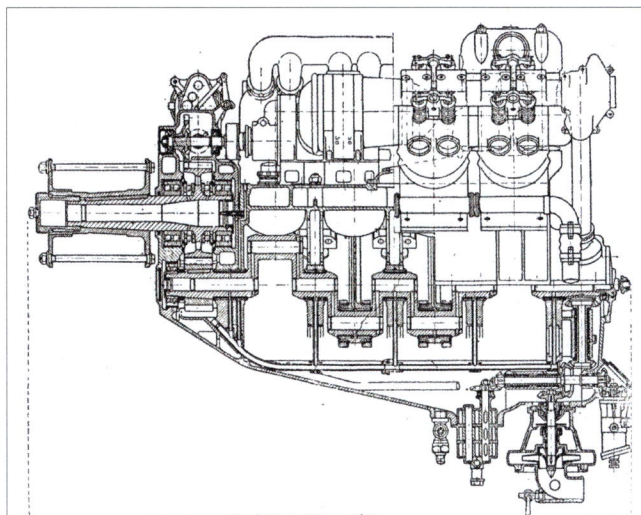

Körting Kg III, eight-cylinder V-type "fast-runner". [B2]

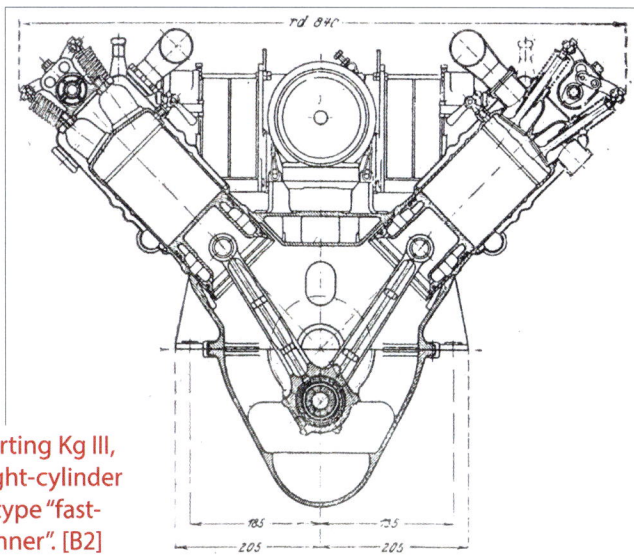

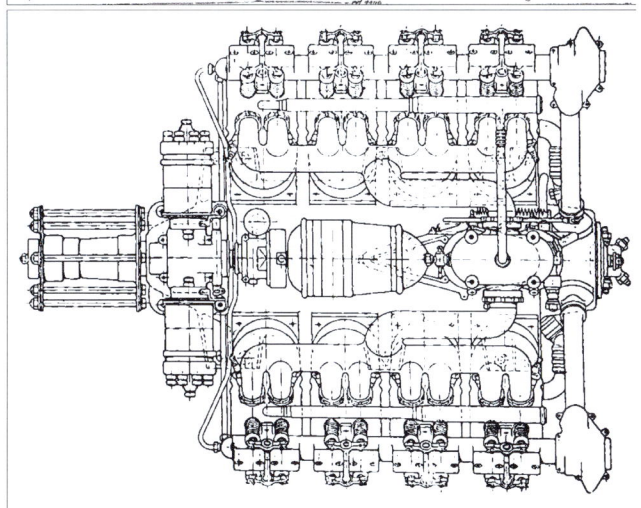

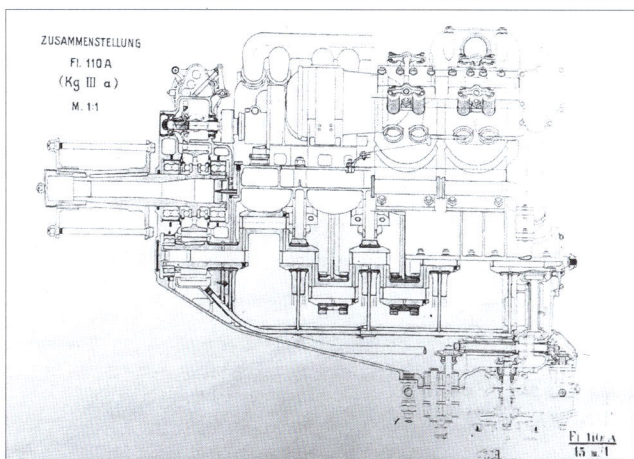

aircraft engine (the internal factory designation was FL.110A) was a high-speed engine and was equipped with reduction gears. It had 4 Pallas carburetors. Before the type approval examination, test engines were delivered to Halberstadt and LFG for flight testing. However, due to bearing damage (lack of high-quality materials and lubricants) the engine did not pass the type approval twice in 1917.

Further test flights were undertaken with DFW Jagdeinsitzer Dr I (only one prototype in 1917).
Bore/stroke 110/140 mm, total cubic capacity 10.6 liters.

V-Achtzylinder 190 PS Flugmotor Kg IIIa

The enclosed Körting drawings allow the assumption that a "pure" Kg III probably did not exist. It must therefore be assumed that the series engines were to be designated Kg IIIa.

3.41.9 250 PS 12-Zylinder V-Motor Kg I

The most powerful V12 engine produced by Körting

Above & Below: Section through Körting Kg III. It had 110 mm bore, 140 mm stroke and produced 185–195 hp at 2150 rpm. It weighed 252 kg including water and oil. The cranks embraced each other similarly to the Hispano-Suiza. [A2]

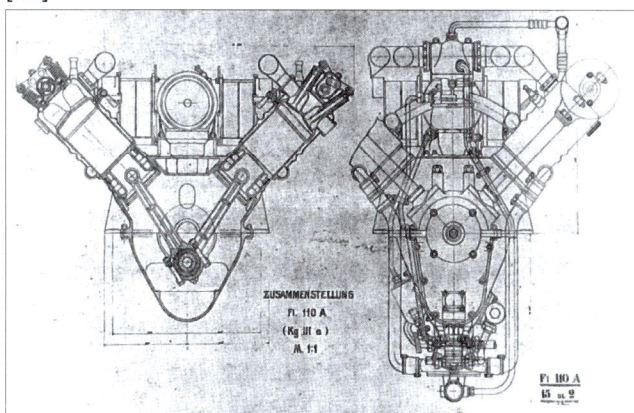

AG was water-cooled, like all previous engines. This time the cylinders were at an angle of 60° to each other. The 260/250 hp were achieved at speeds of 1750/1450 rpm. The company's internal engine

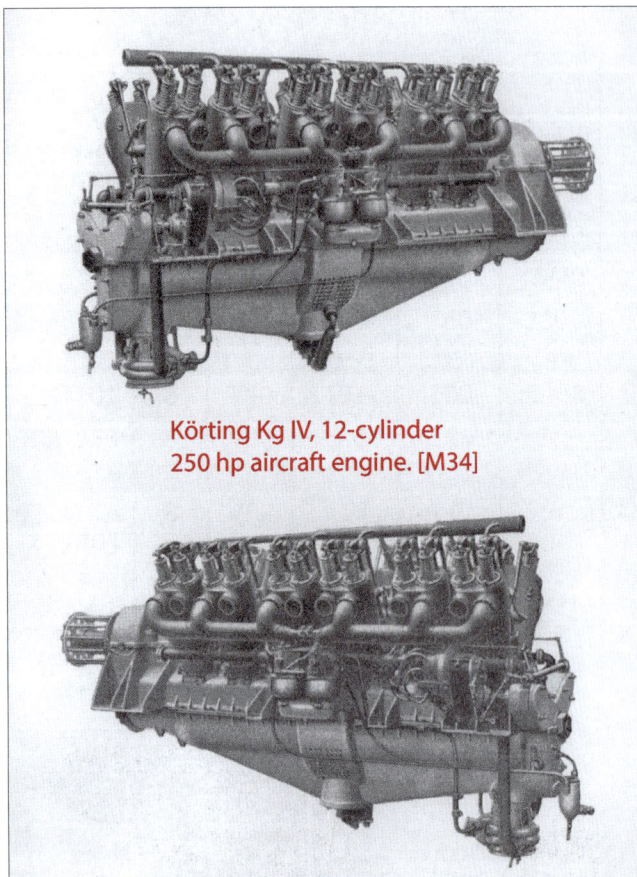

Körting Kg IV, 12-cylinder
250 hp aircraft engine. [M34]

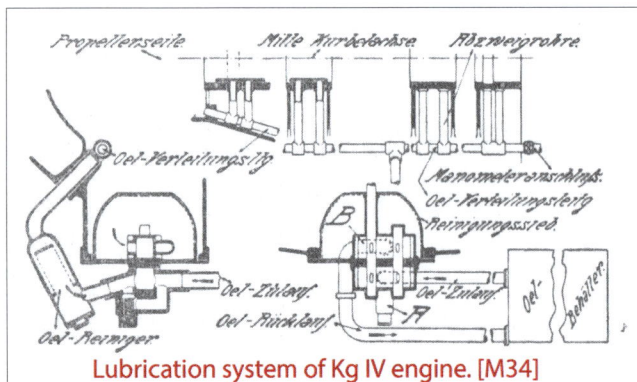

Lubrication system of Kg IV engine. [M34]

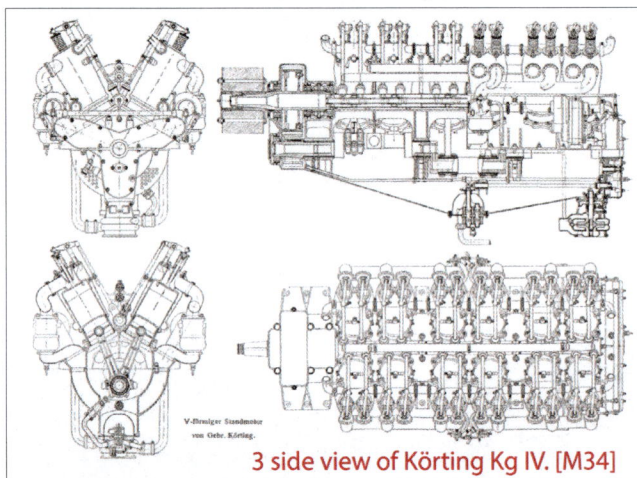

3 side view of Körting Kg IV. [M34]

designation was FL.120. Similar to the FL.110A, this engine had a gearbox with a reduction ratio of 1:2. The camshaft was driven by a drive flange, which was driven by the propeller shaft at the rear. Although the type test was already passed in February 1917, only about 30 units were built.

The engine was characterized by its smooth running and reliability. However, with a mass of over 450 kg, it was found to be too heavy in 1916 and was not approved for series production.

The construction of the valves had some special features. Inlet and outlet valve cones were identical. The outlet valve differed from the inlet valve by a water-cooled valve cover, which should prevent damaging heating of the valve spindle. The valves were suspended and were pressed onto their seats by springs. The spring plate was prevented from loosening by inserted wedges and lock nuts.

A pair of Pallas carburetors were arranged on each side of the engine. So there were 3 cylinders connected to one carburetor. The carburetors were easily removable and were mounted on brackets, which were the continuation of the already mentioned suction channels on the housing. The console's trough, which was equipped with pipe connections, was used to collect dripping gasoline.

The throttle valves of the carburetors were operated simultaneously by a common linkage. By means of an adjusting and regulating screw, an absolutely even operation of the 4 throttle valves was achieved from one lever. The upper part of the carburetors, where the throttle valves were located, was heated with water. An attached tap was used for drainage in case of danger of frost.

The oil circuit 6 in the engine is made by 2 gear pumps, which are mounted together at the lowest point of the crankcase. The oil flows to one pump A from the oil tank and is pressed into an oil distribution line located under the crankshaft bearings. The oil flows through an oil cleaner, which must be cleaned after more or less long operating times, depending on the oil quality.

This gear pump has a circulation channel with a spring-loaded valve, which prevents an unacceptable increase in oil pressure. From the oil distribution line the oil is fed to the bearing points through short branch pipes. The oil is distributed through holes in the crankshaft to the connecting rod bearings and further through special lines in the connecting rods, rising to the piston pins.

By dividing the crankshaft bores into individual chambers, it is ensured that each lubrication point is specially lubricated. On the propeller side, a stream of oil is circulated around the bearing shell and

Above: Kg IV engine on a test bench. [A1]

Above, Below, & Below Left: Jatho IV with 30–36 hp Körting engine 4L111. [3, 1909]

flows through holes to a nozzle which sprays the oil between the wheels of the propeller gearbox.

On the side of the engine opposite the propeller, the oil is fed to the bearings of the magnetic drive wheels in a similar way. In addition, a shunt is connected to the above-mentioned nozzle for lubrication of the gear wheels, which leads the oil to the control shaft of the motor.

The oil distribution line is led outside through the front cover of the housing. A pressure gauge is connected at this point to allow the oil pressure to be constantly checked.

The used oil collects in the lower part of the housing and is pressed back to the oil tank by the second gear wheel ramp B, which is protected by a sieve inside the lower part of the crankcase.

Lubrication of the valve lever pins is done through the oil bushing inside the pin, which is filled with an oil suction agent. During operation, the oil, which has been applied before commissioning, will slowly flow to the surface to be lubricated.

Bore/stroke 120/140 mm, total capacity 19 liters.

Summary of Aero-Engines Made by Gebr. Körting AG									
Desig.	# Cyl.	Type	Bore [mm]	Stroke [mm]	Pwr [hp]	RPM	Rei-Wt kg/hp	Wt	Year
4SL 101	4	R	101	100	28/24	1500/1300	3,6	86	1903/04
4SL 111	4	R	116	126	45/40	1300/1200		130	1908/09
4L 111	4	R	111	126	42/38	1300/1200	3	116	1909 Oertz, Jatho
4L 111b	4	R	116	136	45/40	1300/1250	2,7	116	1908/09
6SL 185	6	R	185 (200)	180	200/180	1000/900	3,0	600	1911, in MIV, PL11
8SL 101	8	V90	101	100	55/48	1500/1300	2,4	125	Wright „Record"
8SL 116	8	V90	116	126	75	1250	2,7	210	1906/07 2 M I; 1908: M II & M III, P
FL.110A Kg III(a)	8	V90	110	140	195/180	2150/2000	1,38	240	1916/17 Type appr. II/18. At 1.15 m, it was the shortest German engine.
FL.120 Kg IV	12	V60	120	140	240	1600	1,7	426	1916, 30 pieces

Above: Jatho IV. [L22]

Above: Jatho IV. [L22]

Left: 6SL185 Körting 6 cylinder airship engine. [B26]

Engine Datasheet	
Gebrüder Körting AG, Körtingsdorf bei Hannover	
Designation	**Körting 4SL 101**
Year:	1903/04
Purpose:	Aircraft engine
Number of Cylinders:	4
Arrangement of Cylinders:	Linear
Bore [mm]:	101
Stroke [mm]:	100
Displacement [l]:	3,2
Compression [Ratio]	
Power [hp]: norm./max.	24/28
RPM [min-1]: norm./max.	1300/1500
Power per displacement [hp/l]	7,5
Carburetor(s)	
No.:	1
Type:	
Fuel consumption per hp per hour [g]:]:	
Oil Pump	
No.:	
Oil consumption per hp per hour [g/PS/h]:	
Ignition No.:	
Type:	
Firing order:	
Cooling	Water
Weight of complete engine (dry) & ext. masses	
Total [kg]:	86
Weight per displacement [kg/l]:	26,9
Weight per hp [kg/hp]:	3,6
Remarks:	

Engine Datasheet	
Gebrüder Körting AG, Körtingsdorf bei Hannover	
Designation	**Körting 4L 111**
Year:	1908/09
Purpose:	Aircraft engine
Number of Cylinders:	4
Arrangement of Cylinders:	Linear
Bore [mm]:	111
Stroke [mm]:	126
Displacement [l]:	4,9
Compression [Ratio]	
Power [hp]: norm./max.	42/38
RPM [min-1]: norm./max.	1300/1500
Power per displacement [hp/l]	7,8
Carburetor(s)	
No.:	1
Type:	
Fuel consumption per hp per hour [g]:]:	
Oil Pump	
No.:	
Oil consumption per hp per hour [g/PS/h]:	
Ignition No.:	
Type:	
Firing order:	
Cooling	Water
Weight of complete engine (dry) & ext. masses	
Total [kg]:	116
Weight per displacement [kg/l]:	23,8
Weight per hp [kg/hp]:	3,0
Remarks: Experimental airship M.V (V – Versuchs-)	

Engine Datasheet	
Gebrüder Körting AG, Körtingsdorf bei Hannover	
Designation	**Körting 6SL 185**
Year:	1911
Purpose:	Aircraft engine
Number of Cylinders:	6
Arrangement of Cylinders:	Linear
Bore [mm]:	185
Stroke [mm]:	180
Displacement [l]:	29,0
Compression [Ratio]	
Power [hp]: norm./max.	180 (200)
RPM [min-1]: norm./max.	900 (1000)
Power per displacement [hp/l]	6,2 (6,9)
Carburetor(s)	
No.:	
Type:	
Fuel consumption per hp per hour [g]:]:	
Oil Pump	
No.:	
Oil consumption per hp per hour [g/PS/h]:	
Ignition No.:	
Type:	
Firing order:	
Cooling	Water
Weight of complete engine (dry) & ext. masses	
Total [kg]:	600
Weight per displacement [kg/l]:	20,7 (20,7)
Weight per hp [kg/hp]:	3,3 (3,0)

Remarks: The numbers in () are related to the advanced version.
Aircraft: Airships: Militär-Luftschiff M IV; Parseval PL 11; Aeroplanes:

Engine Datasheet	
Gebrüder Körting AG, Körtingsdorf bei Hannover	
Designation	**Körting 8SL 116**
Year:	1907 (1908)
Purpose:	Aircraft engine
Number of Cylinders:	8
Arrangement of Cylinders:	Vee-type (90°)
Bore [mm]:	116
Stroke [mm]:	126
Displacement [l]:	10,6
Compression [Ratio]	
Power [hp]: norm./max.	71 (75)
RPM [min-1]: norm./max.	1300 (1250)
Power per displacement [hp/l]	6,7 (7,0)
Carburetor(s)	
No.:	
Type:	
Fuel consumption per hp per hour [g]:]	300 (240)
Oil Pump	
No.:	
Oil consumption per hp per hour [g/PS/h]:	
Ignition No.:	
Type:	
Firing order:	
Cooling	Water
Weight of complete engine (dry) & ext. masses	
Total [kg]:	168 (207)
Weight per displacement [kg/l]:	16 (19,4)
Weight per hp [kg/hp]:	2,4 (2,7)

Remarks: The numbers in () are related to the advanced version issued 1908.
Airships: Militär-Luftschiff M I, M II, M III, M III (Austria), Parseval; Aeroplanes: AEG Z 1 Versuchsdoppeldecker, AEG E 1 Versuchseindecker a.o.

Engine Datasheet	
Gebrüder Körting AG, Körtingsdorf bei Hannover	
Designation	**Körting Kg IIIa**
Year:	1917
Purpose:	Aircraft engine
Number of Cylinders:	8
Arrangement of Cylinders:	Vee-type 90°
Bore [mm]:	110
Stroke [mm]:	140
Displacement [l]:	10,6
Compression [Ratio]	4,9
Power [hp]: norm./max.	180
RPM [min-1]: norm./max.	2100
Power per displacement [hp/l]	17
Carburetor(s)	
No.:	2 x 2
Type:	Pallas
Fuel consumption per hp per hour [g]:]:	226
Oil Pump	
No.:	
Oil consumption per hp per hour [g/PS/h]:	
Ignition No.:	2
Type:	
Firing order:	
Cooling	Water
Weight of complete engine (dry) & ext. masses	
Total [kg]:	240
Weight per displacement [kg/l]:	23,4
Weight per hp [kg/hp]:	1,37

Remarks: 5 engines built.
Applications*: tested on LFG Roland D.XIII and Halberstadt, DFW Dr.I and D.XIII.
* Listing has no claim to completeness!

3.42 Karl Kretzschmar, Dresden

The engineer Karl Kretzschmar was regarded in Germany as a specialist in gas turbines. He published scientific papers on his experiments with this new type of propulsion in various journals, including the 1911 issue of the magazine "*Der Motorwagen*".

Although his theoretical approaches to the new technology were quite correct, he was unable to successfully implement them in practice.

Above: Kretzschmar with his "turboprop-engine" installed in an aeroplane. [J6, 1911]

Left: Gas turbine prepared for test runs under labatory conditions (Kretzschmar 1910/11). [J6, 1911]

3.43 Kruk Motoren-Gesellschaft, Berlin

3.43.0 General

Die Fa. Kruk Motorengesellschaft wurde im Mai 1912 als GmbH in Berlin gegründet. Als Einlage auf das Stammkapital wurden seitens Julius Kruk in die Gesellschaft die Erfindung eines Rotationsmotors für einschließlich der erteilten und der beantragten und der noch zu beantragenden Patente nebst allem Zubehör eingebracht. Die Firma existierte knapp ein Jahr. Nach der nicht erfolgreichen Teilnahme am 1. Kaiser-Preis um den besten deutschen Flugmotor wurde der Motorenbau eingestellt.

Kruk Motorengesellschaft was founded in May 1912 as a limited liability company in Berlin. Julius Kruk contributed to the company the invention of a rotary engine for aeroplane[1], including the granted patents, the patents applied for and the patents still to be applied for, together with all accessories. The company existed for less than a year. After the unsuccessful participation in the 1st Kaiser Prize for the best German aircraft engine, engine construction was discontinued.

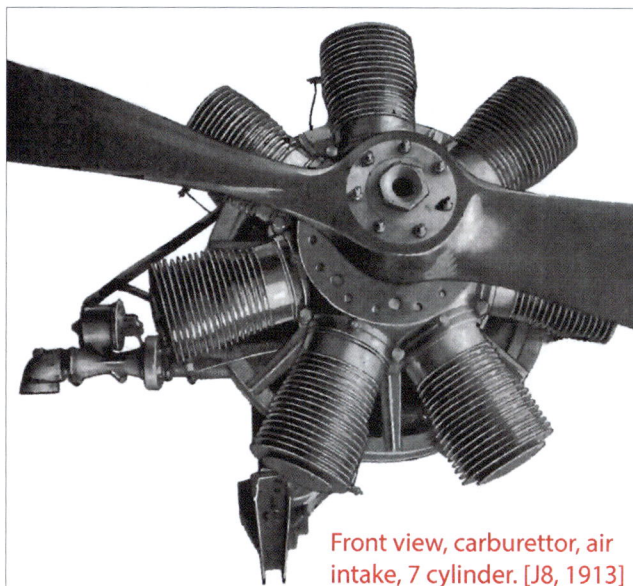

Front view, carburettor, air intake, 7 cylinder. [J8, 1913]

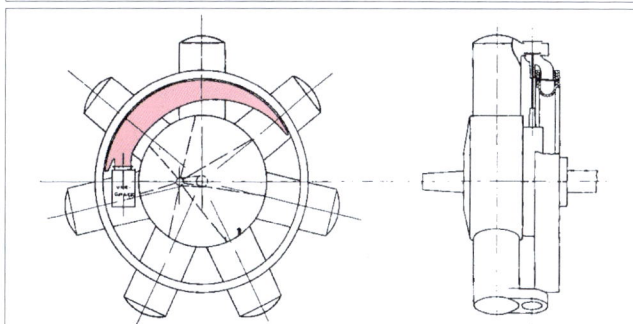

3.43.1 85 PS 7-Zylinder-Umlaufmotor

In the Kruk engine a completely new control method was realized, a combination of valve and ring valve control. There is only one valve on each cylinder, through which burnt gas was exhausted into the open air and fresh gas was drawn in immediately afterwards.

The valve inlet was switched from external air to carburetor connection and vice versa by the rotating cylinders themselves. A ring shaped spigot to spigot end closed off the fixed half-moon shaped gas channel to the outside, which was fed by a normal G.A. carburetor.

The valve had to be alternately connected to the carburetor and the free air. All the valve chambers

Above Right: Working principle of the Kruk rotary engine, crescent-shaped carburetion chamber. [J6, 1913]

Left: 80 PS 7 cylinder aero engine, carburettor side. [J8, 1913]

below the valves opened into a concentric aluminum ring running around the engine, on the inside of which the shell-shaped carburetor housing nestled, extending for about half the circumference.

The fixed carburetor housing was sealed against the rotating ring in the manner of the labyrinth seal by means of several thin steel plates projecting into deep grooves machined into the ring.

Although test runs of the engine gave quite satisfactory results, no practical use had been found for this engine.

Bore/stroke: 130/130 mm
Displacement: 12.0 liters
Power: 85 hp at 1200 rpm

Endnote

1. There is a patent 46a 250 287 "Explosion power machine with rotating cylinders" from the year 1912, which was granted to Selma Kruk. Whether Selma Kruk was the wife of Julius Kruk can only be assumed.

3.44 Robert Kutschinski, Maschinenfabrik, Eisen- und Metallgießerei GmbH, Braunsberg (East Prussia)

3.44.0 Gasturbine Kutschinski

Engineer Robert Kutschinski, as managing director of Maschinenfabrik, Eisen- und Metallgießerei GmbH in Braunsberg (East Prussia) presented a gas turbine for use in aircraft at the General Aircraft Exhibition (ALA) held in Berlin in 1912. More detailed information and illustrations are not known, but in general the technical press doubted whether this could be used to develop a propulsion system for flying machines: *Flugsport* reported in issue No. 9: "Kutschinski's gas turbine is in a class of its own, if it can be counted among the actual aircraft engines at all. The working processes of this propulsion machine are fundamentally different from those of normal aircraft engines and require special constructions, which, however, still require the greatest possible improvement if they are to be utilized for practical applications in aviation."

In 1912, the company was renamed "Braunsberger Motorenwerke, Maschinenfabrik und Eisengießerei GmbH, Braunsberg, East Prussia".

Above: Advertisement placed in the exibition catalog of Allgemeine Luftfahrtausstellung 1912.

3.45 Karl Lindström AG, Berlin

3.45.0 General

In 1917, development began on a large aircraft engine based on the plans of Professor Tuckermann from Helsinki. Karl Lindström AG in Berlin was commissioned with the realization of this project in the spring of 1918, initially limited to a trial order of three units. However, completion was not completed before the armistice.

3.45.1 Twelve-Cylinder 500 hp Aeroengine

The cylinders of this engine were arranged in three rows side by side, of which only the outer row had spark plugs, while the inner row was ignited by the outer ones via connecting ducts. The three pushrods of a transverse row engaged a crankshaft crank, so that only a quadruple-cranked crankshaft was required for the 12 cylinders. With a bore of 120, a stroke of 2 x 70 mm and a speed of 2400 rpm, the engine was to produce 500 hp, with dimensions of only 100 cm in height, 80 cm in length and 70 cm in width, and a design weight of 0.7 kg/hp.

Right: 12 cylinder opposed-piston aeroengine "System Tuckermann". [B4]

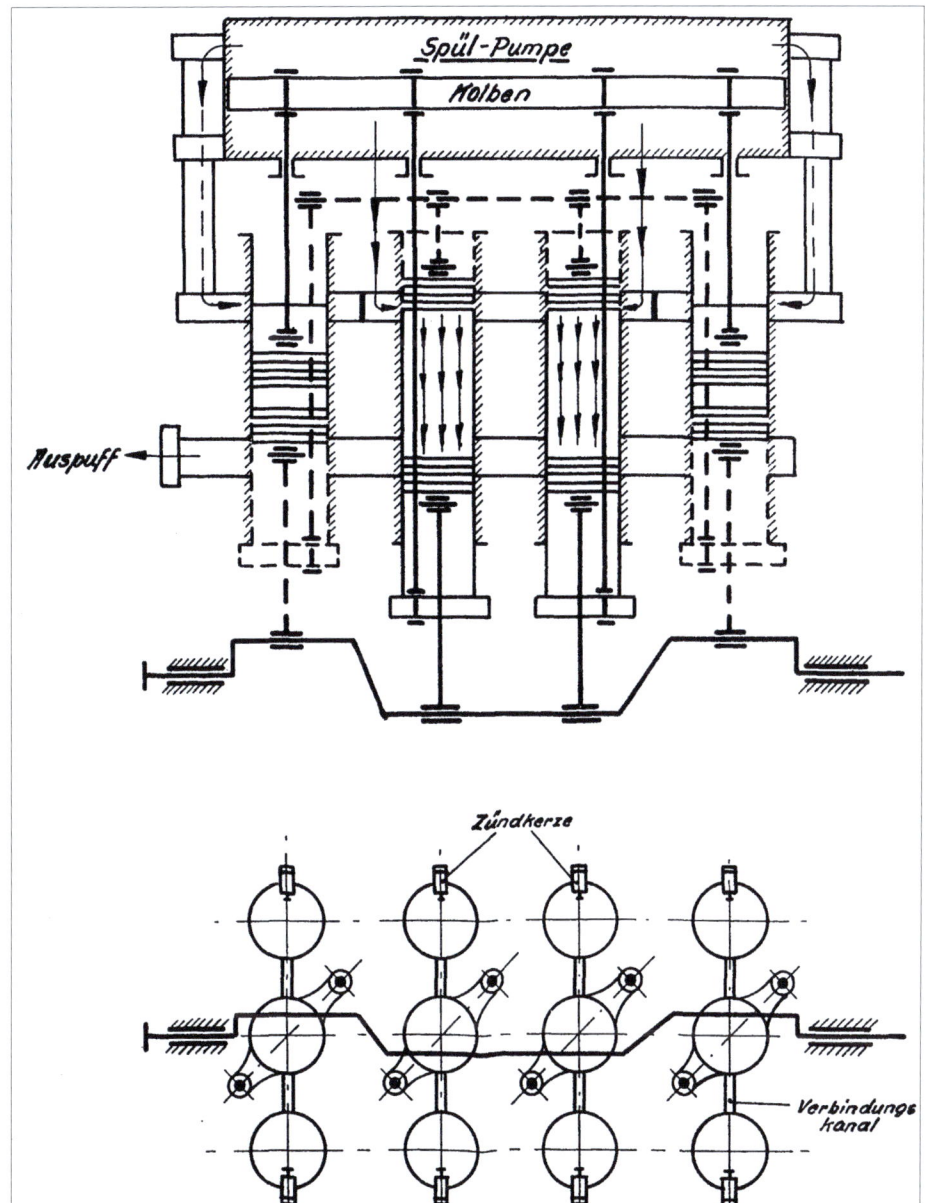

3.46 Loeb-Werke AG, Automobil- und Flugmotorenfabrik, Berlin

3.46.0 General

The company was founded in 1906 as Loeb & Co. by Ludwig Loeb and Dagobert Philip. Initially, it was engaged in the repair of and trade in automobiles of several brands. They acquired representation for Benz, Fiat, Panhard & Levassor and Daimler automobiles. Also gasoline engines of the engine factory Körting in Hannover belonged to the sales assortment.

In 1909, the company began manufacturing its own complete automobiles under the name LUC (Loeb and Co.). Initially, a 12/36 hp model was built with a slide-controlled in-line four-cylinder engine of the company's own design. As early as 1912, four-cylinder 8/22 hp and 16/40 hp models with Knight slide engines were added to the portfolio.

In 1914, the company was renamed Loeb-Werke AG.

3.46.1 Six-Cylinder 230 hp Hiero Aeroengine "Type H$_{IV}$" (1916)

Due to the First World War, automobile production was discontinued. Instead, Hiero aircraft engines were produced under license by Österreichische Industriewerke Warchalowski, Eissler & Co. AG, Vienna. For more information, see section 3.84.

Above: Hiero 230 WNr 34601, built at Loeb in Berlin. [A2]

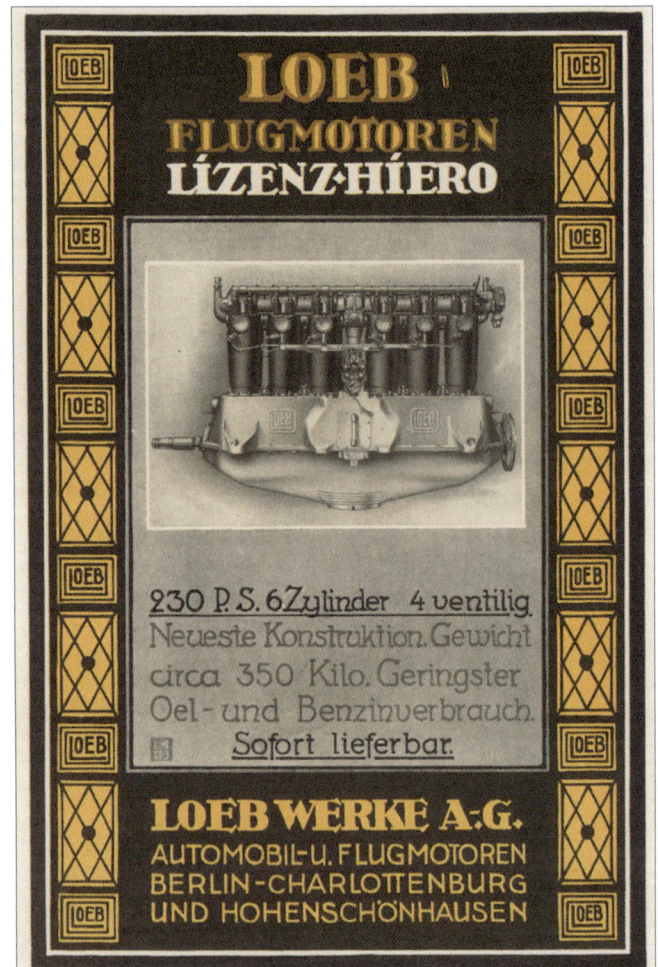

Above: Advertising poster from 1917. [J5, 1917]

Printed in Great Britain
by Amazon